DATE DUE

	DISCARDED		
		PRINTED IN U.S.A.	

HOME IS WHERE THE SCHOOL IS

Home Is Where the School Is

The Logic of Homeschooling and the Emotional Labor of Mothering

Jennifer Lois

NEW YORK UNIVERSITY PRESS
New York and London

NEW YORK UNIVERSITY PRESS
New York and London
www.nyupress.org

References to Internet websites (URLs) were accurate at the time of writing.
Neither the author nor New York University Press is responsible for URLs
that may have expired or changed since the manuscript was prepared.

LIBRARY OF CONGRESS CATALOGING-IN-PUBLICATION DATA
Lois, Jennifer.
Home is where the school is : the logic of homeschooling and the emotional labor of
mothering / Jennifer Lois.
p. cm.
Includes bibliographical references and index.
ISBN 978-0-8147-5251-7 (cl : alk. paper)
ISBN 978-0-8147-5252-4 (pb : alk. paper)
ISBN 978-0-8147-8943-8 (e-book)
ISBN 978-0-8147-5943-1 (e-book)
1. Home schooling. 2. Mothers. 3. Women teachers. I. Title.
LC40.L65 2012
371.04'2—dc23   2012037333

New York University Press books are printed on acid-free paper,
and their binding materials are chosen for strength and durability.
We strive to use environmentally responsible suppliers and materials
to the greatest extent possible in publishing our books.

Manufactured in the United States of America
c 10 9 8 7 6 5 4 3 2 1
p 10 9 8 7 6 5 4 3 2 1

To Marti and Calvin, the two little people who keep me interested in the social construction of good mothering.

CONTENTS

ACKNOWLEDGMENTS

When you spend more than ten years on one project, you have a lot of people to thank. The first round of my deepest gratitude goes to the homeschooling mothers who told me their stories. I would never have understood what homeschooling means to them and their families without their willingness to share their experiences with me. I have tried my best to honor the spirit with which they conveyed them.

Second, I must thank my academic family, the ethnographers who raised me. Patti and Peter Adler, as matriarch and patriarch, have provided me with incalculable support over the years. Like all good parents, they are always there when I need them, and for that I am eternally grateful. I have also had supportive Adlerian siblings for almost twenty years. Alice Fothergill, Katy Irwin, and Adina Nack provide feedback, probe ideas, and share my passion for sociology. Lori Peek gets a special shout-out for reading the first draft of this book with the dedicated acuity she gives to everything—it has benefited immensely from her feedback. Joanna Gregson read draft two and gets extra thanks for using her keen sociological insight to help me sharpen my ideas and her brilliant red pen to help me de-clunkify. My gratitude for her willingness to serve as the other half of my brain for nineteen years cannot be overstated.

I am also grateful to a broader community of scholars who have been generous enough to help this project along: Martha Copp, whose work in ethnography and emotions has paved the way for the rest of us; Michael Flaherty, whose research on temporality provided an analytical epiphany for me and inspired the title of this book's concluding chapter; Maralee Mayberry, whose work on homeschooling was groundbreaking and who has encouraged this project from the beginning; and Jennifer Reich, whose research on mothering helps me think more deeply about my own. The insightful comments of several anonymous reviewers along the way have also propelled this project immeasurably, as have the tireless efforts of NYU Press editor Ilene Kalish and her assistant, Aiden Amos.

The home team at Western Washington University also deserves my gratitude. My colleagues in sociology have given me much-appreciated intellectual support (Mick Cunningham and Laurie Caskey-Schreiber have shown impressive persistence in asking me about this research for more than a decade), and the department has contributed financially to this project. The WWU Office of Research and Sponsored Programs granted me funds for summer research support and interview transcription. Two undergraduate students also helped me locate and interview some of the homeschooling mothers; confidentiality issues prevent me from naming them here, but I greatly appreciate their work!

It is impossible to study motherhood for so long without developing a serious respect for the other family roles that make it so rewarding. Jackie and Joe Lois, Mary Lois, Sara and Gary Brown, Lois and Rollie Reinholtz, Rhonda Reinholtz, and Joseph Colletti have all taught me how important supportive, loving parents are. Sophie, Jacob, and Noah have taught me the same thing from the other end. I am exceptionally grateful to Calvin and Marti, always for allowing me to be their mom, but particularly in key moments for humoring my attempts to be a good one. And finally, my undying love and gratitude go to Tim Reinholtz for his stalwart emotional and family support. I am so lucky that one of the ways his generous nature manifests itself is in sharing the domestic load like no other husband I know.

Introduction

"Won't your children be social misfits?"

"Do you really think you can teach them as well as a professional teacher?"

"What about the prom?"

More than 1.5 million children in the United States are homeschooled. This number, a conservative estimate, represents 2.9 percent of the school-age population[1] and is up significantly from the mid-1980s, when the U.S. Department of Education estimated that fewer than 300,000 American children were homeschooled.[2] Since 1993, every state has provided a legal option for parents to educate their children at home,[3] and although homeschoolers have gained legal legitimacy and visibility with their growing numbers, they have yet to secure mainstream acceptance. Homeschooling is widely misunderstood by the non-homeschooling public, and homeschooling parents themselves feel the stigma sharply each time they are asked whether they are worried about destroying their children socially and academically.

Misconceptions are fueled by national media stories that sensationalize the role of homeschooling in unusual events—either triumphs, such as a homeschooled child who wins the National Spelling Bee, or tragedies, such as a homeschooling mother who, under the influence of postpartum psychosis, drowns her five children in a bathtub. Indeed, in February 2008, homeschooling made national news again, this time in California, when the state was prosecuting a case of child abuse in which the family happened to homeschool. The child welfare authorities argued that the state should require the children to attend public school so teachers could notice and report signs of abuse. During the course of the case, a California appellate court interpreted the state's homeschooling law such that, literally overnight, the parents to approximately 160,000 homeschooled children became criminals. The decision was vacated several months later due to pressure from organized homeschooling groups as well as from Governor Arnold Schwarzenegger, but the event reinforced for many homeschoolers that misconceptions about homeschooling—and thus about the people who choose it for their children—still abound.

What are the realities of homeschooling, and why do people choose it for their children? I asked these questions in September 2000 when I moved to Cedar County, a semirural area in the Pacific Northwest, and immediately discovered that homeschooling was an exceptionally popular alternative to conventional education.[4] Homeschooling's prevalence surprised me; although I had heard of it before, I had never known anyone who actually did it, and I wondered, like many non-homeschoolers (whom I call "outsiders"), what motivated parents to homeschool their children. Wouldn't homeschooled kids be socially awkward? Have gaping holes in their education? How would they learn to deal with diverse populations? And who were these parents who would choose such a radically different life for their children? I imagined they were either staunch evangelical Christians who spent their days using Bible verses to refute established scientific theories or else New Age hippies who taught their children—named Starfire and Chakra—to read auras rather than books. Regardless of on which end of the spectrum their practices lay, surely all of them were irresponsible parents who dismissed the importance of education.

I discovered the exact opposite was true. Homeschoolers are extremely concerned about their children's education, and they homeschool because they see it as a way to be ultraresponsible parents.[5] This applies to most homeschoolers, anyway; the homeschooling community is a diverse one—another discovery that defied my expectations. Homeschoolers come from all walks of life and educate in myriad ways. Likewise, most homeschooled children thrive socially and academically, though some do not, but this is certainly true for conventionally schooled children as well.[6] Meeting a few homeschooling families during my first months in Cedar County quickly disconfirmed my stereotypes, but it also raised other questions about how these families' lives were affected by taking on such an enormous commitment, especially one that is so disparaged. Raising children is hard enough when a family is going with the tide; I could not imagine adding "educate children" to the domestic chore list and, further, swimming upstream to do it. How do parents persevere with such a monumental yet stigmatized family choice? With these questions fueling my curiosity, I decided to investigate homeschooling sociologically.

The issue of household labor and its effect on families is a vast area of study in sociology. With that in mind, I knew any information I gathered about the workload of homeschooling would be complex and interrelated with other areas of family life. In addition, groups or activities that are stigmatized affect people in multifaceted ways, from identities to relationships to social standing and access to resources. No survey of fixed-choice questions emailed to homeschoolers could tap these issues deeply enough to reveal the intricacies of the experience. To study the workload and stigma of homeschooling, I needed to have extended conversations with homeschoolers themselves.

In March 2001, with the intent of learning more about homeschooling from the people who do it, I located Cedar County's primary organization, which I call the Parents' Association for Teaching at Home, or PATH, a homeschooling support group with more than 600 member families. Based on this number, PATH claimed that Cedar County had the highest homeschooling rate in the nation, and though I was never able to confirm that statistic, the number does suggest that our rate was at least twice the national average.[7] PATH's meetings, held one night a month in a public school gymnasium, were open to the public, so I began attending even though I was not a homeschooler, nor even a parent.

The most striking fact I encountered in my early experiences with PATH was that homeschooling "parents" were *mothers*. Cedar County homeschoolers, like homeschoolers nationally, were overwhelmingly mothers in two-parent, heterosexual families, who stayed at home and educated the children while their husbands earned enough in the paid labor force to support their families on one income. Fathers were occasionally involved in PATH, but mothers proliferated the subculture, attending meetings and posting to the email listserv to seek support for or offer advice about homeschooling. I quickly understood that homeschooling was women's work and was closely tied to mothers' identities. The challenges they experienced, such as stigma from outsiders, and the concerns they expressed, such as unmanageable workloads, were filtered through their maternal identities, which influenced how they felt about themselves as mothers, progressed through their mothering careers, and managed power dynamics within their families. Homeschoolers themselves often declared that homeschooling was about being the best mother they could be.

At its heart, then, this book is about good mothering. I present homeschoolers' experiences against the backdrop of the cultural standards for good mothering and show how mothers used homeschooling as a way to live up to those standards. Like many other stay-at-home mothers, homeschoolers are primarily responsible for performing household chores and caring for preschool-age children. Homeschoolers, however, add educating their school-age children, possibly through age eighteen, to their stay-at-home mothering duties. These extended commitments to their children and additional responsibilities to their families significantly shape the way they come to see themselves as mothers. Despite their intense focus on children's education and their willingness to sacrifice a great number of their own interests, homeschoolers are constantly fighting public perception that they are irresponsible mothers for keeping their children out of conventional schools. How do homeschoolers combat the stigma and workload constraints to live up to the norms of good mothering? The answer appears in three conceptual threads, which run throughout this book: *identity*, *emotions*, and *time*.

Sociologists view the idea of identity, or the "self," as distinctly social. We can only see ourselves as we think others see us, and we develop this understanding through our interactions with them—by interpreting their words and actions toward us. Conversely, who we believe we are influences our behavior, so we structure our interactions based on these ideas, which, of course, affects the interactions we have, and circularly, how we see ourselves. For the most part, social interaction shores up our self-perception, but occasionally it drives us to refine or completely revise our identities. This process emerged in the interplay between mothers' identities and their experiences with homeschooling. On the one hand, homeschooling shaped their identities as mothers; they developed certain justifications for homeschooling, which helped them defend themselves against outsiders' negative perception and rebuild their maternal identities. On the other hand, mothers' identities shaped their homeschooling experiences; they continued to homeschool, despite the highly intensive demands, because they saw themselves as certain kinds of mothers. In the pages that follow, I show how mothers' identities both drove and were driven by their homeschooling experiences.

When homeschoolers talked about being good mothers, two additional supporting conceptual threads wove themselves so tightly throughout the narratives that it was impossible to understand homeschoolers' identities without considering the role of mothers' emotions and time. Sociologists view emotions much like they view the self: as interpretive and socially derived. Our feelings are not purely innate or instinctual but rather depend on how we define situations and internalize cultural beliefs about particular emotions. That is not to say that emotions are divorced from biological processes. Indeed, our physiological responses are important elements in experiencing our emotions, but they do not constitute emotions in and of themselves. Instead, we experience emotions "on the template of prior expectations."[8] Through socialization, we learn to interpret these physiological responses by assessing the situation and drawing on our cultural knowledge about emotions. Sociologists are interested in the meanings we create around particular emotions—how we assign value (e.g., jealousy is bad), learn norms (e.g., control anger at work), and label our feelings in context (e.g., he's cute, it must be love). We know that emotions have a robust social component because these beliefs vary across history, culture, and subculture.[9]

One important place we see the social construction of emotions is in gender stereotypes, which yield distinct beliefs about women's and men's capacities for experiencing various feelings. As a culture, for example, we assume that women are "emotional experts," and we stereotype men as having little capacity for emotional self-reflection.[10] Most Americans would readily agree that emotion norms are gendered, and further, that mothering young children is a highly emotional activity. Yet despite these salient understandings in our culture, surprisingly little research has systematically examined the emotional facets of motherhood. I found that homeschoolers' narratives drew on the cultural discourse surrounding good mothering and in doing so exposed particular assumptions about the emotions inherent within it. In the process of examining homeschoolers' struggles to combat the stigma of irresponsible mothering, first to themselves and later to outsiders, this book begins to map out the crucial role of emotions in mothers' identities more broadly.

In addition to identity and emotions, time was the third theme that infused homeschoolers' experiences, and it surfaced in two ways. The first was quantitative and related to workload. Homeschooling mothers talked a great deal about the challenges of apportioning their time to perform their various family responsibilities. Many sociologists have studied the division of labor in the home, finding that women in heterosexual partnerships do the vast majority of household labor and, in light of this inequity, experience more stress and less satisfaction than their male partners.[11] Studying time as a finite commodity, the ways it gets allocated across the different spectra of family life, and how individual family members feel about it tells us something about how we assign relative value to women and men, as well as to paid and unpaid work. This was certainly true for the homeschoolers I studied, who, in their quest to be good mothers, often struggled with the ways they distributed their time over their various responsibilities as wives, mothers, teachers, and homemakers.

Sociologists have also examined qualitative aspects of time. Homeschoolers' "time perspective,"[12] or how they understood the temporal aspects of their lives, was the second way they talked about time. Mothers often felt as though time was passing too quickly, and they talked a great deal about trying to "slow it down" to savor their children's youth and their own identities as mothers. Both of these aspects of time—its objective use and its subjective experience—were central issues for homeschooling mothers, and further, were related closely to their emotions, and thus their identities. The quantity and quality of mothers' time often led to problematic emotions, causing conflict both with their husbands and within themselves. These feelings and the temporal issues from which they arose interfered with their vision of good mothering and their ability to practice it.

In this book, I draw upon data collected from eight years of observing and interviewing homeschooling mothers to examine how homeschooling constitutes a particular type of mothering experience, one that is fraught with what I call "temporal-emotional conflict." Homeschooling mothers try to manage this temporal-emotional conflict by sacrificing more time and investing more heavily in their good mother identities. Although this solution may work for individual mothers in limited ways, it affects their identities greatly over the long run, ratcheting up the standards of good mothering and promoting an ideal that is even harder to live up to than the mainstream version. In many ways, homeschooling is an exaggerated case of stay-at-home mothering; as such, it is useful in shedding light on the cultural ideas about mothering we often take for granted. Thus, throughout the book I argue that these temporal-emotional conflicts are not unique artifacts of homeschooling but rather represent a broader truth about mainstream definitions of good mothering: that the temporal experience of motherhood is emotionally problematic.

Good Mothering

Understanding homeschooling mothers' identities requires laying some groundwork about the cultural standards for good mothering. Sociologists assume that these standards are "socially constructed"—that is, as a culture we have defined good mothering in terms of specific behaviors and attitudes toward children, self, and family. When mothers act in ways that reinforce this definition, they are rewarded with the label of "good mother"; when they challenge it, they are labeled "bad mothers" and reap the consequences. For the most part, we accept this mainstream definition as inherently true; it seems self-evident that good mothers use love and logic, for example, and bad mothers don't, because we don't see the standards as something we invented.

Different groups of people make up different rules, however. This is how we know the norms of good mothering are socially constructed, rather than true in and of themselves, because they are historically and culturally specific. For example, American mothers who did not want to breastfeed in the 1950s were not considered bad mothers, whereas by contemporary rules they are. Even today this belief varies by culture, and even by subculture; for example, in the United States, working-class women and African Americans are more likely to embrace bottle feeding than middle-class women and whites.[13] Although these meanings may vary between subgroups within the same culture, some meanings are considered more valid than others, namely, the ones that belong to the group with the most power. Unsurprisingly, substantial research shows that mainstream notions of good mothering in the United States match those of the middle class; working-class definitions are deviant by default.[14]

These ideas of good mothering, though socially constructed, affect our lives in real ways. Those who adhere to the norms are rewarded, and problems arise for those who deviate. Depending on the magnitude of the deviation (neglecting children's homework vs. physical abuse, for example), violators at the very least get labeled bad mothers by their peers, and in the most acute cases are arrested and lose their children to the state. Mothers' identities, therefore, are heavily influenced by how closely they adhere to their culture's dominant definitions.

In her comprehensive analysis of mothering norms in the United States, sociologist Sharon Hays uncovered what she called the "ideology of intensive mothering."[15] Her historical examination of child-rearing philosophies and interviews with mothers revealed that U.S. culture has raised the standards of good mothering to unprecedented intensity levels, requiring mothers to invest heavily in three main areas. First, the standards dictate that a child's mother must be the primary caregiver. She is perceived to be the best person to raise a healthy, well-adjusted child. Paid caregivers, teachers, and even the child's father are deemed far less suitable for the job. Of course, this belief is not necessarily true. Plenty of fathers, grandparents, and other care providers do a superb job raising children, but this belief is so powerful and pervasive that it compels mothers to sacrifice a great deal for their children.

Second, good mothers must regard their children as priceless, or "outside the scope of market valuation."[16] This tenet strongly encourages mothers to put children's needs above absolutely everything else because they outvalue anything that can be given a price (which is to say, everything). Although the idea that children have a market value sounds ludicrous to contemporary Americans, it is not as taboo across cultures, nor has it been throughout history. The "priceless" child is a social construction. At the end of the nineteenth century, for example, children were valued primarily for their economic contributions to families, and in colonial America children were often sold into indentured servitude.[17] Even in the twenty-first century, parents in some poverty-stricken cultures must choose between selling one child to feed the rest, or having the whole family starve. The fact that it is so difficult for contemporary American parents to imagine selling their children is evidence that this socially constructed idea is deeply entrenched and has immense power in forming our definition of good mothering.

Third, the ideology of intensive mothering is so comprehensive that it encourages mothers to strive for excellence in all areas: child-rearing methods must be "child-centered, expert-guided, emotionally absorbing, labor-intensive, and financially expensive."[18] Yet this idea is also socially constructed. Many fine people have been raised by mothers (or others) who did not spend a great deal of money or consult a cadre of experts during their child-rearing years.[19]

Hays's research found that these three principles—primary caregiver, priceless child, and comprehensive methods—emerge so consistently that they form the foundation of the dominant definition of good mothering in the United States. Furthermore, when taken together, these three principles promote an extremely sacrificial version of mothering, one that asks mothers to achieve near self-obliteration for their children. Yet the increasing sacrifice required of mothers contradicts the key tenets of late twentieth-century feminism, which urge women to maintain an independent sense of self, thus leading to what Hays called the "cultural contradiction of motherhood." American mothers are caught in a paradox: they are asked to be independent women who are financially, politically, and socially liberated, yet simultaneously to sacrifice their time, energy, money, interests, and sense of independent self for their children.[20] These norms not only are contradictory but also are so uncompromising that deviating is inevitable—no one can live up to the opposing ideals—and mothers "can never fully do it right."[21]

But mothers do try. Subsequent research has shown that the ideology of intensive mothering is pervasive, holding across many different populations. Even though most mothers do not unquestionably accept the entire ideology because it is too stringent and requires an unattainable level of self-sacrifice, they are strongly influenced by it nonetheless.[22] Sociologists have demonstrated mothers' adherence to intensive mothering practices across a wide range of activities and life experiences, from paid work to household labor to reproductive choices;[23] however, three previous studies are especially relevant here, as they illustrate how mothers, particularly middle-class mothers, may use children's schooling as a site to implement the principles of good mothering.

Sociologist Annette Lareau discovered two contrasting, class-related parenting ideologies that affect the ways parents think about and invest in their children's education.[24] The middle-class model, the "process of concerted cultivation," drives parents to structure their children's schedules around organized, extracurricular activities that will develop their talents. Working-class parents, in contrast, subscribe to an antithetical ideology, the "accomplishment of natural growth," partly because they do not have the economic means to enroll their children in numerous extracurricular activities, and partly because they place higher value on children's flexible leisure time as well as on their relationships with family and community members. Though both middle- and working-class parents love their children and want them to succeed, schools and teachers embrace the concerted cultivation model, which allows middle-class parents and their children to negotiate the educational system skillfully, while working-class children and parents become alienated from it, never learning to "work the system." In this way, the middle-class notion of sacrificial, intensive parenting is further reinforced by the institution of public education.

Sociologists Alison Griffith and Dorothy Smith followed Lareau in examining how mothers' involvement affects individual children's education, but Griffith and Smith also focused on disproportionate outcomes at the institutional level.[25] They found that mothers who are financially able and so choose to stay out of the workforce—stay-at-home, middle-class mothers—have more time with their children and, thus, more opportunity for the "concerted cultivation" that Lareau identified (more, even, than middle-class mothers who work for pay), which helps their individual children succeed. However, the cultural capital these mothers impart to their children affects the institution as well. When children understand the expectations of a structured classroom and are equipped with self-management skills, the classroom in a middle-class school operates smoothly and teachers' instructional time is preserved. In addition, the extra set of hands mother-volunteers provide in middle-class schools further increases the time teachers can spend on instruction. In this way, mothers' time sacrifice, which is not recognized as "work" either by schools or by mothers, is the hidden yet crucial mechanism that allows middle-class schools to outpace and outperform those in working-class neighborhoods, widening the gap and building systemic inequality into the very institutions designed to eradicate it. Thus it is clear that this intensive, sacrificial version of good mothering has become institutionalized beyond the family; it is an indispensable component of a "good school."

Finally, sociologist Mitchell Stevens has also examined the intersection of good mothering and schooling in his research on the homeschooling movement.[26] The mothers in Stevens's study homeschooled despite the immense domestic burden because it resonated with how they defined good mothering and, additionally, helped them reconcile some of the contradictions inherent in the ideology of intensive mothering that Hays and other researchers have identified.[27] Stevens showed that more conservative homeschooling mothers, often evangelical Protestants, used homeschooling to integrate their traditional gender ideologies with more contemporary definitions of "ideal womanhood," whereas more liberal mothers used homeschooling to come to terms with staying out of the workforce.[28] Homeschooling allowed both groups to be more than "just" stay-at-home mothers. Stevens termed this phenomenon a "renovated domesticity—a full-time motherhood made richer by the tasks of teaching, and some of the status that goes along with it."[29]

The sparse evidence that exists suggests that homeschooling mothers get involved in their children's education for the same reasons that mothers of conventionally schooled children do: because it is part of how they define themselves as good mothers, they feel strongly about it, and they have the time to devote to it.[30] Yet although existing studies of how children's education affects mothers' identities give some attention to several temporal and emotional conflicts, these conflicts are not central analytical foci. The homeschooling mothers in my study talked a great deal about how temporal and emotional tensions affected their decision to homeschool and their identities as mothers, which suggests that delving deeply into these areas will reveal the roles time and emotions play in the social construction of good mothering.

Setting and Sample: PATH and Its Members

I began this research in the spring of 2001 and for two years was actively involved in the local homeschooling community by attending support group meetings and interviewing homeschoolers about their experiences. In 2008–9, I conducted follow-up interviews with two-thirds of my original sample to see how their lives had changed since we first talked six to seven years earlier. In the next chapter, I detail my methodological journey in studying homeschooling, but for now I set the stage by describing the ways individual families' homeschooling endeavors were shaped by the legal, institutional, and cultural factors in our particular geographic region.

There are many ways to homeschool, but one thing common to all home-schoolers is that they do not send their children to public or private school full-time; all of them, to some degree, are in charge of teaching their children academic subjects outside of a conventional educational environment. Part of the reason there are so many ways to homeschool is because, though it is legal throughout the United States, each state has its own laws and requirements, which vary dramatically. Additionally, each state has a different degree of compliance to its homeschooling laws—states with strict laws probably have lower compliance than those with looser criteria.

The parents I encountered usually complied with our state's relatively liberal homeschooling regulations. There were several elements to the law. First, for parents to be considered eligible to homeschool, they had to qualify in only one of the following ways: the instructing parent must have completed at least one year of college; the instructing parent must have taken a fifteen-hour homeschooling course (offered at local community or technical colleges); or the children and parent must meet with a state-certified teacher for an average of one hour a week. The vast majority of parents I talked to met the first requirement, although many enrolled in the fifteen-hour course anyway. In 2001, I did not know of any PATH parents who had their children meet with a teacher once a week. The second legal criterion was that parents had to file an official form with the school district declaring their intent to homeschool (for children age eight or older, the compulsory education age in our state). Third, parents were required to cover eleven curricular subjects: reading, writing, spelling, language, math, science, social studies, history, health, occupational education, and art and music appreciation, but how they did so was entirely up to them. Fourth, the children had to be assessed annually either by a state-certified teacher reviewing their work or by taking a standardized test. And fifth, the law required parents to keep records of the annual assessments but did not require them to submit the results to anyone. In contrast, some other states have much stricter criteria, such as requiring parents to obtain state approval of their curricula, hold teaching credentials, or schedule home visits by state officials.[31]

Homeschoolers in our area were grateful for the flexibility they had under this lenient system. The general consensus was that our state, compared with many others, had very parent-friendly homeschooling laws, which provided a great deal of leeway for parents to direct their children's education with very little intervention from—or accountability to—state authorities. Legally, then, homeschooling was easy to do, which might partially explain the high rate of homeschooling in our area.

While many parents were the sole teachers to their children, some felt their ability to provide certain skills was limited, such as when teaching required a group of children (e.g., orchestra), expensive equipment (e.g., biology lab), or specialized talents (e.g., dance). In these cases, homeschooling parents innovated solutions. One was to utilize the public school district facilities to meet their children's needs; in our state, homeschooling parents had the legal right to do so. Many parents chose this option, especially as their children reached high school age. For instance, the child would go to school for trigonometry or band and then return home to continue with other subjects. Another option was for parents to enlist the help of specialists to tutor their children in particular subjects; they would either pay tutors or barter their own services, such as trading web design skills for Japanese lessons. A third solution was to join institutionalized homeschool co-ops, organizations where they could "enroll" their children in almost any course, usually taught by another parent. Finally, some parents enrolled their children in distance-learning homeschooling programs, where they paid tuition in exchange for curriculum packages, scholastic schedules, testing and evaluation services, and institutional transcripts (Bob Jones University, in South Carolina, for example, sponsors such a program for Christian homeschoolers, grades K–12). Of all these options, the most popular were the least expensive, such as utilizing the public school facilities and trading skills with others. Paying for specialized tutoring in one particular area was also fairly common, but few people I met through PATH were enrolled in organized homeschooling programs, although this option was more common in other geographic regions, depending on state laws.

By 2009, however, the character of homeschooling in Cedar County had shifted. Over eight years, PATH's membership dwindled to approximately 400 member families, despite population growth in the county overall. Part of this decline can be explained by changes at the institutional level: the public school districts began targeting homeschoolers for Parent-School Partnerships (PSPs), in which district-paid teachers met with homeschooling parents one or two days a week to act as "facilitators" in their children's education. Some of these programs had organized classes for homeschooled students, whereas others merely allowed parents to obtain advice from certified teachers. These programs were attractive to school districts, which could count the enrolling homeschoolers and receive increased state and federal funding based on student numbers. In exchange, the program offered to reimburse parents up to

$400 per year in nonreligious curricular costs. PSPs were contentious in the homeschooling community, however. Some parents welcomed the opportunity for advice, networking, and some financial support; other parents eschewed them because they required students to enroll in the public school, and they saw this as a form of "government control" and therefore a threat to their civil liberties. The anti-PSPers often accused the PSPers of not being "true" home-schoolers, though the PSPers did not see it that way. In any case, this institutional-level change made a great impact on the nature of homeschooling in our area over the eight-year span of my research.

At the organizational level, PATH provided a great deal of support for many Cedar County families over the years I studied homeschooling. It connected them with other homeschooling families and provided a venue for sharing curricular ideas, venting stresses, solving problems, and gaining legal, academic, and social information about homeschooling. Despite Cedar County's higher-than-typical homeschooling rate, PATH members' demographic characteristics were quite similar to what the most representative studies have shown.[32] Almost every PATH family was white, and though most appeared to be middle-class, income-levels seemed to range from poor to very affluent. PATH was officially open to all homeschoolers, regardless of religious beliefs; however, many members, at least those who spoke at meetings, clearly identified as evangelical Christians.

Parents typically arrived at the monthly meetings early to browse at the folding tables set up around the perimeter of the room, which displayed the various goods and services PATH offered to members. PATH asked parents not to bring children to the meetings, but many did anyway, so there was always a group of elementary-school-age children running wild in the hallway outside the gymnasium where the meetings took place. The formal meeting activities began at 7:00 p.m. and usually ended around 8:45. Parents then mingled for another fifteen minutes before going home. Meeting activities varied but usually followed a yearly schedule. For example, the September meeting, when attendance was high as many newcomers were exploring the option, always featured a panel of seasoned homeschoolers facing rows of audience members for a question-and-answer session about their experiences. The April meeting always divided participants into smaller groups to discuss concerns and strategies for children of different ages. The number of attendees at PATH meetings also waxed and waned. Some meetings drew hundreds of members, such as when PATH sponsored nationally renowned guest speakers. Other meetings, such as those in the late spring when families were finishing up their year or were burned out on homeschooling, drew only a few dozen.

Portraits of the Homeschooling Mothers

Some of the most prevalent stereotypes that pervade the public's perception of homeschooling parents are that they are negligent regarding their children's education, that their children are socially and academically deficient because of it, and that they are all extreme fundamentalist Christians who believe in government conspiracies. In the aggregate, these are all myths. Of course some of these things are true for a few homeschooled children and parents, but these same things are true for a few conventionally schooled children and their parents as well. By delving deeply into many homeschoolers' lives, this book exposes the diversity among the homeschooling population. In this section, I provide portraits of four mothers to illustrate the ways they might meet some of the stereotypes, but also to show the complexity in the ways they diverge from those stereotypes. I present only the key details here to sketch out general impressions of these four mothers, but because mothers' stories are complex and their motives for and experiences in homeschooling are multilayered, other relevant details surface in later chapters.

Sabrina Hernandez

When I called Sabrina Hernandez to schedule a follow-up interview in the fall of 2008, she answered the phone with the greeting, "Good morning! Praise the Lord!" This was the first time I had spoken with Sabrina. One of my research assistants, who had been homeschooled herself, located and interviewed several homeschooling mothers in 2002, and Sabrina had been one of them. Until I phoned her, I only knew Sabrina through her interview transcript, but I knew I wanted to ask her more about her homeschooling career. A working-class Hispanic American who lived down a long dirt road, Sabrina was fifty-seven years old when I met her in 2008. Her house, a raised ranch, was immaculate, and we sat in her country kitchen to talk over tea and cookies. Sabrina was small—barely five feet tall—but her personality was large. Her dark, shoulder-length hair framed her round face, and her eyes sparked vibrantly when she talked about her passions: her children, her faith, and homeschooling. She had twelve children, ranging in age from thirty-six to thirteen, and had homeschooled all but the oldest.

Sabrina identified as a "born-again Christian," and her faith had influenced many decisions in her life. Born and raised Catholic, she did not "give [her] life to the Lord" until she was in her late twenties. During her senior year of high school, she began dating her (now) husband, Hector, and upon graduation she enrolled in a four-year university, while he joined a branch of the military. After two and half years Hector got stationed elsewhere, so Sabrina "quit" college, and they married and moved to another state. They had three sons over the next six years, during which time Sabrina enrolled in nursing school but dropped out after only one year because her husband resigned from the military and they moved again. In addition, Sabrina and Hector were having marital problems and were "on the verge of divorce" because of his drinking and smoking and late nights carousing with friends. She described her life at that point as "so miserable" that "something had to change." One of Hector's friends had recently returned to his own faith (Pentecostal) and counseled Hector about changing his life by "making a new commitment to the Lord and becoming new in him." Sabrina was skeptical, but after Hector got baptized she saw his behavior change overnight: "From that day on, he has not drank or smoked." Sabrina herself took longer to convert, but she and Hector began attending an evangelical church, and eventually she, too, became born-again.

The Hernandezes' spiritual conversion changed many things in their lives. Aside from saving their marriage, it compelled them to focus on their children: "God really spoke to us on the importance of our children; that was one area that God asked for us to trust him. No birth control, no nothing. We just said, 'Okay, God. Our children are your children.'" Sabrina and Hector enrolled their two school-age children in a Christian school for a few years, until the school closed. The oldest, in eighth grade by then, continued on at a magnet school, while Sabrina began homeschooling the rest (by that time she was thirty-four years old and had seven children). When she was pregnant with her tenth baby, the family relocated again, to our state, where she found homeschooling a great deal easier, in part because of the relatively loose state regulations. When I talked to her in 2008, she was still homeschooling her sixteen- and thirteen-year-olds, the youngest of the twelve children.

Sabrina and Hector believed that "God spoke to our hearts, that if we raised our children for him, he would use them for his Glory"; thus faith was part of everything they did as a family. Sabrina and Hector encouraged their children to pray out loud daily so "we can see what's in their hearts," and Hector led the family in Bible study every Saturday after breakfast. In addition, a Christian worldview permeated Sabrina's curriculum:

[It focuses] on God's viewpoint of the world. History is God's history—you know, how God has used it in the world and in mankind. Even math has a few Christian things in there—you know, God is a god of order and that kind of thing. So all of [the curriculum] has had that basis.

Sabrina also believed strongly in the traditional educational model, so her children gathered around the kitchen table and worked for the whole school day to complete assignments out of textbooks and workbooks. This structured approach to homeschooling not only was necessary, in her view, to cover all the required material, but it also taught her children important character traits, such as responsibility and persistence. Moreover, with so many children to oversee, Sabrina depended on the structured approach to stay organized.

Jackie Bell

The first time I talked to Jackie Bell was in 2002, when she responded to an ad I had placed in the PATH newsletter soliciting interviewees who home-schooled from a secular perspective. After a brief phone conversation, she invited me to her house, which was tucked far away in the woods, to talk about homeschooling. In a cold December drizzle, I drove up a rural, muddy mountain road, every quarter mile or so passing rustic-looking houses, some with blue tarps over farm equipment or trucks up on blocks in the front yard. I arrived at Jackie's log cabin, capped by a green tin roof, where a large dog greeted my car. As I got out, the cabin door opened, and I realized I had been holding certain expectations because they were instantly negated: out stepped Jackie, a thirty-nine-year-old African American woman wearing flowing drawstring pants, a tie-dyed tunic, and dangling beaded earrings. Her hair was cropped to only a few inches, her feet were bare, and her smile was broad. At her side stood her husband, Benny, tall and lean, with hair slightly longer than hers. Also thirty-nine and African American, Benny was dressed as casually as his wife, but his demeanor was more reserved. Their nine- and five-year-old daughters peeked out from behind them as Jackie effusively welcomed me in. Jackie, Benny, and I talked in the living room, surrounded by piles of books, craft supplies, and games, while the girls drew, cut, and pasted at a corner table, periodically interjecting to show us their artwork.

Jackie and Benny, neither of whom identified with any faith, had been married for more than ten years. They met in college on the East Coast but did not start dating until several years after graduation, when Benny was in business school and Jackie was working in a high-level corporate job. Early in their marriage, Benny's career took off, and they moved every few years so he could advance. Jackie was firmly career-minded as well, though she had to start her job search anew with every move. They were pregnant with their first child when they heard about homeschooling and began seriously considering it. They read books and attended homeschooling workshops, where they encountered homeschooled children who were, according to Jackie, "lucid, engaging, and relaxed" and "were with their families in a really comfortable way." Jackie decided to quit work to stay at home with the baby, and she and Benny adopted homeschooling as a parenting ideology, considering everything they did with their daughter to be simultaneously educational and part of their parenting duties. Although Jackie worried in the beginning about whether her daughter was meeting particular developmental milestones at the "appropriate" age, and she was anxious about whether she was providing her daughter, then a toddler, the "right" kind of curriculum. Jackie eventually relaxed and discarded formal curricula entirely, a pedagogy called "unschooling," by the time her daughter was four years old (more on Jackie's pedagogical transformation later).

Embracing this alternative notion of education also changed other things in their family's life "little by little." Jackie told me that she and Benny realized, "Oh, we don't have to do things a certain way. How can we get it to work for us?" Since then, "that question has been applied to everything in our lives." For their second pregnancy, they chose to birth at home instead of in a hospital, as they had for their first baby. They moved to this rural log cabin to be "in a peaceful area of nature," to not feel like they had to "keep up with the Joneses," and to "hear my own rhythm, and be *in* that." When I talked to Jackie and Benny in 2002, Benny was home full-time after leaving his corporate job to pursue his longtime dream of writing a screenplay, which he hoped to (and later did) make into a feature film. The family was living off of their savings and treasuring their time together. Homeschooling, according to Jackie, "was at the forefront of us doing things alternatively."[33]

Patricia Tomlinson

In 2002, forty-one-year-old Patricia Tomlinson walked into Starbucks wearing jeans, a pale blue blouse, and a buckskin jacket, fringed down the arms. Her wavy, light brown hair was pulled back loosely on one side with a decorative comb, and as she introduced herself, I could see that she wore a touch of eye makeup behind her round, wire-rimmed glasses. Laugh lines appeared as she smiled warmly, and we sat down to talk. A former portrait artist, Patricia had a graduate degree in education and was extremely articulate, employing a large vocabulary. She and her husband had two boys, a fourteen-year-old born while she was working as a teacher and "putting my husband through college," and a five-year-old, born only after her husband had finished his master's degree and gotten an industry job in the sciences. Patricia wanted to stay home with the second baby as well as "reconnect" with her older son, so she left her teaching job and decided to homeschool, pulling her older son out of the private school he had been attending (the same school, incidentally, in which she had been teaching).

Patricia's motives (which I will detail later) were multifaceted, but many of the particular reasons stemmed from the fact that her then-nine-year-old was exceptionally "capable" academically. He had been "bumped up a couple of grades," but she was alarmed by the glaring holes she saw in his education. There were "fit" issues as well, since he was so young compared with his class-mates, and given his "introverted" personality, Patricia thought he would fare better if she could individualize his instruction at home. When I talked to her in 2002, she had been homeschooling for five years, and it was going well. In addition to covering the required subjects, Patricia tailored her homeschooling to their family's interests and her children's talents. She infused a healthy dose of art into her curriculum, enrolling her older son in theater classes and piano lessons and nurturing her younger son's imaginative bent. She supplemented her own, less structured approach with structured classes at a private "learning academy" that catered to homeschooled students, and there her older son took classes in U.S. history and geometry. She taught him health, sex ed (which, she laughed, "came up just recently"), and French, but when he wanted to learn Hebrew, she arranged for a private language tutor.

A big focus of Patricia's curriculum was on teaching her children the "moral underpinnings" she thought most important to their growth. She espoused socially progressive views about the roles of women and men in society, and considered herself a "liberal Christian." The private learning academy her son attended was faith-based, and she made it a point to talk to her son about its perspective. She explained to me her view on Christianity and how she wanted to raise her son:

> The people at [the learning academy] are the very strong Christians. I appreciate a lot of the sort of things that they're supporting. I really do. But I also have problems with their stance on diversity issues and sexual orien-tation. And my son, I think, has the same sort of feelings—he's more lib-eral. So he gets religious instruction that's Bible-based, but it's more schol-arly. And then he kind of draws from it what he wants to, and he questions certain things. You know, he'll say things to me like, "What's the deal with these Christian kids not being able to interpret this metaphorically?" That sort of thing. . . . So far he seems to have kind of been imprinted with my husband's and my moral and philosophical standpoint. Which is good because I think that's what you want as a parent. I don't want my child to be totally alien from me.

Whitney McKee

I talked to fifty-year-old Whitney McKee in March 2002, when she had been homeschooling for six months. She lived with her husband, Ray, and their eleven-year-old son, Ritchie, in a small, bungalow-style house in a working-class neighborhood of Cedar County. Heavyset, Whitney moved stiffly as she led me into the living room, where we settled on the couch for our interview. The room had a cozy sitting area and a computer nook, and it adjoined a small dining room where her son's hermit crab cage graced the table. Half self-consciously, Whitney acknowledged the clutter—mostly books and piles of paper—and explained that she often joked with her husband and son by wondering aloud, "When's that maid coming back?" In mock snobbery, she put her nose in the air, tossed back her ash-blond hair, and laughed heartily, blue eyes twinkling. Ritchie was involved in several projects that day, passing through the room often as we talked, but once lingering much longer while he cleaned out his hermit crab cage.

Whitney had become a mother at thirty-nine, later than most, she explained. When she met Ray in her early thirties, he had just come out of a bad marriage, from which he had two daughters. Whitney married him knowing he did not want more children, so she "suppressed all of those emotions for wanting kids." She was thirty-six when "one day [Ray] held a baby" and said, "I want one!" They decided to get his vasectomy reversed, but it "didn't work," so they pursued adoption. After three years, a woman who had just given birth chose Whitney and Ray as adoptive parents, and they brought Ritchie home.

Ray was retired from a blue-collar job and received a small pension. Whitney had always worked, first as a preschool teacher, then, once Ritchie came along, she did "home studies" for an adoption agency "at night while my husband was home" and routinely wrote up reports during the day at an indoor playground while her son played with friends. When I asked Whitney if she would have stayed home if she had been able when Ritchie was a baby, she immediately corrected me: "I did stay home. The first four years, I stayed home." She left the job at the adoption agency and returned to the day care industry when Ritchie was four years old.

For kindergarten, Whitney and Ray enrolled Ritchie in a Christian school, where he had stayed until finishing fourth grade, eight months before I talked to her. Whitney decided to homeschool Ritchie for the first half of fifth grade because they planned to move to Central America; she and Ray had taken jobs through a church program, and though she was reluctant to say the move was going to be permanent, she was "giving it five years," to see if it would work out. The family would move in February, so Whitney thought it would be easier to homeschool Ritchie for the fall semester before they left. She quit her job and began homeschooling, but within weeks, their moving plans fell through. Rather than reenroll Ritchie in the Christian school, and fearing that he was not "streetwise" enough for public school, she continued to homeschool him for his fifth-grade year.

When I talked to Whitney, however, she acknowledged that Ritchie would have to start sixth grade in public school the next year because the family could not afford for her to be out of the workforce. She explained that they were "financially on the low end of life," and that it would be nice to "have a little breathing room." Eight years earlier, a medical condition sent her for two six-week stays in the hospital, where she had "almost died." The condition (which she did not name or explain) left her with lingering health problems and hefty ongoing medical expenses for monthly prescriptions and regular doctor's visits. Though ultimately she thought it was unrealistic, Whitney fantasized about ways to continue to homeschool the next year, such as getting a part-time job with benefits: "Something that at least brings in enough to cover our medical. Then I think we'd be okay. Tight, but okay. You know, I'm not looking for riches." She also predicted that Ray would have to find work as well, but for now, they were focused on enjoying this one year they had to homeschool.

Whitney cried twice, both times tears of joy, during our interview: once when we discussed adopting her son, and again when she talked about her faith. She identified as "Christian," though reluctantly as evangelical because she thought the term carried a stigma of intolerance. Her understanding of evangelism was steeped in love and acceptance—"Christ didn't judge"—and so she ultimately felt proud of her faith and emphasized her "passion for telling people that God desires a relationship with you." Yet despite the importance that faith played in her family's life, Whitney did not use a Christian curriculum. Instead, she followed the public school program and was fairly structured in her daily lessons because she did not want Ritchie to be behind when he began public school the next year.

Overview of the Book

In the chapters that follow, I tell the stories of Sabrina, Jackie, Patricia, and Whitney, as well as those of many other homeschooling mothers. I begin chapter 1 by describing how I studied homeschoolers, the methods I used in collecting and analyzing my data, and the problems and issues I encountered during the course of the research. The next two chapters constitute part I of the book, in which I examine how homeschoolers' emotions were connected to their maternal identities. Chapter 2 focuses on how women's feelings about themselves as stay-at-home mothers influenced their decision to homeschool their children, and chapter 3 illustrates the justifications they developed to fight the emotional stigma of irresponsible mothering that came with keeping their children out of conventional schools. The next two chapters—part II of the book—focus on homeschooling mothers' emotions with respect to time. Chapter 4 exposes the quantitative side of mothers' time, tracing their increasing domestic workloads, rising role strain, and feelings of burnout as their homeschooling careers progressed. The qualitative nature of time is the heart of chapter 5, which shows how mothers, unable to "find" more time, resorted to managing their feelings about it and altering their subjective experience of it to deal with the substantial self-sacrifice homeschooling required. The follow-up interviews form the basis for part III, which shows the changes in homeschooling families and mothers' homeschooling careers over time. Chapter 6 begins by presenting mothers' look back on the time between the interviews. I asked them to tell me about the successes and struggles of their journey since I had last seen them. Chapter 7 continues chronologically and details homeschoolers' evaluations of the present—did they think homeschooling worked for their children, and how did they know? Finally, chapter 8 features mothers' thoughts about the future—where did they see themselves going once their homeschooling careers were over? In chapter 9, I revisit the themes of mothering, the self, emotions, and time, tying them together not only to analyze homeschooling mothers' experiences but to suggest how they can shed light on intensive mothering more broadly.

1

Homeschooling Mothers

Because PATH served as a support group for more than 600 member families and its events were open to the public, I attended my first meeting assuming I would lurk anonymously to get a feel for the issues homeschoolers faced. But when I arrived and saw only a few dozen chairs set in a circle in the middle of the gymnasium, and a like number of people milling about, I knew I was not simply going to blend into the background.

At 7:00 p.m., the moderator and longtime PATH president, Charlie Cooper, herded the group, mostly mothers, toward the circle of chairs. As we sat, he explained that the night's goal was for people to share their experiences and insights, but first we would go around the circle with introductions. After eight people, it was my turn.

"I don't homeschool, and actually, I don't even have kids," I said after I gave my name. "I teach sociology at the university, and I wanted to find out more about homeschooling, so I came here tonight."

Some parents looked surprised, some disapproving, and one mother, a petite woman with carefully styled hair and gold earrings, turned directly toward me and began enumerating the misconceptions about homeschooling, ticking them off on her fingers as she went.

"First of all, our kids are not *unsocialized*. They're involved in more activities than kids who are in school. Second of all, we are our children's *facilitators*. We don't have to know everything, but we sure as heck can find someone who can teach them about a particular subject when we need to. Third," she said, getting increasingly animated, "we believe that kids benefit from having the freedom to pursue the things they're interested in, without some outside authority telling them what to learn and when to learn it. It can be less structured, but that doesn't mean we're just letting them play all day. Homeschoolers are not crazy, irresponsible parents. We love our kids and care about their education."

Her husband interjected with a heavy dose of sarcasm. "Yeah, we make sure they get a 'proper' education, just like if they were in school. Every fifty minutes in our house, we ring a loud bell and tell the kids to stop whatever they're doing and do something else. And to make sure they're 'socialized,' we use foul language and take them to deserted parking lots to teach them how to smoke." The thirty other people sitting around the circle laughed heartily, defusing some of the defensiveness fomenting in the group.

Another woman, whose long, gray braid extended halfway down the back of her denim jumper, earnestly wanted me to understand. She leaned forward, looked me in the eye, and tried to sum it up: "We don't homeschool despite loving our kids; we homeschool because of it." The affirming nods from every one of the other parents told me that this was not the first time they had defended themselves.

I had not realized that merely identifying myself as a non-homeschooler—people I later would call "outsiders"—would trigger these defensive reactions. Though surprised at the fervor of their responses, I tried to look as agreeable as possible, repeatedly nodding in understanding.

Finally, another mother announced, "I wish I'd had a professor like you! If you want to know something, go and find out. That's what homeschooling's all about—I think that's great!"

With that, the tension passed and the group continued with introductions, no longer overly concerned with my presence. The meeting lasted about two hours, and afterward a few members approached me to chat. One mother, Gretchen Forrester, gave me her phone number in case "you ever want to come over and see what a homeschooling family does. Just call first so I can do laundry!" Thus began my study of homeschooling mothers.

Field Research

Field research (also known as "participant observation" and "ethnography") does not conform to the tenets of the deductive scientific approach, which assumes that people can be studied the same way as objects, by formulating hypotheses from established theories, then gathering data to support or refute the hypotheses. Such an approach assumes that there is an objective reality that exists outside of human experience; that the "facts" are out there waiting to be discovered by using a controlled and standardized procedure. While this deductive model is useful in answering certain questions, it would not have allowed me to answer the main questions I had: How do homeschoolers deal with the stigma of their unconventional choice and manage the increased workloads at home? Further, how do these things affect their identities as mothers? The answers depended largely on how homeschoolers made sense of their experiences and understood reality.

People define reality based on their experiences in social life. We assign meaning to social processes and objects, including ourselves and others, then act on those meanings. One way to understand behavior, then, is to investigate the meaning people give to social phenomena. This is best accomplished through field research whereby researchers observe and interact with people in their natural settings and talk to them in depth.[1] The data consist of researchers' written observations, known as fieldnotes, and subjects' detailed accounts of their experiences, solicited via in-depth interviews.

There are several advantages of field research. First, it provides a deep and intricate understanding of how and why social processes happen because it captures the nuanced meanings people give to social phenomena; it uncovers the reality they create.[2] The researcher can examine this reality not by imposing and defining it at the outset of the research but by allowing it to emerge from the data. Contrarily, surveys and experiments, though useful methods for answering some questions about social life, cannot access this depth of experience and therefore are not well suited to answer the questions about the meaning people give to their lives. Second, although field research does not produce findings that are generalizable to other social settings, it does allow the researcher to abstract general social principles and suggest where else they may be applicable, a quality termed "theoretical generalizability."[3] In this way, field research is inductive and produces tentative theories that may later be tested deductively to establish where, when, and how they may be counted on to explain other social phenomena.

I conducted field research with homeschooling mothers because I wanted to explore specific aspects of their experiences: why they chose to homeschool, how they handled the stigma of their unconventional choice, how they managed their time, and how homeschooling affected their identities as mothers. I could only answer these questions by achieving an intimate familiarity with homeschoolers' lives, which required talking to them in depth and participating in their world.

Getting In

Though I did declare my non-homeschooling status at the first meeting I attended, I did not reveal my research interests immediately. Parents reacted so defensively to the mere presence of a non-homeschooler that I was unsure whether they would accept me as a researcher. Because it endeavors to uncover the meanings people give to their lives, field research requires a great deal of trust and rapport between the researcher and the subjects.[4] Without trust, subjects are not very forthcoming, the data are shallow, and we cannot understand the intricacies of their experiences. As a non-homeschooler and nonmother, I wondered after that first meeting whether I could develop enough rapport with this group of mothers, so I waited several weeks to announce my research interests.

The format of the next month's meeting did not provide me with an opportunity to talk to PATH's leaders, but two weeks later, at a homeschooling talent show, I declared my research interests to PATH's president, Charlie Cooper, and paid him the twenty-dollar annual dues to become a member. He welcomed me to join the group, and though he was receptive to the idea of my research, his enthusiasm was guarded. From then on I began telling homeschoolers about my research when it came up in conversation, but I did not gain a great deal of traction because PATH meetings were winding down for the summer, and most of my networking opportunities were put on hold until the fall. Instead I focused my attention on two things: learning about the subculture of homeschooling in the United States by reading homeschooling magazines, websites, listservs, and blogs, and getting a glimpse into the practicalities of doing it by visiting Gretchen Forrester, the mother who gave me her phone number at my first meeting.

Though many families suspend their formal learning efforts in the summer like conventional schools, Gretchen homeschooled year-round. She invited me to her house on several occasions in July and August to observe her homeschooling her three boys, ages eight, four, and two. Gretchen even had me participate, so I would occasionally read to the younger children while she worked with Harry, her eight-year-old, or I would quiz Harry on spelling words while Gretchen nursed the baby or helped the four-year-old in the bathroom. I was struck by how Gretchen was continually moving throughout her day, preparing food and finding new activities for each child. The younger children, especially, required constant attention because each activity entertained them for only five minutes, and, as a nonmother, I was shocked and a bit panicked to learn that toddlers' attention spans were so short. I could see that Gretchen was happy to have me there to relieve some of her burden—homeschooling motherhood was a lot of work, but she truly loved it. In contrast, I was exhausted and drained by the end of these visits. I walked away each time with a solid appreciation for homeschooling mothers' intense and challenging work and knowing that when I did have children, I would certainly not homeschool them.

The monthly PATH meetings resumed in September 2001, and I continued to sit in on them. At one well-attended meeting, Charlie gave me permission to introduce myself to members, discuss my research interests, and solicit interviews. None of the hundred or so attendees objected, and several mothers approached me afterward to express interest in talking to me further. Though my status as a non-homeschooler was clear and seemed acceptable to the people at that meeting, there were other meetings where members probably assumed I was a fellow homeschooling parent; I fit the age, race, and gender profile, so I blended in. PATH was not tight-knit; meetings were high on anonymity because the constellation of attendees was different each time and constituted only a small proportion of the large membership.

I obtained four interviews from my announcement and later grew my pool of interviewees by snowball sampling—asking participants to refer me to others whom I could interview.[5] To increase the diversity of my sample, I also solicited interviews by placing a notice in the monthly PATH newsletter, specifying that I was particularly interested in talking to families with older children, families in which the father was primarily in charge of the homeschooling, or families who homeschooled from a secular perspective. As a result, I secured several interviews with mothers who had high schoolers and who used a secular approach. I received only one call from a father, who initially agreed to an interview but called back ten minutes later to cancel.

Around the same time, a student in one of my university classes, who had been homeschooled until high school, wanted to assist me in my research. She located and interviewed six mothers in a neighboring county where she had grown up. Four of these six mothers were involved in a Parent-School Partnership (PSP), a program run by the public school to support homeschooling families (which I detailed in the introduction). Cedar County's schools did not have such programs in 2001, so these out-of-county mothers' experiences helped me understand early on that homeschooling occurs in a variety of ways. A few months later, another student located and interviewed three mothers who were involved in a similar program in a third county.[6] Thus, seven of my original twenty-four interviewees homeschooled as part of a PSP program in 2001–2002.

The Interview Sample

In the end, the demographic characteristics of my interview pool were fairly consistent with what the most representative research samples of home-schoolers show, though these samples are far from perfect.[7] Twenty-one of my twenty-four interviewees identified with a Christian-based religion, and among those, fourteen held highly conservative and evangelical Christian beliefs.[8] Three interviewees told me they were not at all religious. Twenty-one of the families were white, two were Hispanic American, and one was African American. Parents' ages ranged from midtwenties to early fifties with most in their midthirties to early forties. All interviewees were women, although four husbands participated in their wives' interviews. They home-schooled (at that time or had previously) between one and 12 children (average 3.2), and their years of homeschooling experience at the initial interview ranged from one to 17 (average 6.3). Most families were middle-class, although a few were working-class and upper-middle-class.[9] One subject was single but engaged to be married; one was widowed and homeschooled her grandson, whose father was single; all others were married. Most held four-year college degrees; two worked outside the home (the single mother worked part-time while her son attended a homeschool PSP program; the other worked nights and weekends). (See Table 1.1 for demographic characteristics of my 2002 interview sample.)

My interviewees participated in the homeschooling subculture in different ways, but all of them had an integral understanding of its norms and values. Ten of the twenty-four were actively involved in the monthly PATH meetings, attending regularly to engage in discussion, seek advice, and network with other mothers. Seven interviewees participated more passively in PATH (or its equivalent in the other counties). Though they received the newsletters, were on the email listserv, and visited PATH's website, they rarely attended the monthly meetings, either because they were veterans and no longer needed guidance or because they eschewed the evangelical undertones that were often made salient at the meetings through partici-pants' questions and comments, despite PATH's commitment to be open to homeschoolers of any faith. Seven of the nine who lived in two neigh-boring counties interacted frequently with other homeschoolers because of the PSP programs in which their children were enrolled with other homeschoolers.

Most homeschoolers, even if they were not in a PSP program, also spent time with other homeschooling families, whom they met through their churches, extracurricular activities, such as 4-H clubs, or at particular venues, such as Cedar County's ice rink and public pool, both of which set aside specific times during the school day to cater to homeschooled children (e.g., "homeschool free-skate" took place Tuesdays at noon and "homeschool swimming lessons" occurred Mondays through Fridays in the late morning). Because homeschooling was so prevalent in Cedar County, there was no shortage of children at these activities. Despite the variety of ways my interviewees interacted with other homeschoolers, all of them regularly visited homeschooling websites for curricular advice and moral support, which effectively socialized them to the prevailing norms of the homeschooling subculture in the United States.

Initial Obstacles to Establishing Rapport

Although I regularly attended the PATH meetings and eventually interviewed twenty-four willing participants (twenty-three of them enthusiastic, but more on that later), I did encounter a few obstacles to developing enough rapport and trust with homeschoolers in order to study them. First, some homeschoolers distrust government institutions, such as public education, which they view as a form of invasive government control over their families, thus posing a threat to their civil liberties. Homeschoolers occasionally expressed these fears at PATH meetings both explicitly and implicitly. For example, one nationally renowned speaker at a PATH meeting described public schools as "a poor substitute for family—they're kind of like orphanages" and cast homework as "government intrusion into family life." I quickly understood that there were a few homeschoolers who were never going to talk to a professor at a state-run university, but fortunately most were less resolute in their antigovernment ideologies.

A second obstacle to developing rapport and trust with homeschoolers was that I was not a homeschooler—I did not even have children in 2002— so homeschoolers were occasionally suspicious of my motives for attending meetings and events, though I always tried to explain my research role. On one occasion, a woman I later interviewed (though awkwardly, as I will detail in chapter 2) could not understand why I would attend a homeschool talent show if I did not have children in the production. Even after I explained my research interests, she still seemed suspicious of my motives; I got the

Name	Marital Status	Age	Number of Children	Ages of Children	Race	Social Class	Faith Identification
Alice Lange	Widowed; grandson's father is single	53	1 (grandson)	6	White	MC	Catholic
Annie Agresti	Married	50	3	21, 19, 15	White	MC	Evangelical
Barbara Roberto	Married	Early 40s	2	10, 8	White	WC	Christian
Cassandra Shudek	Married	40	4	9, 6, 3, 2	White	UMC	Evangelical
Darlene Rooney-Henkel	Married	46	2	11, 8	White	UMC	"Progressive Christian"
Emily Ashton	Married	28	3	11, 8, 6	White	MC	Not Religious
Francis Hart	Married	Mid 40s	4	17, 15, 13, 7	White	MC	Evangelical
Gretchen Forrester	Married	35	3	8, 4, 2	White	MC	Catholic
Heather Locke	Married	Early 40s	2	15, 13	White	MC	Evangelical
Jackie Bell	Married	39	2	9, 5	African American	UMC	Not Religious
Kathy Gaven	Married	Early 40s	5	13, 11, 7, 5, 3	White	WC	Evangelical

Name	Marital Status	Age	Number of Children	Ages of Children	Race	Social Class	Faith Identification
Leanna Livingston	Married	Mid 30s	3	9, 6, 3	White	MC	Evangelical
Linda Kelso	Married	Late 40s	3	23, 21, 19	White	UMC	Evangelical
Liz Trudeau	Married	42	4	21, 20, 6, 4	White	MC	Evangelical
Maria Rojas	Engaged to be married	25	2	7, 2	Hispanic American	MC	Christian
Molly O'Donnell	Married	Early 30s	3	6, 3, 1	White	MC	Christian
Nancy Bauer	Married	Late 40s	2	24, 22	White	MC	Evangelical
Pam Rausch	Married	Early 40s	3	13, 10, 8	White	MC	Evangelical
Patricia Tomlinson	Married	41	2	14, 5	White	UMC	"Very Liberal Christian"
Renée Peterson	Married	38	2	10, 2	White	MC	Evangelical
Sabrina Hernandez	Married	51	12	31, 29, 26, 23, 21, 20, 17, 15, 13, 12, 10, 7	Hispanic American	WC	Evangelical
Tracy Chadwick	Married	33	2	8, 4	White	UMC	"Non-religious"
Valerie Scott	Married	43	7	23, 21, 19, 17, 6, 4, 3	White	MC	Evangelical
Whitney McKee	Married	49	1	11	White	WC	Evangelical

Table 1.1 Demographic Characteristics of Interviewee Sample, 2002

feeling she thought I might be a child molester who habitually lurked around playgrounds, bus stops—and, yes, homeschool talent shows—waiting for an opportunity to abduct a child who wandered too far from her mother.

Homeschoolers were also uncertain about what my role as researcher entailed, which is such a common reaction that rapport building in these ambiguous situations is an integral analytic component of the field research methodology.[10] Though I worked hard to establish rapport with homeschoolers at meetings, my opportunities were limited because the meetings were infrequent, were not very interactive, and different people attended each time. Charlie Cooper, PATH's leader, always welcomed me at the meetings but on occasion did explicitly remind PATH attendees that I was a non-homeschooling "teacher" from the local university who was "studying us." In fact, after I solicited the interviews at the one meeting, standing in front of more than 100 people to explain my research goals—a short presentation that went well—Charlie took the microphone back from me and announced: "That was Jen Lois, a.k.a., 'The Spy.'" Then he laughed and said he was only joking. But in jest or not, his occasional remarks marginalized me at some PATH meetings and elicited nervous comments from participants, such as one mother who said, "I should watch what I say. Are you writing this down? Just kidding!" Or as another, leaning in toward my half-zipped jacket, asked, "Do you have a tape recorder in there?"

Thus my status as government employee, non-homeschooler, and researcher engendered PATH members' distrust on several levels. The overly suspicious subset was small, however, and most homeschoolers did talk to me, though some more openly than others. Yet with respect to the overall project, these hurdles were fairly easy to overcome because they stemmed from superficial misconceptions about my identity. It was not very hard to convince most mothers that I was not a government researcher hired to check in on homeschooling parents and report their legal violations to the state authorities. I often directly addressed this fear by explaining that I was not interested in evaluating their children's progress, nor even qualified to do so; I was solely interested in their families' experiences homeschooling.

Ongoing Challenges to Rapport: 2001–2002

There were, however, two hurdles that posed bigger rapport problems, which took longer to overcome because they constituted more salient identity differences between many homeschoolers and myself: faith and motherhood. Both of these identities had deep ideological roots that threatened to keep mothers from fully explaining their experiences, and an outsider from fully understanding their perspectives.

I found it difficult to communicate comfortably with homeschoolers of devout faith, especially evangelical Christians, because I have never had a religious affiliation and, when I began the research in 2001, had only scant exposure to anyone who openly espoused the tenets of evangelical Christianity. I grew up in a nonreligious family, in an area of the country where mainstream Protestantism, Catholicism, and Judaism were the most prevalent faiths. But most of the "religious" people I knew were either very private about their beliefs or very lax in their practices. As a result, I knew very little about the Bible beyond that which is integrated into secular culture. For example, I knew that "let there be light" is a phrase that comes from the Bible (I even knew it was from the first book), and I was familiar with the most well-known parables, but my knowledge of the Christian faith was limited. Furthermore, I felt self-conscious about my ignorance and worried that I would offend my subjects by asking the wrong questions. It took months, for example, for me to understand what, exactly, homeschoolers meant when they talked about hearing "God's call." I finally got up the courage to ask Leanna Livingston during her interview. She could "not describe it in great detail," but then laughed and explained, "It's not hearing God's voice or anything like that, saying, 'Homeschool!' It's just looking at all the factors and all the experiences that we've had and just . . . feeling peace about that." On another occasion I compared Catholic Gretchen Forrester's homeschooling approach to that of "Christian homeschoolers." She sounded offended when she interrupted me to exclaim, "Catholics are Christian!" This type of reaction made me more tentative to ask mothers about faith.

I was also limited by my lack of knowledge of the biblical verses homeschoolers used as shorthand in the subculture. For example, one mother I interviewed was wearing a T-shirt that said, "John 3:16" on the front and "Heaven, yes! Hell, no!" on the back. I later googled the chapter and verse and found that it refers to the following: "For God so loved the world that he gave his only begotten Son that whosoever believeth in him should not perish but have everlasting life." I also discovered that this is one of the most well-known quotes from the Bible. Another example occurred in an interview with an evangelical mother who, in trying to make her point, asked me, "You know how the Bible calls [children] arrows that you shoot?" I typically treated those types of questions as rhetorical, so the speaker continued, and I avoided having to admit my ignorance. But on this occasion she waited for my answer, which was no, and it disrupted our rapport, not only because she had to backtrack and explain but also because it demonstrated that we were not on the same ideological page; it emphasized our difference.[11]

Despite these occasional lapses in rapport, homeschoolers overall were very patient with me and graciously indulged my ignorance (although two interviewees did "want to let [me] know that Jesus desires a personal relationship with [me]"). Eventually I caught up and understood enough of the evangelical discourse to gain a deep comprehension of what mothers were telling me, and, just as important, enough for devout mothers to feel as though I thoroughly understood them.

The second ongoing challenge to rapport at the beginning of the research was my status as a nonmother. As my undergraduate research assistants and I asked homeschoolers questions about their families and themselves, they sometimes gave up trying to explain and told us that we would never understand until we were mothers. (In chapter 2, I will explore how these incidents revealed some features of the ideology of intensive mothering, but for now I focus on the methodological consequences.) This was a frustrating development because it kept some mothers from explaining their experiences to us. Imagine trying to gain a deep understanding of people in a particular group, only to have them claim that their life experiences are so radically different from yours that they completely defy understanding; you *can't* know without experiencing it yourself. It is every field researcher's epistemological nightmare.

Fortunately, the majority of mothers did not revert to this stance, and even most of those who did so obliged us by elaborating when we probed further. When mothers did play the you're-not-a-mother card, my research assistants and I reacted either opportunistically by admitting our ignorance and asking them, the experts, for clarification or by drawing on a similar caregiving identity (older sister, aunt, day care worker), which we hoped might be similar enough to preserve rapport.[12] In the end, I failed to develop sufficient rapport with only one mother, Barbara Roberto, who appeared so reluctant to expound on some of her answers that it resulted in several awkward interview moments (as I will detail in chapter 2).

Gathering and Analyzing Data

For the first two years of this eight-year project, I took detailed fieldnotes of the monthly PATH meetings, the content of members' postings in the email listserv, fourteen presentations at three statewide homeschooling conventions, and numerous informal conversations with homeschooling mothers. At first my notes were quite extensive, since so much was new to me, but as

I developed more familiarity with the subculture, the issues mothers faced, and the rationales for homeschooling, the number of pages I wrote each time dwindled.[13] I also cast a wider net to supplement the data I was collecting in Cedar County. I visited dozens of homeschooling websites, took notes from tape-recorded conference presentations I had not attended, read the two most prominent homeschooling magazines, and collected any news reports I came across that featured homeschoolers. These more global data were integral to my research because they demonstrated the continuity across populations. Homeschoolers all over the United States talked about the same issues that PATH members did—concrete issues such as the stigma of homeschooling and the domestic burden it imposed, as well as more abstract issues, such as motherhood, emotions, and time. In the first year, these became my "sensitizing concepts"[14] around which I focused my observations and developed interview questions.

The twenty-four in-depth interviews in 2002, which ranged from 50 to 140 minutes, provided me with "thick description"[15] of the homeschooling experience. After each interview, I analyzed the data in conjunction with my written observations, and soon patterns emerged around salient topics, such as mothers' identities, emotions, and their lack of personal time. I kept these concepts in mind, refined my interview questions, and continued interviewing, further probing homeschoolers to flesh out the richness and intricacy of the experience. Along the way I formulated tentative theories to explain the patterns. Some new data supported my developing analysis, but when they refuted it, I revised my conceptual framework accordingly. This method of data gathering and analysis was progressive, dialectical, and interactive, a process that aligns with Glaser and Strauss's model of grounded theory.[16] The interviews eventually yielded "diminishing returns";[17] no new patterns emerged, which is a stage in data analysis Glaser and Strauss term "theoretical saturation." After twenty-four interviews I concentrated on analysis, though I continued to attend the occasional PATH meeting or other homeschooling event to reconfirm the patterns that were emerging from my analysis.

The Follow-Up Interviews: 2008–2009

Over the next six years I focused less on other people's families and more on my own. I had two children, and during these early childhood years, I often reflected on what my interviewees had told me about mothering and homeschooling. I thought about their parenting philosophies, their maternal emotions, how motherhood affected their children's education, and, of course, how I would never fully understand their experiences until I was a mother myself. These matters became especially intriguing as my oldest approached school age. In 2008, when my own children were five and two, I decided to check in with as many of my original interviewees as possible, and over the next year I emailed and called them to request follow-up interviews. I wanted to see what had changed in the six to seven years since I had talked to them.

I contacted sixteen of the original twenty-four mothers, and they all readily agreed to be reinterviewed. I met twelve of them in person for the follow-ups, and I interviewed the remaining four over the phone because of scheduling or geographic limitations (two had moved out of state). I also distributed a short survey at the end of the interview in an attempt to collect more precise demographic information on their age, education levels, and income. Although I collected this information for fifteen of the sixteen mothers I reinterviewed, I still lack some of these data for the other eight mothers from my original sample of twenty-four.

I did not follow up with the other eight mothers for a variety of reasons: four had moved, and I was unable to find updated contact information for them; two did not respond to my emails; one tried to fit me into her schedule several times but repeatedly had to cancel; and I chose not to recontact the remaining mother, Barbara Roberto, because of the questionable rapport I had had with her the first time around. The sixteen follow-up interviews were incredibly valuable because they allowed me to trace mothers' experiences over time and hear homeschoolers' stories from a different perspective: I was a mother myself by then.

Relating to Mothers: Time and Emotions in the Field

Because field research focuses on how people construct and act on meaning, we, as researchers, cannot be completely objective and removed from the social world we are studying. We have to interact with our subjects to gain an in-depth understanding of their experiences, and sometimes we choose to participate in the setting to deepen our appreciation of it. Our own skills, knowledge, comfort level with the activity, and demographic characteristics greatly influence the level at which we can operate in the social setting and the role we take, from observer to participant, with regard to the activity.[18] Field researchers do not strive for sterile objectivity for fear of "contaminating" the data, but rather consider carefully how our role in the setting influences the information we are collecting. For instance, taking a distant, peripheral role might help a researcher gain objectivity, but taking a closer, more active role might help the researcher gain a deeper understanding of the meanings within the subculture.[19] There are advantages and disadvantages to any role a field researcher takes, and this is worth discussing because it provides a context for understanding the researcher's relationship to both the subjects and the activity under investigation. My research demonstrates this phenomenon vividly, because becoming a mother deepened my understanding of homeschooling motherhood.

When I had children, I read several books on child-rearing philosophies and later developed friendships with other mothers. I paid more attention to messages in the culture about motherhood because they directly affected me and related to my experiences. The decisions I made about my children's activities, diet, health, and education were momentous ones that I felt, as many mothers do, could have great impact on my children over time.[20] Unlike most mothers, however, I also spent a great deal of time thinking about the ideology of intensive mothering and critically analyzing my experiences. Though becoming a mother was not necessary to understanding homeschooling mothers' experiences, it did enhance it by allowing me to cognitively understand the experience. It moved me from a "peripheral membership role" to an "active membership role,"[21] at least when interacting with homeschoolers as *mothers*, because I was doing many of the activities they had done with their children and was able to relate to their experiences. I remained in the peripheral role, however, with regard to homeschooling because I did not homeschool my own children, and I could not completely relate to their educational experiences.

Becoming a mother did help me experience firsthand the emotional and temporal aspects of motherhood, which increased my affiliation with homeschoolers in some ways but distanced me from them in others. On the one hand, I understood homeschooling mothers better because I related to their intense love for their children, their fears that time was slipping by, and their frustration at the domestic burden motherhood engendered. When mothers and I talked about these topics in the 2008–9 interviews, I contributed my own experiences, rephrased their explanations in ways that made sense to them, and asked relevant follow-up questions that enhanced our communication and rapport. Being a mother was a great asset to the research, probably even more so than if I were a father.[22]

On the other hand, being a mother was difficult on a personal level because spending so much time with intensive mothers occasionally made me feel like a bad mother. For example, at the end of their interviews several mothers asked me whether I was planning to homeschool my own children. I had just spent several hours talking with them about the benefits of homeschooling and the ways they believed it helped them be the best mothers they could be. Yet the instant I declared my intent to send my children to public school, I was convinced I heard disapproval in their voices. Though they always responded with statements such as, "Well, it's not for everybody," or "You have to do what's right for your family," I was nevertheless self-conscious because I felt like I was rejecting their version of good mothering.

The same thing happened when homeschooling mothers found out my children were in day care—and not even at a private home but at a center. I knew from our conversations that they would never have felt like good mothers had they sent their children to day care, but I did. (Of course we did not discuss our different mothering philosophies, but respectfully acknowledged each other's.) I felt that day care provided academic and social advantages for my children that I, personally, did not think I could provide them at home. Day care advantaged me as well, not only giving me peace of mind while I was at work but also effectively socializing me to middle-class mothering norms. For example, I learned to use phrases like "that's not a good choice" to reprimand children for doing something wrong, and "tell so-and-so what you would like to happen next time" to help kids work through peer conflicts themselves. On a cognitive level, I knew that day care was right for me, just as my subjects felt homeschooling was for them. However, the nature of intensive mothering forces mothers to doubt their choices, so despite all the wonderful things I felt my day care provided for my children and me, I still felt some guilt for not "being there" with them for most of the workday.

These feelings were not limited to conducting interviews but also cropped up at other times. For example, occasionally I would feel a wave of guilt when I was at work, alone in my office, writing up my research about good mothering, while "strangers" were "raising my children" in day care. The interview data told me my kids were growing up and I was "missing it"; I would never get that time back. I also wrote about these feelings in my fieldnotes. At times I could not help buying into the ideology of intensive mothering, as this excerpt illustrates:

> Today [my husband] and I had a scheduling mix-up and I had to bring the kids [then 6 and 3 years old] to Tracy's follow-up interview at [the coffeehouse]. We arrived early, and I set them up at the next table with a DVD player, complete with headphones, hot chocolate, and some cookies. When Tracy arrived, she was excited to meet my kids and tried to engage them in conversation, but of course they were entranced in their video, so they just stared at her blankly, then turned their attention back to *101 Dalmatians*. I felt like such a bad mom. She and I then proceeded to talk for an hour and a half about good mothering. The irony was tough to handle!

At other times, I recorded my anger and resentment over feeling judged by this group of intensive mothers. I attended PATH meetings much less often after having my children, but when they were six and three, I went to a presentation by a PATH family who had managed to homeschool through all sorts of family challenges, such as severe financial and medical problems. I recorded the following in my fieldnotes:

> [The presenter] wanted to make another, unrelated, statement at the close of the presentation and Q&A. She said she wanted to "challenge" parents to be careful of TV, computers, and video games. Watching the same DVD over again—"that's not a rich environment!" This really made me bristle, probably because my kids don't mind watching the same thing more than once and because it helps me get things done around the house when they're watching TV. It's not like they watch a lot of TV, but apparently, this is a prime example of horrible parenting, and my kids will lose all of their intellectual capability. It really pissed me off because this was a presentation on homeschooling—what makes these people think they should be in the position to "challenge" us to "improve" our parenting? So parents have to provide a "rich environment," which, according to them, means never exposing your kids to the same thing twice, every second of every day? That's ridiculous.

Granted, my reaction was more than a tad defensive. But these feelings did provide me with insight into the culture of intensive mothering and the great power it exerts over women's lives and mothers' identities.[23] These kinds of experiences helped me understand that emotions interweave themselves into our maternal identities in multifaceted ways.

Despite the degree to which strong emotions are associated with intensive mothering, they have received virtually no sociological attention *as emotions*. Uncovering this relationship will enhance our understanding of both homeschooling and mothering more broadly. The next part of this book lays the groundwork for analyzing homeschooling mothers' experiences through the lens of what scholars have termed "emotional culture."

PART I

The Emotional Culture of Good Mothering

There is a substantial body of research covering many aspects of mothering in the contemporary United States. Some of the main findings with regard to mothers' emotions are important to lay out now, since they provide a framework to understand homeschoolers' experiences and their identities as mothers.

To trace the many contours of the mothering experience, we must give systematic attention to mothers' emotions, both the emotions we think good mothers should feel and those they actually do. A useful concept for understanding these socially constructed ideas is "emotional culture," which refers to a shared set of beliefs about emotions, such as which emotions are valuable, for whom, and how they should be interpreted, acted on, and expressed.[1] Being socialized to a particular emotional culture (or subculture) influences not only the emotions people feel and how they understand them but also how they see themselves, interact with others, and interpret competing emotional ideologies. Different social groups construct different emotional cultures; research has shown that beliefs about emotions may vary by race, gender, occupation, or a host of other identity categories.[2] The particular constellation of emotional beliefs varies, by definition, from one emotional culture to the next. From this perspective, we can see that emotions (like our idea of good mothering) are socially constructed: we give meaning to particular emotions, and then we act on those meanings as though they are inherently true. Our actions, in turn, produce real consequences in our own and others' lives. In this way, revealing the intricacies of emotional cultures is important to understanding human behavior.

Though emotional cultures are multidimensional, one significant facet is the set of norms about experiencing and expressing particular emotions. Sociologist Arlie Hochschild called these "feeling rules" and "display rules" and showed that there are many ways people try to bring their feelings and expressions in line with expectations.[3] She called this process "emotion management" or "emotion work." The homeschoolers I studied talked a great deal about how they tried to manage particular emotions they found troubling. They experienced what sociologist Peggy Thoits called "emotional deviance," which she defined as "experiences or displays of affect that differ in quality or degree from what is expected."[4] Deviant emotions can be the "wrong" feelings as well as too much or not enough of the "right" feelings, but they are always relative, necessarily defined against the backdrop of a particular emotional culture and the rules it embraces. Thus, examining the ways homeschooling mothers evaluated and managed their feelings reveals how they defined inappropriate and, by extension, appropriate feelings for homeschoolers.

As I explored homeschoolers' emotional culture, I saw that it borrowed a great deal from contemporary definitions of intensive mothering. Surprisingly little research has specifically investigated the emotional culture of motherhood, despite cultural stereotypes of women as emotional and the prevalence of emotion norms that are often implicated in the social construction of good mothering.[5] For example, Hays's content analysis of child-rearing manuals revealed that good mothers "instinctively" lavish unconditional love upon their children and prioritize the intense, "natural" emotional bond they share with them,[6] hence the norm that child rearing be "emotionally absorbing." Other research has highlighted the widespread conviction that the emotional bond mothers feel with their children is innate, ubiquitous, and unparalleled. Yet despite the prevalence of emotional assumptions about motherhood, very few studies on mothering have made emotions a central feature of analysis.[7] Emotions are important links to identity because people do not simply feel and manage emotions, they feel and manage "self-in-emotion."[8] Therefore, if we want to understand how mothers construct their identities, we must study their emotional culture.

Though social scientists have not explicitly addressed the emotional culture of intensive mothering, many researchers have uncovered some emotional elements of the mothering experience in the process of studying other aspects of women's lives. One such example is the work-family quandary, which affects most mothers in the contemporary United States. Much of this research focuses on the difficult decisions middle-class mothers make with respect to paid work and family. The studies in this vein highlight, but do not address theoretically, the emotional turmoil mothers experience around their choice to pursue a career (often seen as honoring their own identities) or stay home with their children (often seen as fulfilling their maternal duty).[9] Middle-class mothers seriously question the self-abnegation that ideal motherhood prescribes yet concurrently experience negative emotions, such as intense guilt, for considering meeting some of their own needs before their children's.[10] Working-class mothers feel some of the same pressures their middle-class counterparts do, despite not having the choice to stay home. Most mothers, regardless of social class, feel guilty, selfish, and anxious about possibly failing to raise their children the way good mothers should.[11] It is clear that emotional expectations and the work mothers do to bring their feelings into line with them are central components in contemporary experiences of intensive mothering, and they deserve closer theoretical attention.

This part confronts homeschoolers' emotions directly to shed light not only on their own emotional subculture but also on the larger emotional culture of intensive mothering. Chapter 2 begins by detailing how the mothers in my study decided to homeschool. I present a dichotomy of what I call "first-choicers," or those who wanted to homeschool first and foremost, and "second-choicers," or those who homeschooled because their preferred educational options were out of reach. The two groups relied a great deal on their emotions, which drove them into homeschooling, affected their subsequent experiences over time (which I will detail later in the book), and ultimately shaped their identities as good mothers. Homeschoolers also had to overcome criticism from outsiders; thus chapter 3 shows how they defended their maternal identities by mining the discourse of good mothering to justify their feelings, a finding that suggests emotions play a crucial yet heretofore unexamined role in our cultural conceptions of good mothering.

2

Coming to a Decision

First- and Second-Choice Homeschoolers

The vast majority of homeschoolers are stay-at-home mothers in two-parent, heterosexual families with a husband supporting the family in the paid labor force. That is not to say that homeschooling is impossible when a mother works, when a father is in charge of the children's education, or in single-parent families—indeed, homeschooling happens in all types of family configurations—but because homeschooling takes an extraordinary amount of time and attention, it is much easier to accomplish when the labor is divided so that one parent can be devoted to it full-time. Because mothers are much more likely than fathers to leave the paid labor force to care for young children, this gendered family arrangement is extremely common among homeschooling families, both nationally and in the families I interviewed.[1] As I asked mothers about their reasons for homeschooling, it became clear that their status as stay-at-home mothers was an important factor. This chapter uncovers how mothers' feelings about staying at home influenced their decision to homeschool their children.

Of the twenty-four mothers I interviewed, all but one had wanted to stay at home full-time with their preschool-age children (although not all had been financially able to do so). Nineteen mothers had stayed out of the paid labor force entirely, or very nearly so, during their children's preschool years; two left the paid labor force after their second child was born (in both cases, the second children were considerably younger—eight and ten years—than the first children, who were already in conventional schools); and two mothers had worked unwillingly in the paid labor force, either part-time or full-time, during their children's preschool years (both in low-income families, neither could afford to stay home).[2] Only one of my interviewees, Emily Ashton, willingly worked part-time in a bookstore while simultaneously attending college and juggling day care during her children's preschool years.

Though the research on homeschooling is scant, parents' reasons for choosing it are easily the most commonly studied topic,[3] and over the years several studies—mostly those that allow homeschoolers to express themselves in their own words—have identified five main motivational categories. The "ideologues" homeschool for religious reasons: they oppose the public schools' secular orientation and believe it is their family's right, not the state's, to take charge of their children's education.[4] The "pedagogues" homeschool for academic reasons, though some portion are highly religious as well. They believe the public schools are too inept to teach their children, in some cases, but certainly not all, because their children have special needs or gifts. Homeschoolers who are motivated by "socio-relational" reasons fear negative peer influence in public schools and want to increase their family's unity; these homeschoolers are also highly likely to be religious. "New Age" homeschoolers, the smallest proportion, want to reserve the right to teach their children a globally focused worldview that emphasizes the interrelatedness of all life. Recently, a study of black homeschoolers uncovered the fifth motivational category, which the researchers called "ethnological," reflecting parents' concern about the negative racial environment in conventional schools.[5]

Despite this accepted typology of homeschooling motivations, it is important to keep in mind that some subsequent research—particularly that which quantifies motivations into these existing categories—has severe limitations. One is that people's motivations can be considerably complex; some homeschooling research reflects this complexity, showing that most parents cite several motivations, which overlap at any one time as well as rise and fall in importance over their careers.[6] These overlapping and changing motivations are difficult to capture in a survey respondent's fixed-choice answers. To complicate matters further, a large subset of the research on homeschoolers' motivations has attempted to assess the influence of faith—an infinitely complex concept, which is extremely difficult, if not impossible, to quantify.

(For example, some studies claim that 25 percent of homeschoolers are motivated by faith, while others claim as many as 88 percent.) As such, much of the research on homeschoolers' motivations, especially that which quantifies the effect of evangelical Christianity, must be read critically and interpreted cautiously.[7]

Because quantifying parents' motivations through survey research risks significant validity problems, talking to parents in depth is a more accurate way to tease out the complexity of their reasons for homeschooling. When I did so, many parents gave answers that would have classified them into the categories previous research has uncovered, but the stronger patterns that emerged from my data took a different form, revealing a new dimension of mothers' motivations that may further our understanding of the experience: whether homeschooling was their preferred educational choice or an acceptable alternative to some other unavailable option. I call these groups "first-choice" and "second-choice" homeschoolers.

When I asked mothers about their decision to homeschool, they always framed their answers in terms of their mother identities, rather than primarily as Christians or New Agers, for example, and more than anything else, tied their decision in some way to their status as stay-at-home mothers. I categorized nineteen of the twenty-four mothers in my sample as first-choicers because they believed that homeschooling was a logical extension of their commitment to stay at home with their young children, one that fell into place easily because it "felt right," even as their children aged. The remaining five mothers, however, I categorized as second-choicers because they struggled with the pros and cons of extending this stay-at-home commitment beyond their children's preschool years and frequently wished for an acceptable alternative to homeschooling.

When I sorted mothers by first- and second-choice motivations, I found that these groupings disrupted the previous categories that researchers have identified. For example, many first-choice homeschoolers were ideologues, but I also found them among the second-choicers, who would have preferred to send their children to private Christian school but could not afford the tuition. Likewise, I found some pedagogues who were first-choicers, and others who thought their children's educational needs would be better served in the right school setting. Thus, the distinction between ideologues and pedagogues (or other categories, for that matter) did not hold across my first-choice/second-choice dichotomy. My conceptualization, however, does not invalidate previous categories, but rather demonstrates that alternative classification systems can continue to ferret out the complexity of mothers' motivations to homeschool.

My data suggest that, for many mothers, the decision to homeschool was emotionally entwined with the decision to be a stay-at-home mother. Was staying at home something mothers found rewarding or onerous? Did it build fulfillment or resentment? These emotional conflicts are at the heart of the intensive mothering experience, yet the emotions themselves have yet to take center stage analytically.[8] Revealing this emotional component in homeschoolers' motivations is important because it has significant consequences for mothers' experiences, satisfaction, and identities throughout their homeschooling careers. Later in the book, I will examine how various aspects of homeschooling affected mothers' emotions, but in this chapter, I begin by explaining how mothers' feelings about staying at home influenced their decision to homeschool their children.

First-Choice Homeschoolers: Extending the Stay-at-Home Commitment

First-choice homeschoolers, who rarely, if ever, sought other educational options, talked a great deal about how their powerful feelings for their children pulled them to stay at home full-time, rather than enter or return to the paid labor force. They loved being stay-at-home mothers and considered homeschooling the perfect way to continue being home with their children. However, first-choicers tied their homeschooling decision to stay-at-home motherhood in two different ways. Some had emotional epiphanies upon becoming mothers, which made their decision to stay at home full-time a monumental one; after that, the choice to homeschool was trivial. For other first-choicers, staying at home was a given; the difficult decision came later, when they considered homeschooling.[9]

The Emotional Epiphany of Motherhood and the Logic of Homeschooling

When I asked mothers why they homeschooled, some first-choicers answered by explaining why they stayed out of the paid labor force. Although most did eventually get around to discussing their decision to homeschool, the time they spent recounting their choice to stay at home with their babies indicated that for them, this was an important factor in their decision to homeschool later.

This group of first-choicers talked passionately about the sudden insights they had had upon becoming mothers, which I have called "emotional epiphanies"; the experience of having a child unexpectedly and irreversibly changed them emotionally. These mothers had planned to return to work after some predetermined childbirth leave, but the arrival of their first baby ignited such surprisingly intense feelings that they suddenly felt being apart from the child was unacceptable.[10] These feelings compelled them to rearrange their priorities, quit work, and stay home permanently. Sociologist Chris Bobel found a similar dynamic among the "natural mothers" she studied, who related "shock-shift stories": mothers were shocked by the intensity of feelings they had toward their new babies, and they subsequently "shift[ed] their perspective . . . and restructure[d] their lives."[11] This suggests, as my data do, that mothers often radically recalibrate their emotions in response to their intense attachment to their new babies.

In a few cases, the mothers I talked to had to return to work for some period of time, and the daily separation from their babies was agonizing. For example, Judith Munson, a white, middle-class mother of two college-age children answered the question "What led you to homeschooling?" as she sat on a panel at a statewide homeschooling convention:

> What led me to homeschooling? I had a career that I really enjoyed and was very committed to it, and [my husband and I] had determined that we were going to have children, but it was going to be way down the road. So I enjoyed my job, and it was going very well. And when we decided to begin our family, and our son was born, I didn't anticipate the change that he would bring into my life. So immediately after he was born I knew that I could no longer commit to what I was doing in the workplace. I needed to make a shift. I know a lot of women that can do both, and I'm not one of them—who could do a full-time job and parent. I'm just not made that way. So I can recall [being] in the hospital in 1978 when he was born, calling my boss, and . . . saying I'm not coming back. I'm going to do whatever I can to be home. Well, I arranged all my maternity leave, and I stayed with the company . . . so that I could be vested in the retirement plan. And that was for thirteen months, that I went back to work. And in my recollection—in my adulthood—those were the most *horrible* thirteen months of my life. To leave this little boy every day. I mean, my priorities shifted in forty-eight hours.

Judith traced her decision to homeschool all the way back to the powerful emotional tie she felt to her son the moment he was born. It is interesting that, beyond repeating the question, she did not even mention homeschooling in her answer; yet the link was very clear to her—homeschooling was about her "priorities" as a mother. Several homeschoolers I talked to referred to similar emotional epiphanies upon becoming mothers as a backdrop to explaining their decision to homeschool. They experienced an emotional conversion, whereby they suddenly embraced stay-at-home motherhood and rejected working in the paid labor force. Later, these feelings served as the foundation for them to extend their stay-at-home status to homeschool their children.

Cassandra Shudek, a white, middle-class mother of four boys, also described her emotional transformation into stay-at-home motherhood as an unexpected one, which she saw as the result of a difficult birth and a precarious postnatal period:

> [When I was pregnant with my first son], I assumed I would put my kids in day care and go back to work right away. . . . [But] things didn't go as expected with him. I had a midwife, and I was going to have him at home, [but] I ended up being in labor for three days and getting an emergency C-section. And he and I were both very sick. So we spent some time in the hospital, and [even after we were discharged] he had to keep going back to the hospital for the next two weeks. And by the time we were settled and at home, and I was actually able to nurse him, [I said to myself], "I'm never letting go of him again! Because we barely made it through this!" And I thought, "How could I hand him off to somebody else and go back to work? I can't do it." [My husband] and I had to figure out how we were going to do it on one income. At the time it seemed impossible, and I thought, "I'll go crazy being at home with a little baby all day long; I'll just go crazy." But I didn't, and I never went back to work after that and never felt like I wanted to. It's so funny; I was so sure of myself on some things. I have to eat crow a lot.

Cassandra was emotionally pulled to stay at home, and even though she was initially wary about whether she would be fulfilled, she found it quite gratifying and embraced it quickly. This emotional base made it easy for her to choose homeschooling later.

Because these mothers talked about the sudden onset of their maternal feelings, and cast them as unexpectedly coming out of the blue, I have used the term "epiphany" to describe their experiences. However, it is important to look at the context of mothers' feelings. If we accept that emotions are social constructions, we must assume that social factors, such as social class and the cultural meanings behind motherhood and family, contributed to mothers' emotional epiphanies. Put differently, mothers' epiphanies did not appear spontaneously of their own accord but rather were shaped by a complex interplay among the "natural" feelings from the intensely emotional experience of having a child, the gender and mothering ideologies to which they and their husbands subscribed, and the structural constraints, such as finances and family configuration, on them and their families.[12]

Jackie Bell, the African American, middle-class mother of nine- and five-year-old girls, explained her epiphany in less absolute terms, which allows us to uncover some of these complexities. Jackie identified as a first-choice home-schooler but recounted her difficult emotional journey to embracing stay-at-home motherhood, starting her story long before she was even pregnant:

> JACKIE: I was working in [a big city] doing textile trade negotiations—and I liked that job a lot—and so to give that up, for me, was challenging because I always thought I was going to be this career woman. I was going to be, I don't know, a CEO or [*laughs*] you know, president of a corporation. . . . I mean, I was always like, "Oh, yeah, I can't wait until I'm a mom," and [Benny and I] would talk about [whether I would go back to work or stay home with a baby someday]—but I didn't have a real draw to be home until I was pregnant. And then all of a sudden it was like, "Oh, I can't imagine not being with the baby!" I couldn't imagine it! And the pull was really strong for me.
>
> JEN: Did it intensify when she was born?
>
> JACKIE: It really did. And breastfeeding [increased that bond too].

Jackie's description up to this point revealed the epiphany moment that other mothers experienced as well, where she suddenly felt the intense "pull" to be home with the baby. Yet she continued, explaining the conflict she felt over staying home, and in doing so, explained how she "learned" to value the "pull" to be at home:

> But then I found myself *home*, you know . . . and it was an adjustment for me. . . . I hadn't really learned to value the worth of a mother. And I've got to give Benny a lot of credit for this. . . . He would just say, "You know, you're doing an important job," and "Wow, it feels so good to know that, when I'm away at work, that the kids have you here." And over the years, I started to appreciate myself that way, too. And for me, too, the transition of not making a financial income [was hard] and, again, he'd be really supportive. You know, whatever he makes is ours, and he helped me see that I was working too. I was working. And it was a lesson for me to understand that this is as valuable as working outside of the home.

Although Jackie talked about her emotional epiphany for wanting to be with the baby, her emotional transformation into accepting stay-at-home motherhood took longer to complete. She explained that Benny played an integral part in the transformation; through joint emotion work, they helped Jackie embrace the emotional culture of middle-class, stay-at-home mothering.

Benny sat in on my interview with Jackie and explained his take on her transformation, emphasizing its duration by using the word "evolution":

> It was an interesting evolution for me. I remember having the discussions about, "Okay, what do you really want to do after the baby is here? Do you want to take some time off? Do you want to go back to work in six weeks? What is it?" [Jackie had such] ambivalent feelings about it. "Is it important?" or "What am I missing out on? What trade-off have I made?" . . . And it was really clear to me that . . . this is our legacy for the world, just [raising] two great people. So I saw such value in what she was choosing to do. And found that it was lasting and important in ways that what I was doing every day [at my job] wasn't. And then, over time, for Jackie to decide, "Yeah, I want to stay home"—it's been quite an evolution for us to reach where we are now.

Despite Benny's conviction that there was great value in being home with the children, neither Jackie nor Benny mentioned the option of Benny quitting work to be a full-time parent, though when I talked to them in 2002, he had left his paid job and was home pursuing his dream of writing a screenplay. The full-time at-home-parent decision, and the emotional turmoil that accompanied it, was Jackie's, a gendered pattern that other research on mothering has also uncovered. Indeed, sociologist Pamela Stone found that the mothers in her research felt their husbands' support on the surface— "it's your choice"—but they interpreted the subtext of that message as "it's your problem."[13] Assuming that husbands' careers trump wives' forces the "choice"—and its accompanying emotional dilemmas—into women's lives. When mothers have clear emotional "epiphanies" about staying at home with children, these dilemmas are eradicated.

These epiphanies, then, serve an important function in the emotional culture of intensive mothering. For mothers in general, they provide validation that they have made the right decision. Mothers appeal to their "instinct" and "know" that they have made the right choice. Homeschoolers relied on the same feelings when it came time to homeschool their children. Once they had the stay-at-home epiphany, homeschooling was just a logical extension of the important work they were doing as stay-at-home mothers. Thus, an early conversion to the emotional subculture of stay-at-home motherhood gave them the tools they needed later to "know in my heart," as several mothers told me, that homeschooling was the right choice.

The first-choicers who had emotional epiphanies about staying at home with their children often tried to express their particular feelings and explain how motherhood had changed them. These mothers seemed to understand that others might not share their emotional entry into motherhood, perhaps because they were intrigued by their own unexpected emotional shift. They seemed to have thought a lot about it, and they earnestly tried to convey their feelings when I asked. Though they often naturalized these emotions, they did not universalize them; they talked about their feelings as an inherent part of motherhood *for them*. In fact, every mother who related a stay-at-home epiphany to me used the first person in her emotional account, trying hard to explain how "I felt" and how the feelings arose "for me." Yet they still traced their feelings to when their babies arrived, and they experienced the surprising emotional jolt of motherhood.

This is not to say that non-homeschooling mothers never have similar emotional experiences, or that having these emotional experiences necessarily leads to homeschooling. Rather, my data suggest that some homeschoolers' careers may begin with their unexpectedly intense emotional draw to be stay-at-home mothers.

The Emotional Assumptions of Motherhood and the Epiphany of Homeschooling

The other group of first-choicers also talked about the intense emotions of motherhood as the reason they chose, first, to stay at home full-time and, later, to homeschool. Yet this second group differed because the intensity of their maternal feelings did not surprise them. They had "always known" they wanted to be full-time, stay-at-home mothers, thus (if they thought they could manage it financially) they planned in advance to stay at home after the birth of their first child.[14] Stevens's research with homeschooling mothers revealed that the majority of his subjects were predisposed to staying home with children full-time.[15] This was also true for my sample, though recent research has demonstrated that this pattern does not exist for all groups of homeschoolers.[16]

Some of the mothers who were more financially strapped talked about their negative feelings upon returning to their jobs for a short time after their babies were born. At first these mothers' experiences seemed to parallel those of other first-choicers, such as how emotionally difficult it was to leave the baby to go to work. For example, Barbara Roberto was a white, working-class mother of two children who told me she had never wanted to be a working mother. She explained that for financial reasons, she had had to return to work for a short period after the birth of her first child:

> I've always wanted to be a stay-home mom [so once my daughter was born], working wasn't okay; I didn't want to work. [But] I worked for about three, four months after she was born, and I just hated it. I remember once I went for a job interview, and my sister was babysitting, and all I could think about at this interview was my baby at home. And I remember I came home, and I just grabbed her from my sister, and I started to cry.

Given that previous interviewees had told me how surprised they were to discover they suddenly had these intense maternal feelings that pulled them to stay at home, I asked Barbara if her feelings at the job interview took her by surprise. What followed was a very awkward exchange:

> BARBARA: What do you mean "take me by surprise"? When you say that, it's like I didn't have any emotions or something.
> JEN: Like, did you think, "Oh my Gosh, I can't believe I miss her so much?" Or—?
> BARBARA: No. [Pause]. Do you have a family? Do you have children?
> JEN: No. I don't have kids.
> BARBARA: It's very hard to—it's one of those things you have to experience to know how emotional you'll get attached to this child. And it's not just through birth or biological, it's through adoption or whatever. It's—I don't know. I don't know. It's another one of your family members that you really love. It's just—you get emotionally attached. It's just part of life; it's the way life is supposed to be. It's hard to explain how that love for your child is, and how you would give anything for them. It's very, very hard unless you know.

Like the other group of first-choice homeschoolers, these mothers attributed their choice to stay at home to the intense emotions of motherhood. Unlike the others, however, they were not surprised that they felt this way and, furthermore, seemed unable (and in some cases unwilling) to elaborate on their emotions. They assumed that all mothers feel intense and immediate emotional attachment to their children, and this belief was so deeply embedded in these homeschoolers' understandings of motherhood that asking them to trace the source of their feelings did not make sense.[17] It was nature; it was biology; it was motherhood. Indeed, I offended Barbara when I asked if her intense attachment took her by surprise, as though I were suggesting she was an emotionally unfit mother who did not have the "normal" emotional response to her child. She deduced that my "inappropriate" questions stemmed from ignorance; I didn't know because I wasn't a mother.

Barbara was not the only mother to deflect questions about where these feelings came from or whether they had always been there (though she was definitely the most insulted). For these first-choicers, the particular feelings and their intensity were so hard to put into words that they often concluded that the emotional experience of motherhood was ineffable.[18] Although a few mothers tried to explain, they gave up quickly, telling me that only when I became a mother would I understand. One mother told me that having a child is "like having your heart walking outside of your body. It's a really different sort of feeling. I don't know what else to say. You're not a mom yet, so you don't understand." And another waved me off with a smile after a brief attempt to explain: "You'll see. It's not something you can explain to someone who hasn't been through it. There's no other way to know."

These mothers not only believed that their intense feelings of attachment were naturally part of motherhood, but they also universalized them to all mothers. Sociologist Mary Blair-Loy has noted that because the "family devotion schema" is naturalized in U.S. culture, it yields such power that we can "barely imagine an alternative," and it "becomes the default master script" in women's lives.[19] Unlike the mothers in the first group whose epiphanies ushered them into one emotional reality of motherhood ("I felt so strongly"), these mothers used the second person to talk about *the* emotional reality of motherhood ("*you* feel so strongly"). Due to this emotional absolutism, these mothers held more rigid and less emotionally complex definitions of motherhood than those who had been surprised by their feelings upon becoming mothers.

Because all the mothers in this group knew in advance that they would want to stay at home with their preschool-age children, their intense emotional attachment was expected, and staying at home was a given, provided finances allowed. There was no decision to be made. Therefore, when I asked them why they decided to homeschool, they addressed the question directly (as opposed to the previous group of first-choice mothers, who recounted their decision to stay at home). These first-choicers explained that as their children approached school age, homeschooling became a momentous decision, fraught with substantial deliberation. Like the first-choicers in the previous group, these mothers' decisions took the form of emotional epiphanies, though in contrast, they occurred later on the mothering time line and were about homeschooling rather than about staying at home with preschoolers.[20]

Many of these mothers had epiphanies because they asked for them. Several told me that they were called by God to homeschool their children after "praying about it." Here again the epiphany played an important role in the emotional culture of mothering—it relieved mothers' uncertainty and instilled a sense of confidence that they were doing the right thing for their children. Angela Welch, a middle-class, African American mother of four, and a session panelist at a homeschooling convention, explained her moment of clarity:

> Thirteen years ago on a Sunday night I was sitting there in church, and . . . the message that night was, "What does God want you to do?" And I sat there pretty arrogant, when I think back on it. I was thinking, "Well, I'm married, I think I'm a good wife, and I am a stay-at-home mom. So what *else* could he want me to do?" [*audience laughs*]. So I thought, "I'm there!" But the question never did leave me. It stayed in my heart. What does God want me to do? And as I pondered that, I had no peace, I kept pondering. . . . And [not long after] I heard these two moms talking about homeschooling, [and] I had such a burst of enthusiasm within me! I stopped them, I said, "How can you do that? How do you get involved?" . . . I tell you, there are days when I cry; there are days when I think, "What am I doing? Did I really hear from God or what?" But I keep going. . . . My son—he's fourteen now—has never been to school, and he thinks he's missing something . . . so he'll say, "Mama, can I go to school?" And I say "Yes! When God releases me, you can go!" [*audience erupts in laughter*]. Every so often he'll say, "Did he release you yet?" [*more laughs*]. I'll say, "Not yet! Not yet!" And I'm hoping God doesn't release me—that we'll go all the way.

Angela's story is typical of this group of first-choice homeschoolers. She knew that her status as a stay-at-home mother was what God wanted—that was a given—but her revelation came later, when he led her to homeschooling.[21]

Other first-choicers explained that God revealed homeschooling to them as part of a larger plan for their families. In 1978, Sabrina Hernandez was a twenty-seven-year-old mother of three boys when she and her husband became born-again Christians (a conversion I detailed in the introduction). Over the next few years, her sons attended both private Christian and public schools, but all the while "God was working with my own heart." Recall that Sabrina and her husband felt that God wanted them "to trust him" with their children, so they gave up birth control, had nine more children (for a total of twelve), and homeschooled all but the oldest. By the time I talked to her in 2008, Sabrina had been homeschooling for twenty-three years and still was not finished with her two youngest. She explained that she homeschooled because she "really felt a calling from God" and that her "focus has been mostly in raising up our children to serve God."

Not all mothers asked for God's guidance, so the call to homeschool was unexpected for some. Valerie Scott, who identified as evangelical Christian, explained her epiphany. She knew she was going to homeschool the first time she heard about it. It was in the early 1980s, and conservative Christian James Dobson had a guest on his radio show:

> [My husband and I were] listening to the radio station, and Dr. Raymond Moore came on, and he was talking about homeschooling. And we listened to it, and we knew right then and there—he and I both—that's what we're going to do because we could not think of any—how can you *not* [homeschool]? What else would we do? I mean, we never even thought of homeschooling because we'd never heard of it. We really felt called to do it. I mean, we really felt like the Lord wants it.

It is interesting that fifteen of the twenty-four mothers I talked to fell into this subset of first-choicers, and all of them identified as Christian (thirteen evangelical, two Catholic). It is likely that these mothers' identification with Christianity (especially evangelical) gave them more traditional ideas about gender; therefore it makes sense that they were more likely to have "always known" that they wanted to stay home with their children.[22] However, it is important to note that there were some Christian mothers in my sample who fell into the previous first-choice category, and some Christians for whom homeschooling was second choice.[23] Thus, it seems that Christian gender ideology, while probably an important factor, was not the sole influence on the mothers' decision to homeschool.

In addition, the mothers in this group—those who had always wanted to stay at home but had their epiphanies to homeschool as their children got closer to school age—were the only ones who talked about being called by God to homeschool. Seven of the fifteen in this category (first-choicers who had always wanted to stay home) explicitly mentioned a call from God. Evangelical mothers in other categories did not seem as likely to understand their entry into homeschooling as a call from God (or at least none of them discussed it with me). Furthermore, neither of the two mothers who had been financially unable to stay out of the workforce full-time—both evangelical Christians—mentioned their call from God.

This pattern suggests that God's will was an explanation that best fit the experiences of homeschoolers who could achieve it: those who had always wanted to be stay-at-home mothers and who were financially able to do so. Though not every mother who fit these two criteria used God's call as a rationale for homeschooling, the only ones who did were traditionally minded, middle-class Christians. This divine-call template simply did not fit the experiences of other first-choicers, who had originally wanted to return to work, the second-choicers, who struggled with their status as stay-at-home mothers (as I will discuss momentarily), and working-class first-choicers, who had not been financially able to stay at home full-time. It seemed that God called only those who held certain beliefs about motherhood and could afford to act on them.

Second Choice Homeschoolers: Struggling with the Stay-at-Home Commitment

Homeschooling was second choice for five of the twenty-four mothers in my sample, all of whom expressed real difficulty with the idea of staying at home with their school-age children. Four women in this group had chosen to be stay-at-home mothers for at least one child's preschool years, but all had planned to send their children to conventional schools at age five (some did so) and return to the workforce. However, at some point their conventional-school choice became unavailable, and they chose homeschooling as an alternative, which meant extending their commitment to stay at home with their children. The adjustment was hard on them, and they often talked about it at length. In contrast to first-choicers, who fully embraced stay-at-home motherhood, second-choice homeschoolers struggled with equating the intense love they had for their children with their commitment to stay at home indefinitely, so their emotions were often contradictory and problematic.[24] Furthermore, second-choicers did not explain their reasons for homeschooling with the overwhelming and "natural" emotions of motherhood, as first-choicers did. Of course, this does not mean that second-choicers did not feel these overwhelming emotions—in fact, it was clear to me that all the mothers I interviewed felt deep love for their children. Second-choice homeschoolers, however, did not see homeschooling as love's logical manifestation, or as the only way to demonstrate their identities as mothers. Therefore, it was harder for second-choicers to come to grips with extending the stay-at-home commitment.[25]

Second-choicers explained their decision to homeschool in two main ways, despite feeling it was not ideal. Three mothers resorted to homeschooling because their children were not thriving in their conventional schools but the alternatives were out of reach, and two felt pressured by their husbands to embrace the extended, homeschooling version of stay-at-home motherhood.

The Child's Progress

Three second-choicers homeschooled because they wanted a particular educational experience that would fit their children's individual needs, but their preferred conventional options were not available. Although some first-choicers arrived at homeschooling through similar paths, they soon discovered homeschooling was ideal, and they embraced it. Second-choicers differed, however, in that they remained somewhat dissatisfied with homeschooling, verbalized their dissatisfaction, and continued to consider alternatives that might meet their children's needs. For example, Darlene Rooney-Henkel was a forty-five-year-old white mother of two children: an eight-year-old daughter who attended public school and an eleven-year-old son, Paul, whom she homeschooled because his Asperger's syndrome prevented him from succeeding in a conventional classroom. Paul had attended first grade in 1996, and although he was gifted academically, he "would fall apart by one o'clock" because the classroom was too structured and the activity was overstimulating. Darlene pulled him out of first grade and homeschooled him until fourth grade, when (in 1999) she tried again to put him in public school and procure an individualized education program (IEP) for him. However, the school district was unfamiliar with his disorder (first recognized in the *DSM-IV* in 1994), and the school testing failed to qualify him for an IEP. Darlene told me that when she met with the school counselor,

> he apologized and said, "I feel like we've failed your son. He's one of those who are falling through the cracks. Gifted, but can't be in a gifted program because he has certain processing problems so he can't work independently, but yet doesn't qualify for the special-needs IEP, because he's gifted."

Darlene was frustrated because she felt Paul needed practice socializing with other children (impaired social skills were one way his Asperger's manifested itself). Furthermore, she wanted to enter the workforce to contribute to the family income and pursue a career that she was passionate about. She did not want to continue to stay at home full-time but felt that her son's needs warranted homeschooling him.

Another mother, who sat on a panel at an annual convention, explained that she homeschooled her son because he had developed learning disabilities from chemotherapy treatments to his brain when he was an infant. She said that, as he began to develop, she could see he had "great disparities" in his abilities:

> He had some things he could do better than most kids his age. He had an unbelievable memory. . . . At age six he was using words like "turbulence" and "cumbersome." . . . But at the same time he couldn't—and still can't at age twenty—tell the difference between a nickel and a penny. And so with these disparities in his ability, I knew that he would never survive in a regular classroom, and special ed would destroy him. And so I didn't see that I had any other option but to homeschool.

Because these second-choicers' motivations revolved around the individual child's needs, they often sent their other children to conventional school. In contrast, all the first-choicers I talked to homeschooled all their children who were still school-age because they defined homeschooling as something that was in the best interests of the whole family; it allowed them to remain stay-at-home mothers and wives (I will return to this issue in chapter 6).

Patricia Tomlinson, the white, forty-one-year-old mother I profiled in the introduction, had two boys, ages fourteen and five when I talked to her in 2002. Patricia was also a second-choice homeschooler. Recall that a few months before her second son was born, she decided to leave her job as a teacher and homeschool her older son (then age nine) who had been attending a private school. Although Patricia cited numerous reasons for choosing to homeschool, the most important stemmed from the school's inability to accommodate her son's very high academic capability. Although he was "bumped up a couple of grades," this accommodation had "created a little damage," affecting him physically, socially, and academically. Being in a class with older children had physical consequences:

> He was kind of like a little mascot. Because the middle school kids thought he was really cute—you know like a little professor-type or something— and they physically poked him. I mean, physically would kind of maul him. I would take this kid's clothes off every night and see his body covered with little pokey bruises. And it got really bad actually; it got to the point where he developed a systemic staph infection. All these little networks of bruises and scrapes just add up—he got seriously sick. From the poking.

And social concerns kept her son from challenging himself academically:

Because my son is highly capable, he did this thing in school where, even though he was younger than everybody, he would kind of look to his right and look to his left and figure that if the [older] kids didn't know [the answer]—well, he didn't want to stand out academically. Didn't want to hurt anybody's feelings by blowing everybody out of the water with what he knew. So he'd just politely let the teachers think that maybe he didn't know. And then they would give him a test, or he'd write a paper, and they'd wonder if I wrote it for him.

Patricia also began to notice alarming holes in her son's academic foundation, which she believed would hamper his learning later:

His teacher in second grade . . . recognized that he was a talented person and immediately started giving him things like division and multiplication with absolutely no concept development at all. So for years . . . he could continue to do every task that was given to him, but he didn't have any understanding in it. When I decided to homeschool him, we just backed right up and started working on concept development so that he understood why he was doing what he was doing. Understood the base ten [*laughs*]! So that's really one big reason. One. That's not the only reason, but that was a pretty big reason. I wanted to be in control of his education.

Patricia felt that her son's unique situation made a conventional classroom a poor fit for him, so she homeschooled and continued to do so until he went to college. In her follow-up interview seven years later, her first son was in college, though she was still homeschooling her second son (then eleven). When I asked if she had been happy with her decision to homeschool, she responded:

If I lived elsewhere, and I had more financial funds, you know, I think it would not be the first choice. Like, for example, [famous school for the arts] has an academy, and I would've had my [first] son go there for high school, definitely. But that would've meant boarding school. In retrospect, I think he wanted to go, but he was too shy to ask me about it, and he thought it was too expensive. So we didn't even pursue whether or not he would get a scholarship or anything like that. But in retrospect [*shrugs*].

Of all the mothers I interviewed, only one did not want to stay home with her children, even when they were preschool age. Emily Ashton, a self-described "very unconventional person," had three children, ages eleven, eight, and six, when I talked to her in 2002. Because she had had her first child when she was seventeen years old and single, but wanted to continue her education, she had brought him to class with her at the community college she attended. Her relatives helped her with child care in the evenings and weekends so she could work part-time in a bookstore. Within a few years she married, had two more children, and continued attending classes (again, children in tow), working and juggling child care schedules with her husband until each child reached kindergarten age, when she sent them off to private Catholic school ("for the education," not the faith orientation). When the family moved to our state, however, Emily and her husband decided not to enroll the children in private school, though Emily worried that the adjustment to public school would be difficult. She reasoned that a year of homeschooling would ease the transition:

> I wasn't sure about the transition from private to public school, because I did that when I was little, and it was really traumatizing, to get thrown in to this worldly place when you are very sheltered. So I thought, "Well, I'll homeschool for a year and transition them." It only took like a month and a half and my oldest son [then ten] was like, "No, thank you, I'd rather go to school. I don't care what they do to me there; I don't want to be here anymore!" [*laughs*]. So we put him into school, and he was so brave. I cried for like three weeks, every day. "Did you make a friend?" "No, not yet, but maybe tomorrow, Mom," and I'm like, "Oh, God!" [*mock crying, then laughing*]. But [my younger son] is such a different temperament. He's very painfully shy and a really abstract thinker. . . . And I was scared, so I chose to homeschool because I didn't think he'd be able to handle [the move to public school] [*laughs*]. And so we finished homeschooling the first year, and it worked out pretty well.

In addition, her son was academically advanced for his age—he had been "skipped one and a half grades" in the private school—so after one "transition" year of homeschooling, Emily tried to register him for public school one year ahead of his age peers. However, the school district would not allow it. Emily told me about the conversation: "I'm like, 'But he's not learning at that level,' and they're like, 'Well it doesn't matter; we don't do that in this district,' and I'm like, 'Well, sorry [*laughs*], I'll just keep him at home.'"

Second-choicers never attributed their homeschooling decision to their desire to stay at home with their children, something that distinguished them from first-choice homeschoolers. Whereas first-choicers often introduced—unsolicited—the emotions they felt as stay-at-home mothers when asked about their reasons for homeschooling, this group of second-choice homeschoolers were often emotionally conflicted about staying at home, but they homeschooled because they thought it was in their children's best interests, given limited alternatives.

The Husband's Pressure

The other group of second-choicers homeschooled because of their husband's pressure on them to embrace an extended, homeschooling version of stay-at-home motherhood. There were only two mothers in this category, but their stories expose several facets of the emotional culture of intensive mothering. Renée Peterson and Tracy Chadwick had serious misgivings about homeschooling, although both at times said they were glad they were doing it. Their narratives wound around and back on themselves, revealing a great deal of conflict, vacillation, and ultimately reconciliation of their own feelings with their husbands'. Because their explanations were multilayered, I present larger chunks of their interviews to illustrate the complexity involved in their decisions to homeschool.

Renée was a white mother of two children, ten-year-old Taya, whom she had as a single parent, and two-year-old Andrew, whom she had with her husband of five years, Brian. Renée, who identified as Christian fundamentalist (though she was not raised in that faith), had always been a very active and adventurous person. She worked as a whitewater raft guide and captained a sailboat across the Pacific Ocean. She had backpacked throughout the world and served as a city police officer for several years. Having Taya in the midst of all this "barely slowed me down"; shuttle van drivers for the rafting company would drive her daughter from the beginning of the raft trip to the end, and other officers would watch over Taya when it was Renée's turn to enter a mock hostage situation to complete a training exercise. As a single mother, Renée kept working and relied on her friends and family for child care. In retrospect, however, Renée "really regret[ted]" bringing up her daughter in that way. At some point after marrying Brian, she decided to stay at home. As we talked through her decision, however, it became clear that Brian's traditional expectations heavily influenced her choice to stay at home, and it seemed to me that Renée was struggling to bring her own beliefs and feelings into line with Brian's, at least to some degree. I quote our conversation at length here because her explanation is quite nuanced:

RENÉE: I *never* thought I'd be at home. My mom worked. It seemed like the thing to do when I was a kid; it was really cool to have moms work. I just always figured I'd be working. And it seems like a different trend now, to have one parent at home. It's like this new thing which is—it just seems so good for the kids. . . . So now I think [staying at home] is important, and now that I've been doing it for a few years, I am really glad that I'm doing it. Whereas before we had kids, I was like, "uuuhn" [*makes unsure sound like she doesn't feel entirely comfortable with the idea*].

JEN: So once you had Andrew, you decided to stay home, and you developed more of a liking for it?

RENÉE: Um, actually it was probably since I got married [three years before I had Andrew]. . . . [I didn't decide to stay home] until I got married, when it seems—see, Brian grew up with dad working and mom always at home, and so I've been kind of adapting to that kind of lifestyle. It's been a real eye-opener. But I married him partially because of how neat his family is and the dynamics there. And so to kind of follow that as a role model has really good. But very different from the adrenaline rushes of sailing over to Hawaii a couple times, traveling Europe, backpacking North Africa and Asia [*laughs*]!

JEN: And you don't get that adrenaline rush from homeschooling.

RENÉE: Oh! It is the hardest thing! [*Sigh.*] Very different from the adrenaline rushes [of police work]. You don't get the pats on the back like you do when you're wearing a badge [*laughs*]! You get lots of accolades from the public and from others around you. But it's almost like you're an invisible person when you're at home. And so that's been interesting to deal with. My first couple of years at home, I probably should've been on antidepressants [*laughs*]!

When Renée described her "eye-opening" experience, feeling like an "invisible person" who should be on "antidepressants," it was clear she was conflicted about staying at home.[26] When she contrasted her experience—growing up with a "cool" working mother—with Brian's traditionally gendered family's "neat" dynamic, I suspected there was more to the story. I asked Renée why she did not return to work if staying at home depressed her. It was here that she clarified Brian's pressure on her to stay at home:

[I was working in the police department] while Brian and I were getting married. But then it soon came down to either the career or our marriage—within the first six months—and so I figured I could do my job a good ten years, but hopefully Brian and I would be around for a good fifty years [*laughs*]! But, yeah, it was really hard to give up the police department after working for it so hard.

Renée was a second-choice homeschooler primarily because being a stay-at-home mother was her second choice. She stayed home, however, to try to meet Brian's expectation of the ideal wife and mother, and homeschooling became part of that. When I talked to Renée, she had only been homeschooling for about four months, but one of her main reasons was to increase "family bonds" and encourage "relaxed family time." She told me that Brian had complained about the conflict between her and ten-year-old Taya over homework, which made evenings unpleasant. Renée's hope for homeschooling was to get Taya's work done during the day "to make the evenings, when Brian gets home, much more harmonious."

Whereas Renée felt a great deal of pressure from Brian to embrace stay-at-home motherhood, Tracy Chadwick, a thirty-three-year-old, white, middle-class mother of two children (ages eight and four), felt pressure from her husband to embrace homeschooling. For the Chadwick family, education was a central family issue, so Tracy invited her husband, David, and his father, George, who lived with them, to participate in the interview as well. The Chadwicks were very proud of their educational heritage. More than thirty years earlier, George had founded and run a private school and was quite well known in the local educational community. Both Tracy and David had attended an alternative, interdisciplinary college program (where they met) and held staunch beliefs about particular pedagogical truths, which were often a topic of conversation among the three adults in the home.

When we talked in 2002, Tracy's daughter, Sydney, was enrolled in pre-school part-time, and Tracy had been homeschooling her son, Jacob, for two years. Though Tracy explained that she had wanted to stay at home with her children when they were young, she was much less committed to home-schooling them, constantly weighing the pros and cons of other educational options. Her husband and father-in-law, however, were very committed to having Tracy homeschool. An extended segment of our conversation, peppered with interruptions and contradictory opinions, reveals the intricacies of David and George's pressure on Tracy:

TRACY: For me, private school is the ideal. Why homeschooling over private schooling? Can't get into Montessori; that would be my first choice. Wish we were doing that. You have to start out in preschool pretty much, to do Montessori. If I could do it over again, we'd be doing Montessori. We wouldn't even be homeschooling.

DAVID: You think that, but you don't know that.

TRACY: I feel like homeschooling is second-best to that, because [Montessori's] with a group of other kids, multiage environment, self-directed

learning. I just—I love it; I think it's great. It's holistic education instead
of being piecemeal.

DAVID: But you don't know that. Because it might not work for Jacob.

TRACY: It might not have worked for Jacob, but anyway, we can't do Montessori. And the other alternatives haven't worked for us. They're either too
far away—a thirty-minute drive each way—or it costs five thousand dollars a year. That's a lot of money, and with two kids, you can do the math.
So, I would dream of that. At this point, we just can't afford it. A lot of
our friends go to the Waldorf School, but—you know, if you ever want to
know anything about the schools in [this town] you should come to me
because [*laughs*] I know *everything* about each one because I've looked
into each one! Which is interesting, because most homeschoolers believe
so much in what they're doing. That's not the case for us. Well, for me.

Tracy's conflict about her children's education was clear, along with how her
feelings departed from other homeschoolers' and from the other adults in
her family; indeed, when she corrected her last words, she showed that she
was the only one in the family with reservations about homeschooling. Later
in our conversation, however, Tracy swung back to the pros of homeschooling, which George and David obviously endorsed:

TRACY: Putting Jacob in school six or seven hours a day seems a bit—it's
probably not a good idea.

GEORGE: Cruelty!

JEN: Because of the structured—?

DAVID: —Yeah, absolutely. I mean, it's not exactly cruelty, but he's got such
a good far-ranging mind and is interested in so many things, and it's
the way we learned. . . . We're hyperlearners, and we don't do classes,
we learn on our own. And that's part of my personality, from day one.
And pretty much that's the way Tracy has been—well, since leaving
Catholic school.

Eventually our conversation turned to their four-year-old, Sydney:

DAVID: Sydney just started with [pre]school and we're not sure what—

TRACY: —She loves it.

DAVID: Yeah, she does love it, yeah, absolutely. But I still hold out hope that
she'll—

TRACY: —It will be a very interesting process, because she loves it—I knew
she would—and she will continue to love it. . . . It has been great for

her. I'm so glad we're doing it. She needs a life away from her brother who is rather overbearing at times. And she needs a life away from me, and I could totally see her going to school. In some ways I feel like it would be hard for her to be homeschooled, but on the other hand, I think it might be very good for her. So I don't know.

GEORGE: She would learn a lot more [being homeschooled].

DAVID: Um-hmm.

TRACY: Yeah, but is intellectual learning everything?

GEORGE: No, but it's something.

DAVID: It's certainly not everything,

TRACY: What about the gratification? When I'm with my friends, or when I go to town, for example, to her school and I interface with other adults, I am *very* jazzed. That is a *great* part of my day.

DAVID: But is that everything?

TRACY: No. But I'm sure glad I have it. And —

DAVID: —Well, it's not as though she would not have a social life.

TRACY: No, but—

DAVID [TO JEN]: —As my wife has made clear to you, we're what are often called lifelong learners. . . . And it would be a pretty special school to help a child to be interested in so many different things and have that freedom to study as widely as they wanted to and delve as deeply into whatever their interest is. And when thinking about Sydney going to school and Jacob being homeschooled, I think of her situation as being more impoverished. You can even see we have a divide in the way we think about it.

Clearly the Chadwicks wanted their children to get the best education they could provide. The family's pedagogical legacy, however, was weighty and reverberated through many different realms of their lives: the children's education, of course, but also their peer relationships, family finances, and the interpersonal dynamics among the three adults living in the house. In later chapters, Tracy will discuss how she felt about the impact of homeschooling on her own time and responsibilities, but for now, suffice it to say that she was a second-choicer who homeschooled, in part because her husband and father-in-law preferred it, and in part because the alternatives were financially out of reach.

This brings me to a note about finances. Some mothers discussed money, or lack of it, as one factor in their decision to homeschool. However, no one gave it as their primary reason for homeschooling (Tracy came closest). Money is worth mentioning, though, because it so principally affected families' ability to have one parent at home full-time. Some families had little financial trouble with only one wage earner, whereas others had to tighten their belts considerably to make it on one income. But these families had enough financial wiggle room to make the choice, whereas two of the mothers I talked to (Whitney McKee and Maria Rojas), both first-choicers in spirit, simply could not afford to homeschool full-time. In that sense, homeschooling is a privilege reserved for families who earn enough to keep a mother at home. Yet my data also show the class issue in reverse: homeschooling may be a concession for those who cannot afford private school tuition. Therefore, homeschooling is a class issue from above as well as below.[27] (I will return to this issue in subsequent chapters.)

This chapter has shown that first-choicers were content with their decision to homeschool, whereas second-choicers, less content, often sought alternatives. This distinction has revealed how emotions may influence mothers' maternal identities and, thus, their decision to homeschool. All the mothers I talked to said they homeschooled because it was in the best interests of their children, and knowing this allowed them to internalize good-mother identities. However, friends, family members, and strangers were not always convinced that homeschoolers were responsible mothers; thus they frequently had to defend themselves against critics' accusations. In the next chapter, I examine how mothers drew on the emotions inherent in the ideology of intensive mothering to demonstrate their good-mother identities to outsiders.

3

Defending Good-Mother Identities

The Homeschooling Stigma

Non-homeschooling strangers, friends, and family members, whom I have called "outsiders," frequently criticized homeschoolers for keeping their children out of conventional schools, often implying—and sometimes stating outright—that they were irresponsible mothers for doing so. The criticism was constant, and over time homeschoolers became adept at defending their parenting choices and fighting the stigma of homeschooling.

Commonly understood, a stigma is a negative label applied to people who have broken a social norm, suggesting they are somehow inferior or immoral for deviating from society's rules. Sociologists' view of stigma, however, is slightly more nuanced because of our perspective that reality is socially constructed—that our beliefs about what is real drive our actions, and these actions have real consequences in our lives (as I discussed in the introduction). When we examine stigma closely, we see that it is not caused by a person's rule-breaking behavior but rather by others' *perception* of that person's rule-breaking behavior. Howard Becker was one of the first sociologists to reveal that the crucial feature in being labeled deviant was not committing deviance but being accused of it. Plenty of people break rules, but if they are not caught, they do not incur a stigma. Conversely, rule followers can incur a stigma from being wrongly accused of deviance. Therefore, when studying how stigma affects people's identities, some sociologists are more interested in the accusations and management of deviance than in the deviant behavior itself. Many studies have shown that when others treat us as deviant, whether or not we have broken a rule, we are prone to internalizing this view of ourselves and eventually come to think of ourselves as deviant.[1] The label actually has more impact on our identities than the rule-breaking behavior.

One way people deal with stigma, and one of the things homeschoolers did, is to influence others' perception by making statements to cast themselves in a positive light. These verbal strategies, called "accounts," help people "bridg[e] the gap between action and expectation" in order to neutralize the damage to their identities.[2] Conceptually, there are two types of accounts: "excuses" accept the wrongfulness of the act but deny responsibility for it (e.g., "I didn't know I was using marijuana; I thought it was a cigarette"); "justifications" accept responsibility for the act but "den[y] the pejorative quality" of it[3] (e.g., "Sure, I used marijuana, but I wasn't hurting anyone"). Both types of accounts help deviants "save face," align their conduct with cultural expectations, and reconstruct respectable identities.[4] Yet because of their conceptual distinction, excuses and justifications neutralize stigma differently. Excusers present their behavior as regrettable and distance themselves from it; they show they agree with the social rules but deny the deviant identity their behavior suggests. Inversely, justifiers endorse their behavior under the circumstances; they admit to committing the act but oppose classifying it, and thus themselves, as deviant.

The homeschooling mothers I studied used justifications; instead of claiming their homeschooling was irresponsible but beyond their control (which would be an excuse), homeschoolers avowed their decision to homeschool and denied that it was irresponsible. In doing so, they rejected the accusation of maternal deviance and cast themselves instead as hyperresponsible mothers.[5]

When I examined outsiders' accusations and homeschoolers' justifications more closely, however, I discovered that mothers cast them in emotional terms, which implies that homeschoolers' stigma as maternal deviants was rooted in what outsiders perceived as their *emotional deviance*.[6] In this chapter, I uncover the four justifications mothers used and show how each one helped them defend their good-mother identities by drawing on the "appropriate" emotions embedded in the discourse of intensive mothering. Analyzing the clash between critics' and homeschoolers' definitions of appropriate maternal emotions helps us see not only the significant impact it had on homeschoolers' identities but also the robust emotional expectations inherent in the emotional culture of intensive mothering.

Justifying Maternal Emotional Intensity

Many outsiders disapproved of homeschooling because they believed it would harm children in multiple ways. Critics often accused homeschoolers of irresponsible mothering and challenged them to account for their decision.[7] Although some fathers also had to defend their decision to homeschool, mothers received the brunt of the criticism because they were with children more often and were primarily in charge of the homeschooling. In addition, when outsiders did criticize fathers, they rarely attacked their paternal responsibilities, whereas when they criticized mothers, they clearly questioned their maternal identities. Therefore, mothers quickly learned to defend themselves by invoking particular justifications to neutralize the stigma of irresponsible mothering.

Although on the surface, outsiders wanted mothers to explain the deviant *behavior* of homeschooling, each accusation underneath targeted mothers' deviant *emotions*—specifically their excess emotional intensity—which outsiders assumed underlay mothers' motivation to homeschool. Mothers were cast as deviant not for homeschooling per se but for allegedly letting their maternal emotions spin out of control, which led to the irresponsible behavior of homeschooling. Homeschoolers defended themselves in four specific ways, each justification aimed at a particular charge of excessive maternal emotional intensity.

Academically Arrogant

Homeschoolers were commonly accused of feeling arrogant about the academic demands of homeschooling. They were cast as smug, irresponsible mothers who thought they could do a better job teaching their children than credentialed teachers in conventional schools. Outsiders often expressed this view to me when they discovered I was researching homeschoolers, but they also confronted homeschoolers directly. Linda Kelso, whose three homeschooled children were in college when I talked to her in 2002, said, "When I told my mother I was going to homeschool her grandchildren [*laughs*], she went ballistic. She was yelling at me about how I didn't know the first thing about being a teacher and that I was going to destroy their lives." Many mothers related stories like this, about how their own families reacted to their decision, perhaps because as family members, they felt some ownership in the children's lives, an idea implied in Linda's choice to refer to her children as "her [mother's] grandchildren" rather than as "my children."

The charge of academic arrogance did not stop with family members, however. Mothers also explained how even their friends felt they had the right to criticize their parenting. Valerie Scott, the white, middle-class mother of seven children, decided to homeschool in the mid-1980s, when the movement was new (recall from chapter 2 that she heard about homeschooling from a radio program). She explained how her friends reacted to her decision, implicitly accusing her of feeling superior and overconfident about her ability to teach her children: "They all said, 'Who do you think you are, that you think you would be able to teach your children school at home?' . . . I was just very taken aback."

Strangers, too, seemed to feel unusually free to questions mothers' ability to teach their children. Over the years I heard countless stories of the ways these confrontations occurred. A common scenario went something like this: a homeschooling mother would bring her children with her to grocery store in the middle of the day. Another customer, perhaps behind them in the checkout line, would strike up a conversation with the children, usually asking them why they were not in school. The children would respond that they were homeschooled, at which point the stranger would cast a disapproving look at the mother or make a snide remark about how it must be nice not to have any homework. Then, frequently (according to mothers), the stranger would start quizzing the children, usually in math: "What's two plus two?"

So many mothers reported these experiences, in which children were forced to perform to substantiate their mother's teaching capability, that it was a common discussion topic at meetings, on websites, and on listservs. In fact, a list titled "Top-Ten Answers You Should NEVER Give to the Question, 'What?! No School Today?'" circulated on the Internet and made its way to our local listserv. It contained witty comebacks for mothers to use against strangers' accusations in public places. Among the suggestions were "No, we homeschool. We're just out to pick up a bag of pork rinds and some Mountain Dew, then we gotta hurry home to catch our soaps," and "Noooooope. Me 'n' Bubba jes' learns 'em at home. Werks reel good!"

Most mothers interpreted others' criticism as an indictment of their parenting ability. The message was that homeschooled children would suffer because parents arrogantly dismissed teachers' expertise. Many mothers understood this accusation because they had held the same perspective when they had first heard of homeschooling. Before Pam Rausch, a white, middle-class mother, had considered homeschooling her two children eight years earlier, she thought, "This homeschooling thing is not the right way to go. All these people [are] out there thinking that they know what they're doing, and they don't have a clue; they're probably ruining their children."

To combat the perception that they were arrogant, homeschoolers invoked a justification: they admitted feeling a great deal of confidence that they could provide the best education for their children, but they denied that this confidence was excessive or problematic. Valerie said, "I felt confident in my conviction that this was for our family; on how to do it, I wasn't that confident. I knew I *could* do it, I just wasn't sure *how*." Mothers anchored their confidence in their intimate knowledge of their children's interests and motivational currencies; they argued that it truly did place them in the best position to advance their children's education. Parents discussed this idea at one of the PATH meetings I attended, which I recorded in my fieldnotes:

> We talked about individuality in kids—how each is different, but schools don't honor that. "Standardized curriculum is for standardized kids!" one mom declared, and another asked how teachers could possibly know how each kid is different. "But a mother knows!" she said. "A mother knows how her kids are different and what they need to learn in their own ways."

Thus, homeschooling nurtured each child's individuality. This rationale effectively countered charges of maternal arrogance because it drew on cultural ideas of good mothering: good mothers know their children better than anyone else (including fathers), and because of this, they can—and should—respond to all of their children's individual needs as they arise.[8]

Some homeschoolers, though not the majority, neutralized the stigma of arrogance by explaining that a conventional classroom was ill suited for their children because, relative to their age peers, they were advanced and would not be challenged, or were delayed and would fall behind.[9] Mothers justified their confidence in homeschooling by detailing the great lengths they went to in finding the right fit for their children. Gretchen Forrester, my first research participant, explained how her oldest, Harry, learned to read at age three, and as he approached kindergarten age, she and her husband, Tyler, explored the options. They first visited a Catholic school:

> Although I'd heard all good things about their kindergarten, what I saw when I walked into the room was twenty-five or twenty-six kids with one adult. And they were coloring in dittoes. They were *coloring*. And at that time, we weren't quite sure how we were going to cover the two hundred

dollars a month in tuition, and so when I saw those dittoes I thought, "Man, I could make a lot of dittoes for two hundred dollars a month!" [*laughs*]. And I had what I can only describe as kind of a physical reaction. It was like a spiritual experience. I thought, "I can't do this! I *can't*!"

Gretchen felt that because the school's standards were so low, it would be easy for her to exceed them. By talking about her "physical reaction" and "spiritual experience," she justified the degree of confidence she felt; she knew—via an epiphany—that classroom was not the right place for her son.

Later, Tyler met with one of the teachers and asked what the Catholic school could offer their child in particular, given that Harry was already reading. Tyler related the conversation:

> I'm saying, "Our child reads by sight, yet you are having him color in a ball. How's that advancing his education?" And it was almost like [the teacher said], "Well, I'm the early childhood development expert, you're not." You know, kind of like that. And I [thought], "That may be so, but I'm the Harry expert, and *you're* not."

Gretchen and Tyler justified their confidence in homeschooling their child by focusing on their intimate knowledge of him—they were the experts. This account neutralized the charges of arrogance and irresponsible parenting; choosing the right academic fit was highly *responsible* parenting.

Some mothers knew they could better provide for their children's education because conventional schools are gender- and race-biased. Because children must mold to the institutional demands, many mothers explained that school inhibits their "natural" development. Cassandra Shudek, who decided to stay home after a precarious postnatal period (see chapter 2), had four young boys, ranging in age from nine to two when I talked to her in 2002. She had been homeschooling for three years when she told me how conventional schools did not mesh with young boys' biorhythms:

> Six- and seven-year-old boys [are] just not wired to sit at a desk for five hours a day. I've found with my boys, that they need time—a lot of time— just to climb and run and dig holes and break branches and tear leaves off of trees. . . . Once they get some of that out of their system, then I can sit at the table with them for a good hour. . . . But if they haven't gotten those wiggles out [*laughs*], then it's like pulling teeth to try and get them to listen to a story or to practice penmanship. And it becomes a power struggle at that point. So I just figured, why fight nature?

Cassandra drew on what "everybody knows"[10]: young boys can't sit still. Their education suffers because the system does not honor their biology; thus Cassandra confidently asserted that homeschooling would better maximize their academic potential.

Jackie Bell, the African American mother of two young girls who liked "doing things alternatively," also opposed the way conventional school was structured, explaining how her children would be "stifled":

> My kids ask a lot of questions in a day. *A lot* of questions [*laughs*]! In a school setting, a child does not have the opportunity to ask all the questions they want to ask, and my belief is that that somehow stifles a child; they think they *can't* ask. . . . I think that [my kids have] learned that it's okay to talk. That's a big part of what I want them to learn.

Jackie's concern—that her daughters learn it was "okay to talk"—reveals two interesting themes. First, this philosophy parallels that found among the middle-class parents Lareau studied, who promoted an emerging sense of entitlement in their children (rather than the sense of constraint that working-class and poor children learned).[11] Second, Jackie's concerns paralleled those of other black homeschooling families, who often homeschool because they do not want to expose their children to the racial bias found in conventional schools.[12] Jackie and her husband said that these race- and gender-related reasons underlay their motivation for homeschooling; they had read about studies showing that racial and gendered stereotypes in conventional school discourage African American girls from being assertive, vocal, and academically oriented.[13] Jackie framed her account convincingly and cast herself as a responsible mother, who knew she could do better.

Mothers talked about the conventional school system as a threat to their children's education and identities. They homeschooled because they, not professional teachers, were the experts on nurturing their children, working with their learning styles, and ensuring that they would blossom into the unique people they were meant to be. All the mothers I talked to invoked this powerful justification and, in doing so, neutralized others' accusations of them as feeling arrogant about providing for the academic needs of their children.

Socially Overprotective

A second way outsiders charged homeschoolers with emotional deviance was by labeling them as overprotective, a maternal feeling that would prevent children from developing the skills to function in society. Indeed, the second most common question (after "Why homeschool?") was "What about socialization?" In eight years, I heard this phrase hundreds of times. Homeschoolers themselves heard it even more, and their annoyance at constantly having to defend themselves unified them. Rolling their eyes and distorting their voices, they mimicked outsiders: "How will they learn to work with others? Aren't you worried they'll be social misfits? What about the prom?" One mother told me that her own parents were concerned that her children were "kept in a bubble" and would not "learn to cope" or "know how to get a job." They feared she was "robbing" them of their chance to learn how to navigate social life. These accusations cast homeschoolers as irresponsible mothers who, because of their uncontrollable overprotectiveness, were failing their children by sheltering them from reality.

Homeschoolers justified their feelings by admitting they felt greatly protective but denying that the degree was extreme. They argued that homeschooling appropriately shielded their children from the real dangers present in conventional schools. Rampant bullying was one example. Most mothers feared the ridicule and ostracism their children could experience in school (although some with boys who were small for their age were concerned about physical bullying), and though a few mothers discussed their own victimization, most expressed how heartbroken they felt when remembering their own class scapegoats. One mother said, "Kids can be so cruel; why would I put my son in that situation?" and another compared a conventional classroom to "*Lord of the Flies* . . . [where] all the kids just kind of take over," and teachers were helpless to monitor peer interactions. Mothers drew on the maternal norm of feeling fiercely protective: good mothers are willing to "kill and die" for their children.[14] By framing school as an environment where cruelty would inevitably damage their children, mothers justified the need to protect them by homeschooling.

Another danger homeschoolers identified was that "labels" might be applied to their children, damaging their self-esteem. Ability tracking, or grouping students by aptitude scores, often concerned mothers whose children were academically behind their age peers. In school, "everyone knows who the dummies are," as one mother told me. "But with homeschooling," as another explained, "she doesn't have to know that [she is behind]. And I feel she's better off—more confident." Others feared their children (especially active boys) would be stigmatized as "problem children." Maria Rojas, a Hispanic American mother in her midtwenties, pulled her son out of public school after his kindergarten year. She told me that homeschooling "built up his self-esteem. In kindergarten he got sent to the office a lot. . . . So at home he's . . . not labeled the 'problem kid' . . . who disrupts the class; . . . he's my son who's smart. I didn't want that [negative label] to have to follow him through his whole life." In framing their concerns in this way, homeschoolers relied on well-recognized threats to children's self-esteem such as being bullied or labeled stupid. Responsible mothers should want to go to great lengths to protect their children from them.

Many homeschoolers were also suspicious of teachers' and schools' motivations to assess their children's behavior, which they feared would result in their children being "medicated" for "behavioral problems" and thus given a formal diagnosis through the school system that would follow them for the rest of their lives. (Schools cannot legally assess or diagnose children without parental permission, but nevertheless, many mothers feared it could happen.) Patricia Tomlinson, the white mother of fourteen- and five-year-old boys and a former middle school teacher, believed that, at times, schools convinced parents to overmedicate their children. She told me that the parents of her former students occasionally called to tell her that the new teacher was encouraging them to evaluate their children for conditions that might require medication:

> So the parent phones me up and says, "Now when my child was in your class, did he seem to have Asperger's [syndrome]?" Or "Did he seem to have attention deficit hyperactivity disorder?" Now, it's not to say that ADHD and Asperger's aren't real entities. But I think teachers have way too much on their hands, and it's way too distracting to have a rugged individualist in your class. It's easier to medicate them, I suppose. That sounds a little paranoid, but I think that happens, and it really concerns me as a parent. . . . I didn't want my child to go into a setting where the teachers thought if he went on and on about a topic, maybe he had Asperger's. Or if he wiggled in his seat, he had attention deficit, or whatever. It's like a candy box of neuroses from which to choose.

Although Patricia admitted that she sounded "a little paranoid," she used her teaching experience to argue that her concern was indeed justified, and that children need a great deal of protection.

Mothers also identified the dangers of educational bureaucracy, seizing on a state-level debate about instituting mandatory academic benchmarks, which required standardized testing starting in the fourth grade. Whitney McKee was only halfway through the one year she planned to homeschool her eleven-year-old son when I talked to her in 2002. She explained his experience with the stress of standardized testing in school:

> I was always very careful not to make Ritchie feel bad about himself. But it just naturally began to happen when he went to school. . . . All of a sudden the [statewide standardized achievement] test came up. And I don't know why his teacher said this, but she said, "If you don't pass this, you don't get to pass fourth grade." And he just came home sobbing, and scared of it, and the night before the test he couldn't sleep. And on the way to the test he cried, and I finally looked at him and said, "If you don't pass, then I'm homeschooling you. And I don't want you to worry about it. I don't really care how you do on this test. Just go in and do it." Well, he did fine. But just that kind of pressure—it's more than the character of the child can handle. He's a great kid, and I hate to watch that kind of pressure on him.

Ritchie performed adequately on the test, but Whitney decided to home-school him anyway (in part because of their plans to move to Central America, which I discussed in the introduction). She presented his experience as a dramatic example of how schools pose real dangers for children, which helped her neutralize the stigma of being overprotective. Her protective feelings seemed justified against the backdrop of contemporary definitions of motherhood, which assert that children are "entitled to a prolonged, carefree, innocent time,"[15] and that it is "a mother's job to ensure that they encounter [the] world in just the right increments."[16]

Homeschoolers also gave examples of unlikely events such as natural disasters, murderous rampages, or terrorist attacks that could threaten their children while in school. Studies have shown that protecting children's physical safety and health is a highly salient feature of good mothering; thus home-schoolers neutralized the stigma of maternal deviance by referring to horrific yet rare events, such as the attacks of September 11, 2001, and the Columbine High School murders, to legitimize the "real" dangers conventional schools posed.[17] In fact, the day after the 2007 mass murders on the Virginia Tech University campus, one mother posted an inquiry to the listserv with the subject line "distance learning for college?" Her message indicated that she was sincerely thinking of ways she could homeschool for college, something I had not heard any homeschooler suggest previously.

Morally Self-Righteous and Extreme

The third type of emotional stigma homeschoolers bore was that they were self-righteous and morally extreme, feelings that led them to teach their children values that would forever position them at the margins of society. At one extreme of the moral continuum were the liberal parents or, as one mother called them, "granola people," whose homeschooling was seen as "some weird hippie thing" and whose feelings toward the environment, politics, and social justice were cast as self-righteously leftist. At the other extreme were the evangelical Christians who, as another mother explained, "sign their emails with 'devoted servant to [their husband, God, and their children]' and wake up at 5:00 a.m. to do their daily devotions, . . . their morning chores, . . . and make breakfast before their children sit down to eat." They were also cast as self-righteous and morally extreme: "That's like totally June Cleaver! It's crazy!"

Although many homeschoolers I met held some philosophies that were out of the mainstream, most did not consider themselves radical, as they perceived others did. Thus, they reacted to the stigma of moral extremism in two ways. First, they offered "traverses"[18] wherein they denied some of the extremism attributed to them, and they invoked, at least at times, rationales that held mainstream American appeal and meshed well with politically moderate rhetoric. For example, they argued that values such as self-discipline and deferred gratification were not nurtured in conventional schools, which stripped individual children of the tools to achieve and created a generation with many social problems. Mothers felt it was their ultimate responsibility—not "the state's"—to ensure that their children embraced appropriate morals and developed the corresponding character traits. Maria Rojas, the twenty-five-year-old Hispanic American mother of two young children, explained: "I just want my children to have successful lives. To be good community members: pay their taxes, have good jobs, function in the community, and just be good individuals. . . . I'm taking responsibility, and in the end, if it turns out they didn't [adopt those values], it was on me; I didn't leave it to someone else."

Thus, homeschoolers neutralized charges of extremism by emphasizing the mainstream view that responsible mothers cultivate their children's moral development and raise upstanding, productive citizens.[19] Homeschooling provided them with more time to do this, as Leanna Livingston, a mother of three young boys, told me: "We can have 'round-the-clock input into their character development. I think the parents that have their kids at public school, and only see their kids for a couple hours a day, have a lot harder job trying to do the character-development kind of issues than we do." This rationale, emphasizing that good mothers need to "be there" for their children, draws clearly from the ideology of intensive mothering.[20]

The second way homeschoolers responded to the charges of moral extremism and self-righteousness was by acknowledging their intense emotions but denying they were problematic. Unlike the traverses mothers offered, these justifications drew from politically partisan rhetoric. Conservatives, or those who espoused dissatisfaction with what they perceived to be the lack of moral agenda in public schools, dominated PATH membership; the vast majority of this conservative group held evangelical Christian ideologies and traditional beliefs about gender. As I discussed earlier, these perspectives are common among homeschoolers, especially the group of first-choicers I identified (see chapter 2).[21] These conservative mothers believed that "the hub of society is the family" and accused the state of overstepping its bounds by "teaching morality" (or a misguided form of it), because it prevented parents from doing so. Thus, they disagreed with antiprayer laws and opposed curricula that taught children about drugs and sex, the theory of evolution, and homosexuality. Renée Peterson, whose husband pressured her to stay home with their children, said, "We have a gay uncle, and it's talked about, and we love him, but acting out on that is just not what we value. So for the public school system to say we have to accept it all—I have a hard time with that."

Some homeschoolers were more politically active in promoting this morality message. For example, one of the emails I received on the homeschooling listserv directed me to the website of an evangelical Christian homeschooling mother with a PhD in education, who had self-published several books about homeschooling. One was titled *Onto the Yellow School Bus and through the Gates of Hell*, and the other was *God-Free School Zone: Reclaiming Our Children for Christ* (which was "available for a donation of any size!"). Both of these books promoted her self-proclaimed agenda of "spiritual warfare" against the public school system, which she believed Christians, homeschoolers or not, were duty-bound to pursue. Her website explained her motivations for writing the latter book:

> She wrote the book for those public school parents who would like to understand what is happening in the school system and make informed decisions about how to return Christ to the center of their children's education. [The author] makes a strong case for either returning Jesus to His proper place as Lord inside the system, or getting all of our children out.

And yet, mothers denied that such views were morally extreme and self-righteous. Though I was not able to read this homeschooling mother's book, I did wonder what "strong case" she made to justify proposing such a radical change to the public school system. I suspected it relied on the assumptions inherent in conservative Christian ideology.

Many homeschoolers relied on this evangelical line of moral reasoning, that they only needed to answer to God, the definitive moral authority.

Valerie Scott, the white, middle-class mother of seven children whose friends had criticized her homeschooling decision, explained how her husband suggested she respond to their remarks: "He said, 'You really don't need to answer their questions anymore. This is between you and I and the Lord. And we've decided. *We* are answerable for our children.'" She continued, explaining how she viewed her children in a way that many Americans would consider extreme:

> These [my children] were gifts from the Lord to me, and he was entrust-
> ing them into my care. You know [how] he calls them "arrows that you
> shoot"? . . . I knew I was going to shoot them. I could not give anything
> better to mankind than a well-adjusted, loving, serving, human being.
> Who love[s] the Lord. I felt like I was molding and making these chil-
> dren, and God entrusted me enough to be able to do that. With his help, of
> course, and covering all my mistakes. That's a big deal; to me it was a big
> deal to realize that that's *important* that I put my life into these kids, and to
> see them grow up to do bigger and better things than I ever did. Which is
> their higher calling in the Lord.

Many mothers expressed similar nonmainstream views, citing passages in the Bible that explained that their children were merely "on loan" to them from God.[22] By stressing not only the family's but also God's authority over children's moral development, homeschoolers justified their extreme opposition to public education by appealing to "higher loyalties."[23]

Regardless of political leaning, most homeschooling families believed strongly in helping their children develop a solid sense of right and wrong before exposing them to "negative" social influences, a prominent feature of good mothering other studies have uncovered as well.[24] Conservative home-schoolers, however, like evangelicals in the United States, believed in their own moral superiority because they were following "God's path," which they characterized in absolute terms.[25] Valerie continued, explaining how her seventeen-year-old son, the fourth of her seven children, encountered temp-tations to stray from God's path when he joined a public school basketball team:

> He wants to be a light to the world, and sometimes he gets sucked in by
> the worldly stuff before him. I can tell. . . . I'll talk with him, and then it all
> comes out that he's not doing what's right, and so he's not happy with him-
> self. He says, "Mom, it's real difficult to keep your priorities when you have
> so much coming at you. You know, the guys [on the team] are really into

girls, and the way they talk in the locker room—I'm hearing that. And they swear. Even the *coaches* swear!" And it's difficult; it's a battle. So he comes home worn out from that battle. . . . [If I had sent him to public school] I would've been sacrificing [him].

Using militant evangelical rhetoric, Valerie cast her son's experience as a "battle" in which his peers tried to lure him away from the universal path of righteousness.[26] By stressing the danger of losing him to the forces of evil, she justified her self-righteous extremism.

At the other end of the spectrum, and far fewer in number, were the liberal homeschoolers, who were often labeled self-righteous extremists because they, like their conservative counterparts, believed their children's character and values would be negatively affected by the curricula and people in public school. Unlike the conservatives, however, most liberal parents were not religious, and those who were distanced themselves from evangelical politics by characterizing their beliefs as "progressive Catholicism" or "liberal Christianity." Thus, they justified their self-righteousness not with appeals to moral absolutism but rather with appeals to moral relativism, pointing out the lack of it in public schools. They wanted their children to think critically, question the social order, and embrace diversity but thought public schools only gave lip service to these values. Other research has revealed similar motivations for some groups of homeschoolers.[27]

Recall that Patricia Tomlinson, the white mother of two boys, had pulled her highly capable nine-year-old son out of the private school he had been attending because she saw glaring holes in his education. Though that had been a "pretty big reason" for homeschooling him, she also explained another one:

I started getting really concerned about how my son was being kind of culturalized to be a typical, insensitive male. When he was a little boy, he was really able to couch his feelings in words and *loved* music. . . . And what I found [at his private school] was that . . . [boys learned about] being "cool," just sort of being closed. Just not being very emotive. And it really hurt me that my son was becoming like that. So I just said, "Forget it. You're not going to be around this. I really want you to do things like paint and move your body, play a musical instrument, and sing." And I made him do that. I *forced* him to do it. . . . When you're raising a child, you're not just educating, you're trying to give them some moral underpinnings, too. I really want him to be a good partner when he hooks up with a life partner; I want him to be a constructive, decent person who's not just expecting somebody to mop up after him. And so I give him the running commentary about men, women, and relationships.

Patricia held beliefs that some would consider radical, such as challenging traditional masculinity (striving to get her son to be more "emotive") and relationships (talking about his future "life partner"), yet she justified her moral extremism by claiming that gender stereotypes are truly a problem, and that schools not only overlook gender inequality but in fact promote it.

Other liberal parents justified extreme beliefs such as naturalism ("High-fructose corn syrup as the main ingredient in food is not okay!") and anti-consumerism. David and Tracy Chadwick, the upper-middle-class parents who lived with their two children and David's father, George, justified their extreme views on mass media:

DAVID: We don't watch TV . . . [so] we don't expose [the kids] to ads on television and a lot of things about this culture, like video games and that kind of stuff. We *question*, I guess is what I'm trying to say. I find that critical thinking—which is one of the most important things you can ever learn, and you need to have [in order] to live in a democracy—is not really taught in the schools, as far as I can tell.

TRACY: Quite the opposite. Which is why we don't have a democracy here [in the United States]!

The Chadwick family's lack of exposure to TV and their assertions that the United States is not a democracy certainly made them statistical outliers. Yet they justified their extremism by invoking leftist political rhetoric to deny that their views and practices were wrong. In these ways, parents of all ideological persuasions justified their extreme moral beliefs and self-righteousness by pointing out mainstream society's moral inadequacy and its consequences.

Relationally Hyperengaged

The fourth type of emotional deviance outsiders directed at homeschoolers was that they were hyperengaged with their children—that their abnormally strong desire to be emotionally and physically close to their children caused them to be excessively involved with every aspect of their lives. Outsiders claimed that these intense feelings, allegedly the result of mothers' own psychological "issues" (usually cast as codependency or something similar), led to an unhealthy mother-child bond that prevented children from developing independence. For example, many mothers said that they could not bear the thought of sending their children to school because they would "miss them too much." Such statements quickly spawned the stereotype of hyperengagement and called mothers' feelings into question; they were accused of forfeiting their children's well-being to fulfill their own emotional needs.[28] Whitney McKee, the working-class mother who homeschooled her eleven-year-old son for only one year, told me that her sister raised "concerns" about her homeschooling, saying suspiciously, "I didn't realize you and Ritchie were so close." Whitney, feeling judged, responded, "What did you think we were? We're mother and son!"

Most mothers responded to the charge of hyperengagement the way Whitney did: they justified it by avowing the close bond with their children while denying it was unhealthy. They argued that homeschooling fostered these close family relationships, which were in their children's best interests, and this neutralized the stigma of irresponsible mothering. As one convention speaker said, homeschooling was about "the four R's: reading, writing, arithmetic, and *relationship*." Indeed, other studies show that fostering strong family bonds is one common reason parents give for homeschooling.[29]

One way mothers justified their engagement with their children was by questioning cultural norms. They thought that American culture coerced parents into believing that early mother-child separation was good for children's independence and maturity, yet they had seen firsthand the damage (they believed) separation could do to the mother-child bond. Cassandra Shudek reached this conclusion after sending her oldest son to preschool, a decision she later regretted:

> [Preschool] is the norm in our society. So I just went along with it without thinking and put him in, and he hated it. He hated being away from me. He thought he was being punished. . . . The only thing he could think of was, "Why doesn't she want to spend that time of the day with me? Why is she making me go to this? She knows I don't like it; I cry." All the kids were crying when they left their mothers. But we're told they need to do this for their social development, and they have to detach from their mothers and all of that.

Cassandra justified her close bond with her son by showing how her experience challenged cultural assumptions about the mother-child relationship, rhetoric that also exists in some alternative mothering movements, such as the international pro-breastfeeding group La Leche League. Such rhetoric often emphasizes that mothers should rely on their intuition, even if it means disregarding "expert" advice; the "instinctual" emotions of motherhood serve as a superior guide to child rearing.[30] For example, one mother said that the idea of homeschooling "answered what my heart felt," which was to keep her children with her rather than enroll them in school.

Mothers explained that homeschooling would allow them to spend more time with their children and stay emotionally connected to them. They said that school disengaged children from their families during "their best hours of the day" and interfered with the mother-child relationship in which they had invested so much. Judith Munson, the mother who had had her stay-at-home epiphany immediately after giving birth to her son, explained this rationale as she sat on a panel at a statewide convention. Recall that she phoned from the hospital to resign from her job:

> [I quit work because] I wanted to do nothing but be with this little guy. So I did everything I could to learn about becoming a good parent; I wanted to be a good mom. And I'll skip up several years: homeschooling became a part of that because I didn't want to give him up—not just to the school system per se, but . . . I really was enjoying the time that we were having together. . . . And that's when I heard about homeschooling . . . and I said, "There's my excuse to be able to keep him home: I'm gonna homeschool him."

Judith's rationale—that homeschooling is good mothering—allowed her not only to neutralize the stigma of maternal deviance but also to construct an identity as an extremely responsible mother, who did not want to send her children to school to be, as many homeschoolers said, "raised by someone else." Like Cassandra and Judith, many homeschoolers stressed their intense emotional bond with their children and their desire to be good mothers—highly noble feelings by contemporary U.S. standards and an integral part of the ideology of good mothering. Sociologist Linda Blum referred to this ideal as the "exclusively bonded mother-child dyad," which promotes the belief that children need their mother's physical presence, especially during the preschool years, (otherwise they will unbond and detach from them), and that the mother is the *only* person suited for this job.[31] This idea is rampant in popular discourse, which warns of disengaged mothers during children's "formative years."[32] Homeschoolers borrowed this rationale and extended it, redefining the formative years as lasting well into adolescence, which helped them justify keeping their children out of school.

Another way homeschoolers contested the stigma that they were hyper-engaged was to emphasize that childhood was finite, and most parents, as one mother said, "look back and regret not having enough time with [their children]." Homeschoolers contended that they were not squandering their time. Dramatic life events could punctuate this rationale. For example, one mother decided to homeschool after the terrorist attacks of September 11 "to build our family bonds closer." And Barbara Roberto, the white, working-class mother of a ten-year-old and an eight-year-old (whom I offended with my questions about her maternal emotions; see chapter 2), said that she homeschooled because a tragedy validated her bond with her children:

> My girlfriend's kids were both killed in a very, very sudden accident, and when you go to a friend's funeral for their children, you really think [about] what's really important here in life: it's your children. I remember [my daughter] was about four when that happened, and that really had quite an impact. Just really, "What's important?"

Mothers also fought the stigma of hyperengagement by showing how homeschooling enhanced children's relationships with other family members. Fathers, for example, could spend more time with children because homeschooling provided scheduling flexibility, so vacations were planned around the father's work schedule rather than determined by the school calendar. The quality of family members' time together was also enriched. Renée Peterson told me how her home life had changed dramatically after she pulled her ten-year-old daughter out of conventional school (at the behest of her husband, Brian, because he wanted evenings to be "more harmonious"; see chapter 2):

> When [Taya] was in school we'd be having battles after school to get home-work done, and a twenty-minute assignment would take her three hours. I'd be tired, end of the day, needing to get food on the table, Andrew [the toddler] was fussy. Evenings were just a bad, chaotic time. There just was not much time left for family time. . . . [Homeschooling] makes the evenings when Brian gets home just much more harmonious. We can do family games, we listen to books on tape—we just have much more relaxed family time. And at eight o'clock the kids are in bed. Taya's reading for another half hour in bed; Andrew goes to bed with his books. They're both content, and it's a nice evening.

Thus, mothers cast homeschooling as a way to resist having their family time dictated by the demands of school. Another mother said: "All these statistics . . . about the American family [show] the way families splinter apart into all their own activities, and they hardly ever eat together anymore. When you are homeschooling, you are together." Sociological research has documented several ways in which institutionalized education encroaches on family life, particularly for middle-class families.[33] Thus, this mainstream rationale, that family bonds were preserved and protected from the dictates of outside forces, resonated not only with homeschooling mothers but also with outsiders who disapproved of their educational choices.

Mothers also claimed that schools drove wedges between siblings, noting that the age-stratified structure of conventional school taught older children to reject their siblings because it was not "cool" to play with younger children. Cassandra pulled her oldest son out of kindergarten for this reason. Homeschooling had reversed the dynamic, and she hoped it would continue:

> I think about how great it is that I have four brothers growing up who know each other, and who spend so much time together, and really enjoy each other's company. They're probably going to be close the rest of their lives. . . . I've seen it with some of my homeschooling friends whose kids are older, and I think [to myself], "That's how I want my family to be."

Under mothers' watchful eyes, family relationships were maintained and nurtured, which is a key element in cultural definitions of good mothering.[34] Homeschoolers justified their hyperengagement by showing how family relationships can never be too close, which helped them construct identities as good mothers.

These four ways of justifying their intense maternal emotions helped homeschoolers fight the stigma outsiders applied to them. By drawing on the discourse of good mothering, they gave credence to their claims that they held the "right" emotions, and by drawing on the fears inherent in the emotional culture of mothering, they justified their level of emotional intensity. They were not arrogant; they were categorically confident that they knew their children's needs best. They were not overly protective; their children needed protection from the real threats inherent in conventional school. Their moral self-righteousness was not extreme; schools actually promoted mediocre (and some thought wrong) cultural values. They were not hyperengaged with their children; they recognized how schools artificially and prematurely severed the family bonds that were imperative for children's development. Thus, homeschoolers' vision advocated feeling more of the emotions that good mothers feel—confidence, protectiveness, moral conviction, and engagement.

These justifications benefited homeschooling mothers by allowing them to maintain good-mother identities in the face of harsh social criticism. To mothers' detriment, however, the justifications intensified the already inten-sive model of good mothering, ratcheting up the standards and ultimately promoting an emotional culture of intensive mothering that was even more difficult to live up to than the version typically promoted in mainstream cul-ture. If intensive mothering already strips mothers of their time and energy, how did homeschoolers find the temporal and emotional resources for this even more intensive version of good mothering? The next part deals with the significant temporal tensions homeschoolers encountered in the emotional culture of good mothering.

PART II

The Temporal-Emotional Conflict of Good Mothering

In the previous chapters, I explained how the emotional culture of intensive mothering affected homeschoolers' lives dramatically. The beliefs about how mothers should feel, along with how they should demonstrate their commitment to their children, drove homeschoolers to extend their commitment to stay-at-home motherhood for an additional twelve years. In addition, I showed how homeschoolers actively drew on the ideology of intensive mothering to justify their decision to homeschool, neutralize outsiders' criticism of their emotional deviance, and maintain their identities as good mothers.

As I explored the emotional culture of homeschooling motherhood further, I discovered that the issue of time also played an important part in mothers' lives, directly conflicting with some of the feelings related to intensive mothering. This temporal-emotional conflict occurred in two distinct ways, which are the subjects taken up in this part. To frame the discussion, I will first review some of the ways sociologists have examined mothers' time.

Research has shown that how much time mothers have, along with the ways they use it, significantly impacts their experiences and identities as mothers. Much of this research has focused on the gendered division of labor in the home, quantitatively examining the "second shift" of household work that women perform relative to their male partners. Studies find that, in general, women do between two and three times more housework and child care than their male partners, though women have redistributed their efforts in recent decades.[1] Mothers feel more time stress now largely because more of them (mostly middle-class mothers) have entered the paid labor force than ever before, and men, as a group, have been extremely reluctant to increase their domestic contribution. The result is that married mothers feel strapped for time and become emotionally exhausted from trying to juggle all their domestic responsibilities with very little husband support.[2]

In addition to documenting this time stress, sociologists have tried to uncover the ways mothers deal with it. In analyzing the period from 1965 to 2000, sociologist Suzanne Bianchi and her colleagues found that as married mothers have dramatically increased their participation in the paid labor force, they have (unsurprisingly) decreased the time they spend on housework; in fact, they seem to have "swapped paid work for housework almost hour for hour," and since men have not substantially increased their contributions, less housework is getting done.[3] Since mothers' lack of time has caused them to cut back substantially on housework, it would seem that their tighter schedules would also reduce the time they spend with their children.

Contrary to popular belief, however, contemporary parents—particularly mothers—spend more time with their children than in earlier decades. Bianchi and her colleagues showed that both mothers and fathers have accomplished this by multitasking and including children in their own leisure activities. Yet unlike fathers, mothers have also sacrificed their leisure time, experiencing a significant decline in "pure free time" (time "uncontaminated" by family caregiving) and "child-free time" (with or without other adults), whereas fathers' free time has remained stable over the same period. Bianchi and her colleagues posit that the ideology of intensive mothering is at work here, driving employed mothers to sacrifice their own interests for their children.[4] Indeed, their data showed that employed mothers have fifteen fewer hours of free time per week than their nonemployed counterparts, and that they are still more likely than fathers to feel as though they do not have enough time with their children, despite spending more hours with them. This research demonstrates that mothers' lost discretionary time has become an important factor in sustaining gender inequality in heterosexual families as well as triggering problematic emotions, such as anger and resentment toward their husbands.[5]

Clearly, time and emotions are highly salient features of mothers' identities; furthermore, these two concepts seem to be intricately connected—discussion of guilt and anxiety abound in the research on mothers' time. Yet existing studies have neglected to explore the temporal and emotional intersection of mothers' identities. The homeschoolers I talked to, however, explained several ways the temporal and emotional dimensions of motherhood were in direct conflict; disentangling this relationship will enhance our understanding not only of homeschoolers' lives but also of the social construction of good mothering more broadly.

This part reveals how the intensive demands of homeschooling left mothers strapped for time, which led to problematic emotions that had to be managed. Chapter 4 begins by presenting the stages mothers passed through in trying to add the teacher role to their other family responsibilities. They became quickly overwhelmed and burned out with the amount of work required, so they managed these problematic emotions by using their time differently, trying to find a balance among their various domestic responsibilities. Chapter 5 continues this temporal theme, exploring how homeschooling caused mothers to forfeit their personal time, "me-time" they had previously used at their discretion to pursue their own interests. Mothers first tried quantitative solutions by allocating their time differently to free up space in their schedules. This strategy inevitably failed, however, and mothers resorted to managing their feelings by manipulating their subjective experiences of time.

4

Adding the Teacher Role

Domestic Labor and Burnout

The way household labor is divided in most families disproportionally taxes mothers, affects their time greatly, and influences their feelings about their husbands and families. Not only do mothers do more work than fathers in the majority of heterosexual, intact families with children, but they are more likely than fathers to become run-down and emotionally drained.[1] The mothers I studied reported that homeschooling added so much extra work to their already busy lives that it often pushed them into "homeschool burnout."

Burnout is an emotional and temporal phenomenon: it occurs over time, when people deplete their emotional resources more quickly than they can replenish them. Research has addressed this phenomenon in two distinct ways. Hochschild proposed that burnout is common among workers in service-based industries because they are asked to access and manipulate their private emotions as part of their occupational duties. This type of emotion management for a wage, which she termed "emotional labor," is most prevalent in jobs where workers must engage in close contact with clients, produce particular emotions in them, and have their own emotions evaluated as part of their job performance, for example, as flight attendants or customer service representatives.[2] When professional transactions elicit negative emotions, whether in workers or customers, it is always workers who are obligated to smooth over the situation by manipulating their own emotions. This intense emotional labor is stressful, which leads workers to devise ways to manage it, such as numbing their feelings so that the unpleasant emotions on the job do not affect them as intensely. The consequence, however, is that workers may become self-alienated, unable to distinguish their private feelings from those they manage on behalf of the company.[3] These workers become emotionally burned out; they feel drained and exhausted from their emotional labor.

Other conceptualizations of burnout have delineated similar processes. The most well-known model in the psychological literature is the Maslach Burnout Inventory (MBI), a quantitative tool that measures job-related burnout along three distinct dimensions, which workers experience sequentially.[4] "Emotional exhaustion" occurs when people feel emotionally "used up" from their work and dread facing another day on the job. With few emotional resources left, they begin to engage in "depersonalization," becoming callous and less emotionally involved with clients. Workers may then experience a sense of "reduced personal accomplishment": because they have stopped caring, they feel they are not adequately doing their job. Despite the conceptual importance of emotional exhaustion as the catalyst that begins the burnout process, most of the literature using the MBI does not examine how workers try to manage their problematic emotions once they appear, which, according to Hochschild's sociological theory, is a key element to understanding how people experience burnout.

A drawback of both theories, however, is that they focus only on the experience of paid workers and do not address the possibility that burnout can happen in private life. Hochschild acknowledged the importance of private-life emotion work, noting that "in the most personal bonds . . . emotion work is likely to be the strongest,"[5] but she specifically applied her theory of emotional labor and burnout to workers in the service industry to highlight the exploitive process of co-opting a worker's personal resources (emotions and private emotion work) for company gain. In any case, it seems plausible to suggest that burnout can also happen off the job, in private life and personal relationships. Although some research has demonstrated the intense emotion work that family relationships involve, only a small subset has addressed the possibility that this private-life emotion work may specifically lead to burnout—that people may become emotionally drained and exhausted from their interactions with their family members.[6]

A second weakness of existing models of burnout is that they focus disproportionately on the emotional components of the experience at the expense of the temporal dimensions on which it hinges; both Hochschild and Maslach argue that when people develop burnout, they experience emotions that intensify over time, occur in a particular sequence, and are problematic because the person's emotional resources have been depleted faster than they can be replenished. Clearly, succumbing to and overcoming burnout depends, in part, on time.

I found that burnout was a common experience for many homeschoolers because the teacher role was such a considerable time investment. Mothers experienced what sociologists have called "role strain," where they had difficulty meeting the demands of their other family roles, such as wife, homemaker, and mother to other children (e.g., preschoolers whom they were not yet officially schooling).[7] Yet homeschoolers also reported progressing through a series of problematic emotions arising from their role strain, which often culminated in emotional burnout. Some mothers were able to overcome their burnout, while others were not. This chapter examines the ways mothers managed their emotions in order to manage the role strain of homeschooling their children.

Progressive Role Strain and Emotion Management

Mothers who taught their children at home had to adjust to the demands of adding the teacher role to their repertoire of other family roles. Although a few mothers had previously been professional teachers, for most the role was entirely new. As they adjusted to the demands, many women experienced various types of role strain, which typically led to problematic emotions. Mothers commonly used a set of strategies to try to alleviate these feelings, but most eventually burned out.[8] Some of them overcame burnout, while others stagnated in this emotionally draining stage.

Homeschoolers passed through four stages when adjusting to the teacher role. These stages were marked by the type of role strain they experienced, the emotions they felt, and the particular strategies they used to try to manage these feelings.

Role Ambiguity: Insecurity and Structure

Parents in my study decided to homeschool at different points. As I discussed in chapter 2, some decided years before their children were ready for school (in a few cases before they were born), some decided once their children reached school age, and others removed their children from the public or private schools they had been attending. Once they committed, however, mothers entered the first stage of homeschooling, where they felt a mixture of excitement and insecurity about their decision. They were excited because they thought this was the best option for their children, yet they remained nervous that they would not succeed, a common concern among new home-schooling mothers.[9] As Cassandra Shudek, the white, upper-middle-class mother of four boys, explained:

> Kids come out of school not knowing how to read, so you just expect that if the teachers can't do it, then it must be really, really hard. And when there are twenty different [books] offered on how to teach your kids to read, . . . you're convinced that you're going to need a master's degree and five years of experience teaching in classrooms to do it. And it can be terrifying.

Most mothers doubted their ability to become their children's primary teachers, especially if they had no formal teaching training. Yet even some who had been teachers were insecure about their ability. Molly O'Donnell, a white, middle-class mother and former high school teacher who had recently begun homeschooling her six-year-old son, reflected on her "terrible" confidence level:

> It was really, really bad! . . . Despite [my] being a teacher. Because if it had not been my child, it would have strictly been a professional thing. But this has emotional and professional and long-range impact to our child. So I was very nervous about it. I really did not think I could really do it well.

It was not that Molly did not know how to teach; rather, she did not know how to teach a child to whom she had a deep emotional attachment—her own. She felt unable to approach this assignment solely as a professional teacher because of the personal investment she held in her son's education. Such role ambiguity has been shown to be an important factor in burnout among professional teachers and other service workers, perhaps because role ambiguity may lead to emotional insecurity, as it did for these homeschool-ing mothers.[10]

To reduce this role ambiguity, and thus their insecurity, mothers researched different pedagogies and curricula. Most, but certainly not all, felt an intense desire to structure their curriculum and plan out a yearlong schedule that would keep their children on track with their conventionally schooled peers. Some mothers first sought curricular advice from the public school district, which was of little help, so most eventually looked to experienced homeschoolers.

The most common advice veterans offered was to embrace more flexibility in teaching styles and curricula. Veteran homeschoolers often talked about their own disastrous experiences starting out with "too much" structure (which they called the "school-at-home" method), in which they simulated a conventional classroom in their home, complete with blackboards, desks, and subjects separated out by minutes of the day. Veterans tried to convince newcomers that homeschooling was not simply bringing structured ideas about school into the home but rather about holistically educating their children according to their interests and needs. They constantly told newcomers to relax and explained that their children would learn if parents made learning fun.

Angela Welch, the African American mother in her late forties who had started homeschooling her four children twelve years earlier (when she realized that God wanted her to homeschool; see chapter 2) recalled the first weeks after she decided to homeschool. She explained that she had attended a statewide homeschooling convention where she sat in on an introductory seminar led by Judith Munson, the homeschooling veteran who was well known around the state for her homeschooling political activism. Judith's suggestions for curricular choices gave Angela pause. She had expected authors and titles of classic texts, but instead Judith encouraged her audience to take an unstructured approach to education. Angela explained how Judith's advice made her nervous: "I listened to Judith, and she said things that were blowing me away! Things like, 'Let [the kids] play; let 'em play!' And I raised my little timid hand and said, 'What do you mean by, "Let 'em play"?' And she [repeated], 'Let 'em play!' And I thought 'Ooooh boy!'"

Experienced homeschoolers tried to redefine inexperienced mothers' emotions for them, exposing them to the "feeling rules"[11] of the homeschooling subculture. They suggested that the inexperienced homeschoolers should relax (both their curricula and their emotions), that they should not be terrified about their abilities to teach their children, and that children learn best through enjoyable, playful engagement—at times even suggesting children's everyday play be the main curriculum. A few mothers implemented this approach, but most became very nervous at such suggestions, which heightened their sense of role ambiguity and insecurity. They did not believe their children would learn without a formal curriculum, and as a result, they ignored the advice. When I asked newcomers whether they would consider an unstructured approach, they made statements like, "I'm too terrified to try that right now," and "I can't gamble with my son like that." Instead, they bought expensive curricula and scheduled the entire year by dividing the chapters in the books by the number of weeks in the traditional school calendar. Despite constant warnings against such rigidity, most newcomers felt much less anxiety about homeschooling in this way.

Once mothers began homeschooling according to a predetermined structure, most experienced a honeymoon period (anywhere from six weeks to five months) when they stuck to their schedules—even getting ahead in some areas—and their children happily absorbed the knowledge their mothers imparted to them.[12] Renée Peterson, the white, middle-class mother of two children, ten and two, described her first few weeks of homeschooling after pulling her daughter, Taya, out of a private Christian school in hopes of making their evenings "more harmonious":

> The first six weeks of homeschooling were *fantastic*,,,, Oh! She was just a delightful kid! She was *wonderful* to be around! ... We got all our work done when I was at my strongest and not as tired, and we weren't bouncing off each other's emotions as much [as when she was in school]. ... Both [my daughter and I] are much more comfortable with structure, so we had our schedule. We both like to check things off, see how much we can get done in a day.

Homeschooling originally brought the relief Renée was hoping for: more relaxed family dynamics and a more academically productive child. She attributed her success, in part, to the structure they followed. Mothers like Renée, at this point, thought the demands of the teacher role seemed clear, which reassured them that homeschooling—and their structured approach to it—was the right choice. It also made them feel competent in the teacher role. When Sabrina Hernandez's first kindergartener taught himself to read during her initial year of homeschooling, she thought, "What's there to teaching kids? It's so easy, they teach themselves! What do teachers complain about?"

Role "Failure": Anxiety, Interpersonal Emotion
Management, and Intensification

For the vast majority of structured homeschoolers, the honeymoon came to a crashing halt when they encountered two challenges: children's low motivation and their lack of progress relative to parents' expectations. These impediments made mothers feel like they were failing as teachers, which marked the second emotional stage of adjusting to the teacher role. They experienced extreme anxiety, fearing they were ruining their children. To counter these feelings of role failure, mothers tried to manage their children's negative emotions and help them catch up academically by intensifying the curricular structure.

LOW STUDENT MOTIVATION AND MANAGING EMOTIONS

One challenge mothers encountered was their children's poor attitude toward schoolwork. Many children quickly learned that it was no fun to complete a workbook assignment at the kitchen table before they could play. I asked Renée what happened after her initial six weeks, during which ten-year-old Taya had been "just wonderful to be around":

> I don't know *what* happened [*laughs*], but she would [say], "No, I don't want to do this! . . . No, I *won't* go to my room!" [I] just [had] no control over her. [She was] slamming doors—you name it. We just couldn't get through. It was a huge crisis point. [She] just didn't want to do anything. . . . She *hates* writing, so we started out the school year doing some calligraphy, but I think she overheard me saying that we call that "penmanship," too, and she hasn't done it since [*laughs*]! So I'm needing to work on ways to motivate her. To make it interesting to her. . . . To push through it.

The majority of parents I talked to described having experienced similar problems, though not always as severe. Like Renée, most tried to "push through it" because they saw doing so as a way to instill important values in their children—traits that they, like many Americans, saw as necessary to succeed in life, such as discipline and delayed gratification (see chapter 3). Parents' fear was that if they allowed their children to perform only the activities they liked at the expense of those they did not, they would develop a poor work ethic and not become successful adults. Thus, not only was "pushing through it" a strategy mothers used to try to manage their children's emotions, but they also used it to manage their own anxiety about ruining their children.[13]

However, when pushed, some children "dug in their heels," as one mother told me, and parents felt they had to hold firm. Alice Lange, a white, middle-class grandmother who was in her first year homeschooling, explained that her six-year-old grandson did not understand that school time was "serious," not "playtime with Grandma": "If he's not in the mood to cooperate fully, we have a test of wills, and I won't give in [*laughs*]. That is the hardest part for me, because some days it seems like it's an all-day process." As a result, Alice set up a classroom in her spare bedroom to try to manage her grandson's emotions—to keep him from "goofing around," as she said—by changing the setting and thus the definition of the situation. In this way, she engaged in "tight" interpersonal emotion management[14] by rigidly and unilaterally directing what emotions her grandson should feel, and thus how he should behave. Her artificial classroom, however, did little to help him become more serious, and despite her best efforts, Alice became emotionally drained from the constant interpersonal emotion management.

Yet mothers who pushed their children academically also struggled with some of the basic philosophies of homeschooling, which they initially found attractive, such as providing their children with an individualized education. The experts claimed that children's lack of motivation in a certain area was a clear indication that they were not developmentally ready to learn that particular skill. Forcing them would only further decrease their motivation. Experienced homeschoolers, again, recommended more flexibility. They often used their own pasts as examples. Louise Griggs, a white, middle-class mother who had homeschooled four daughters over the course of nineteen years, explained her early experience to a large audience as she sat on a panel at a statewide homeschooling convention:

[When I first set up my classroom and started homeschooling] with the heavy curriculum and all the structure and, you know, blackboards and everything, my oldest daughter especially . . . pretty soon just dug in her heels (being that kind of personality anyway) and would not—*would not*— do anything as far as academics. You know when they say, "I hate"—fill in the blank: reading, math, you know, whatever—then that's the time that you should probably back off for a while.

Renée, Alice, and Louise, like many others, soon realized that one of the most exhausting aspects of homeschooling was the sheer amount of interpersonal emotion management they had to perform to gain children's cooperation. Research has shown that managing others' emotions, whether for a wage or not, can be draining, which sets the stage for burnout.[15] Experienced homeschoolers understood this, which is why they recommended reducing the structure. Trying to change children's feelings about a subject was a losing battle; indeed, the strategy could backfire, reducing motivation in other areas or, worse, extinguishing children's love of learning entirely.

"INADEQUATE" STUDENT PROGRESS AND INTENSIFYING STRUCTURE

Another challenge many homeschoolers encountered was that their children were not progressing as quickly as they had planned. Although mothers were happy to devote extra time to teaching when their efforts were successful, when children did not improve, mothers felt like they were failing in the teacher role. Whitney McKee, the working-class mother who was halfway through her only year of homeschooling, was unsure about how well her eleven-year-old son was keeping up with his conventionally schooled peers:

> I look at his math book and how far we've gone and how much more we have to do, and [I say to myself], "There's no way we're going to get done by the end of May or middle of June!" I mean, there's just *no way*. And then Ritchie keeps saying, "But mom, [my class] didn't finish our book last year [in private school]." And I'm like, "Okay, okay." But why didn't *we* finish? Why aren't we further along?

While Whitney explained this to me, her son, Ritchie, who had been listening to our conversation as he cleaned his hermit crab cage, interrupted: "We already finished the science book."

"Yeah," she conceded. "We finished that quickly." Although Whitney suspected they were making adequate progress when her son confronted her with the facts, she was unable to shake the feeling of failure: that he would suffer academically with her as his teacher.

When children were "slow" in an area, parents experienced a reduced sense of personal accomplishment, which is one of the main dimensions of the burnout syndrome.[16] Mothers felt extreme anxiety and blamed themselves. Twenty-five-year-old Maria Rojas, for example, told me that she lay awake some nights crying, thinking, "Oh my gosh, I'm never going to be able to teach my child to read. I don't have any [training]. He's going to be retarded." The sudden realization that their children were "behind" panicked them. Gretchen Forrester, the mother I observed homeschooling her three boys on several occasions, was a former high school teacher. Unlike many mothers I studied, she had always homeschooled in an unstructured way, which worked for her first son, Harry, since he had started reading at age three. Gretchen had never experienced any worries or frustrations with Harry's academic ability until one day when she attended a gathering with other families and realized, "we've really got to get to work" on one of his skills:

> It was writing. I [saw] what kids his age could do, [and] I had the feeling like he was *behind*, even though he was reading giant, hardback chapter books, I'm thinking, "Oh man, he's really behind." So I decided we were going to do "school at home" for writing. I never really said it, but I just

thought, "We are going to write every day." I tried to really make it official. . . . And, you know, I didn't want to stand for him holding his pen-
cil the way little kids color. I wanted him to hold it [the right way]. I got
one of those pads that has upper and lower case lines so you know how
your letters are to be formed. And I told him, "You can practice writing the
alphabet or whatever you need to do, but every day you need to practice
your letters." . . . And he would cry, and he would fight when it was time to
do the writing.

Even mothers who had previously used an unstructured approach found
it difficult to follow the experts' advice to drop the subject for a few months,
or even years, until the child was "ready for it." Thus, mothers reacted to
their children's struggles and to their own role-failure anxiety by intensifying their structure; they assigned more work in the "problematic" area,
which decreased the child's motivation and, in turn, often led to lower performance. When performance and motivation dropped again, many mothers responded by increasing the structure once more. This process illustrates
an "emotion line," a "series of emotional reactions to a series of instigating
events."[17] In this case, the emotional reactions created an intensifying loop
for mothers, which led to a cycle of relentless planning and stress. Many
mothers ended up using even more time to plan the next day's lessons, and
this became emotionally draining.

Renée Peterson, whose daughter had started slamming doors and quit
working on calligraphy, found herself caught in this cycle of relentless planning. She described the toll it took on her:

I get tired. Gosh, there's a lot of times where I just crawl into bed at eight-
thirty after the kids are in bed, and I'm just like [big sigh], read my book,
roll over, go to sleep. But then I'll wake up at two [o'clock] in the morning and start thinking, "Okay, what do we need to do here?" and just—the
wheels [in my head] are turning. It seems like if you're a schoolteacher,
you focus on a certain grade level and you have all your materials, and you
know your subjects, and once you get it down, you can kind of expand
your teaching on those things. But with this, it's a continued thing—I'm
constantly maybe just half a step ahead of Taya in some areas, feeling like
I'm maxing out in fifth grade [laughs]!

Anxious about role failure, Renée decided to intensify her structure.
Although her deep emotional and physical investment in the teacher role
exhausted her, and the stress was chronic, she continued because it reduced

her anxiety about failing. The emotional exhaustion she and many mothers described is the first step to burning out.[18]

Role Conflict and Overload: Burnout,
Compartmentalization, and Reliance on God

As mothers intensified their curricular demands and tried to combat their children's low motivation, they burned out, which marked the third stage of mothers' emotional adjustment to homeschooling. Homeschoolers often feel stress and overcommitment because of their immense "physical and psychological workloads."[19] However, the mothers I studied described the deleterious effect of the substantial emotional workload as well, which took its toll in the form of role conflict and role overload, depending on which roles were involved. Role conflict arose because the goals of the teacher role often contradicted those of the mother role; the homemaker role, however, brought about role overload because mothers had too much housework to do in the time available to them.[20]

Some mothers felt the conflict between their roles as teacher and mother. Whitney McKee, the mother of eleven-year-old Ritchie, described this tension in detail:

> When you go from being a mother to being a mother-teacher it's a real hard adjustment for both of you. My son, who teachers think walks on water and is considerate and polite and kind, . . . becomes much more demanding. And things [that] he would never do in school, he's very comfortable [doing] with me. . . . He falls apart. [He says], "I can't do it," and "I need you." He knows that I won't reject him, and that my love is unconditional for him, so he can push a little further. His teacher would never tolerate that kind of behavior. He never is rude [to me]. He never says mean things to me. But emotionally, yeah, a little more outbursts. But you just have to keep plowing ahead. . . . The easy thing would be [to say], "Let's just close the books." But that's what he wants me to do. So you just keep pushing. And then you think, "Why did I do this? Why am I here?"

Whitney was torn between acting as a teacher, who would not tolerate such behavior, and as a mother, who would tend to her child's emotional needs. Mothers often reported that emotional dynamics made a typical teacher-student relationship impossible; note that Whitney did not go from "mother" to "teacher" but to "mother-teacher." At home, children could use their emotions to manipulate their mothers (not necessarily consciously), and mothers spent a significant amount of time trying to combat it. This seemed especially true for mothers who embraced the school-at-home method, presumably because they also embraced the traditional idea of teacher, which in many ways requires a degree of affective neutrality that conflicts with the ideals of intensive mothering.[21] To manage the drastically different emotional requirements of each role, mothers compartmentalized mothering and teaching, which is a logical response to role conflict.[22] However, homeschoolers who tried to be emotionally available mothers at some times but professionally distant teachers at others often burned out. Juggling both roles separately did not adequately alleviate their conflicted feelings.

Many mothers also felt strain in the form of role overload with regard to their role as homemaker because of the sheer amount of time that homeschooling took from their daily schedules, a finding that has been supported by other research on homeschooling parents.[23] I heard countless mothers express anxiety about having no time to do "my housework," which they considered solely their responsibility because they were stay-at-home wives and mothers. Homeschooling often overloaded them, upsetting the delicate balance of household responsibilities, which distressed them. Many mothers made statements like, "Ah! A messy house! How can I homeschool?"

The families in my study varied in the number of duties they considered necessary to keep their households running; thus role strain was exacerbated for families with heavier chore loads. Tracy Chadwick's white, upper-middle-class family was committed to "whole foods," which meant that Tracy bought the raw ingredients to cook much of the family's food from scratch. For example, she would buy a large bag of wheat berries, grind her own grain, and make the family's bread. She noted that when they made "porridge pancakes" in the mornings, "it's not a quick breakfast!" This commitment only furthered the role overload she experienced.

One way mothers adjusted to the increased demands placed on them was by trying to juggle it all—performing every role in their repertoire to the utmost of their ability. Tracy stayed up late and got up early to do chores. I asked Tracy and her husband, David, about housework:

> TRACY: Our standards are fairly high in that department. I can't live with a messy house. And so we're picking up constantly. It's just part of having kids. Yeah, if they were in school, that would be super-duper—but [because we're homeschooling] the engine is revved up a little higher. Which is good because we're revved up higher anyway. So we don't go

to bed until it looks [spotless] like it does right now. And so I pick up every night. We all pick up—well, everybody but David picks up every night. David does the sensible thing and reads the *New Yorker* and then goes back to work.

DAVID: No, that's not—

TRACY: —It's okay, honey, you do other things. . . . And I have to say that both David and I have an unusual amount of energy that other people comment on. Most of my friends could not do what I do, the way I do it. It's not a fault or a blessing or anything, it's just that, you know, they go to bed at night.

Tracy, a self-described nonreligious, "liberal, environmental, left-wing" woman, felt responsible for most of the daily housecleaning. When David tried to contest her characterization of him as no help in this department, she acted as an "emotional buffer,"[24] absorbing some of the difficult emotions that could arise for him when confronted with the unequal division of labor in their home. Tracy protected his privileged emotional status by justifying why she did so much more. First, the overall division of household labor was fair (he did "other things"); second, housework was not an imposition because she had such an unusually large store of energy (compared with other people who "go to bed at night").[25] With these rationalizations in place, Tracy was able to feel good about juggling her roles as teacher, mother, and homemaker and deny that she was overcommitted.

However, Tracy was burning out. Homeschooling in a structured, school-at-home way added too much work for most mothers (though not all) to comfortably fold into their daily lives, an observation that has been supported in other research on homeschooling.[26] Mothers' immense role overload made them feel inadequate in all their roles and led to burnout.[27] When I interviewed Tracy, she sounded busy but committed to homeschooling. Several months later, however, things changed. She found homeschooling to be increasingly draining because she could not keep her son learning on a predictable schedule, and the more she tried, the more he rebelled. Her friend Gretchen Forrester, who used an unstructured style because Harry read at age three, advised her to be more flexible, but Tracy resisted. Gretchen told me about Tracy's frustration:

She was hitting a wall. She was like, "I have to tell you, I've been interviewing schools." I'm like, "What?!" See, she got this idea of what homeschooling was like from another family who has a very structured curriculum, and the children are *very* well behaved. And she decided she wanted more of that, so she did school-at-home, and it was awful. Jacob fights, cries, screams, you know, the whole dynamic just fell apart. . . . And she didn't tell anyone until it was too late—at least anyone who could have helped her see how unimportant it was that he be on some imposed course or whatever. But I said, "Tracy, he's doing math when you—" and gave her several examples of how we just do math in our everyday life. And so that day she said [to Jacob], "I need help. I don't know how we're going to pay these bills. Can you show me how we can?" and she said it was the best day they'd had in weeks. She put the curriculum aside and just let him do it. And he didn't realize he was doing math. He didn't realize he was doing his writing. And he did it willingly, and he had a good time doing it. . . . But she just said, "It's so exhausting to always have to go in the back door, rather than just sit down and say we're going to do math, and we're going to do reading, and we're going to do writing, and then we can play and have fun."

For Tracy, going "in the back door" involved integrating her teacher and homemaker roles so that her son could learn while the bills got paid. But her desire to compartmentalize the roles made her resistant to this approach, and with David's scant domestic contribution, it was too much for her to juggle. She burned out and shortly thereafter enrolled Jacob in public school (more on Tracy's journey in subsequent chapters).

Leanna Livingston, like Tracy, was also burned out from homeschooling. She used a very structured curriculum and revised it often, which made her teacher duties seem relentless. When I asked her whether she had considered a less structured approach, she said she was "not comfortable being that hands-off with it." Yet constantly revamping her curriculum took a great deal of time, exacerbating her feeling that she was not accomplishing enough, a common progression of the burnout syndrome.[28] Furthermore, homeschooling was not her only source of stress. She also reported feeling strapped for time to do "my chores," though she made a conscious effort every afternoon. Her husband worked full-time as a public school teacher and had trained for five marathons in recent years. Leanna told me that he had very little energy to contribute to household and family duties, which meant the housework, child care, and homeschooling of their nine-, six-, and three-year-old boys fell on her.

Like Tracy, Leanna juggled the competing demands of teacher, mother, and homemaker, yet unlike Tracy, Leanna overcame burnout periodically by relying on her faith:

I think [you can overcome burnout] if you have a clear feeling that this is what you're supposed to do. You know, we *know* why we're homeschooling. We know it's the right choice for us. And that makes all the difference. Having the clear-cut call. Feeling that this is what God wants us to be doing with our children. This is what he's called us to. And he's gonna help us do what we need to. That's a huge thing. Knowing that we're not really in this alone. We've got the help of somebody that knows a lot more than we do [*laughs*]!

Leanna was able to overcome burnout because she was confident that she was following God's plan, a pattern other research has uncovered as well.[29] She not only used her faith in God—"knowing" it was the right path—to alleviate her feelings of overcommitment but also used language to obscure the unequal burden she carried in the family: "God wants *us*" to homeschool. By recasting her individual effort as a collective endeavor, Leanna concealed the fact that she was solely responsible for the housework, parenting, and teaching.[30]

Other Christian homeschoolers, too, gave examples of how they relied on God to manage their emotions. At one statewide convention I attended, I sat in on a session titled "When Reality Hits, How to Keep Going." The presenter identified herself as "dyslexic, from an abusive, alcoholic home and was 'saved' by 'the Lord' after her first year of college." She talked about what homeschoolers should do when they experience the "TFS," which I recorded in my fieldnotes:

It's the "Total Failure Syndrome." This happens when homeschoolers end up feeling like a failure in all areas: as a mother, teacher, and wife. She gives us a handout, and in it she says that annually, she has a "pity party" for herself. She tells us that when that happens, her husband says she should take a few days off, but she gets back to work instead, and plows through the discouragement. "Don't make decisions based on emotions!" she advises. She hasn't felt like cooking dinner for her family for the last twenty years, but she's "done it every night!" In the handout, she provides some words of inspiration: "*Hooray for the little red hen. She can do the work of ten. And when she's done, she does it again.*" She also advises us to "play the 'glad game' because we are far from earth's needier creatures; we need a lesson in poverty."

This presenter recommended dealing with the stress of homeschooling by suppressing the problematic emotions (mothers should not "make decisions" based on them, nor should they take time off to address them); transforming them through cognitive shifts (in this case, mothers should change their feelings of relative deprivation by comparing themselves to less fortunate groups); and persevering despite the discouragement that comes from role overload.

In addition, the presenter evoked numerous biblical themes throughout her session and anchored further advice in the foundation of the patriarchal hierarchy that most versions of evangelical Christianity espouse (husband answers to God, wife answers to husband, children answer to parents). She described one occasion when she had had a particularly hard day homeschooling. I recorded her story in my fieldnotes:

> Her husband came home and asked, "How was your day?" She responded by saying it was awful: all this bad stuff happened, and one child said such-and-such, and the kids fought, and so on. Her husband said—and she tells us this as though it was just what she needed to hear—"I think that was wonderful day! It's a homeschooling mom being humble to her children." Her husband prays that "God will encourage me to encourage," but also that God "fills" her to replace what she gives in encouragement. "You see?" she says, hoping we understand her point. "My husband sent me forth to use my gift of encouragement."

The attendees in this session seemed fairly responsive to her message, though some of the audience questions suggested that not everyone felt completely confident that this information could solve their homeschooling problems. One audience member asked for the presenter's advice on her particular situation, saying, "I started having chest pains in [another] session [earlier today] when I thought of all the things I wasn't doing. I have older parents who I have to drive around and kids who have to get to orthodontist appointments. I've lost focus in the homeschooling. What would you suggest?" The presenter responded by advising this woman to try to do it all anyway, and to celebrate her subordinate position: "Do it with a servant's attitude and a joyful heart. It's an opportunity for us to serve. There's only one place to get focus, [God]." Thus, some factions of homeschooling's emotional culture, particularly the most evangelical ones, blatantly dismissed mothers' problematic emotions, encouraging them instead to embrace their suffering and accept their overloaded lives.[31]

Role conflict and overload took a strong physical and emotional toll on homeschooling mothers, burning them out despite their best emotion management efforts. Christian and secular homeschoolers' burnout arose from the same sources: an overly structured curriculum and an unwillingness to acknowledge, or at least be angry about, their husbands' insufficient participation in household chores.[32] Yet Christian mothers, like Leanna and the session presenter mentioned earlier, relied on the tenets of evangelical Christianity (and on the unequal gender roles therein) to help them more easily justify their husband's sparse contribution, whereas Tracy's secular and progressive ideology perhaps prevented her from adequately explaining away David's lack of involvement. It was more difficult for Tracy to manage her discontent because the way her family's labor was divided contradicted her ideas about gender equality, a dynamic found in other research on married couples' division of labor.[33] As a result, Leanna persevered, but Tracy enrolled her son in public school.

Role Harmony: Prioritization, Support, and Integration

Although some mothers became trapped in the burnout stage of homeschooling, some moved beyond the role conflict, overload, and juggling that homeschooling engendered. One way they did so was by "bowling." I heard this term from an experienced homeschooler at one of the monthly PATH meetings. She was fielding questions from the audience and someone asked, "How do you juggle it all?" She answered, "You can't juggle it all. With homeschooling, it's more like bowling!" Though she did not elaborate, everyone laughed because it was such a descriptive analogy: jugglers fail when they drop one ball; bowlers knock down what they can at each opportunity; they do not always need a strike to do well—it all counts.

Mothers who bowled relieved the emotional stress of role overload by prioritizing mothering over the homemaking. They lowered their standards for housework so they could spend more time with their children, a philosophy that research has documented among some other groups of mothers as well.[34] Gretchen Forrester, the mother of three young boys told me:

> I have to constantly remind myself that I have the rest of my life to have the house be perfect. . . . This is a pretty small window of time that I'm going to have this opportunity to be home with the kids, and if the laundry waits because we're reading out loud and doing watercolor and taking nature walks, then we can dig through the laundry pile to find clean socks. And we do, often, because the priority isn't on the house.

Gretchen's roles were not equally important, so she did not juggle them as though they were.

Yet it was difficult for homeschoolers to prioritize motherhood without help from their husbands because, although some housework, like folding laundry, could be disregarded, there was still too much, like meal preparation, that was essential. Mothers who overcame burnout almost always had husbands who supported them with housework and some aspect of the teaching or child care, though it was very rare that mothers reported fathers who shared these responsibilities significantly. Cassandra's husband supported her by being an "involved" dad and taking charge of some of the teaching, though his contributions paled in comparison to hers and were related to playing with the children rather than focusing on their academic skills. He also agreed with her that the housework was unimportant. She told me, "Joel knows what it's like to be home with the four kids, and he's glad that I'm playing with them and not feeling like I need to have the house be a social showpiece or anything. He doesn't have that expectation of me. The house is just where we live." It is interesting that this form of husband help with the housework, however, involved releasing his strict standards for it rather than pitching in to get more done. Mothers perceived that husbands who shared some of the work, whether teaching, housework, or child care, were integral to their success. They helped alleviate stress and burnout by reducing the overload, which helped mothers keep their heads above water (the picture was not all that rosy for most mothers, however, as I will discuss in the next chapter).

Mothers also overcame burnout by heeding the advice of experienced homeschoolers and relaxing the structure of their curriculum. Jackie Bell, the middle-class African American mother of two girls, told me that she was very anxious early in her homeschooling career, trying to make sure she assigned the right kind of work for her oldest daughter, then four years old. She read many books on age-appropriate skills and pedagogies, becoming progressively overwhelmed until one book helped her redefine her idea of being a teacher:

> All of a sudden, everything came into focus. "Okay, I don't have to know everything in order to be able to help her. I just have to be a facilitator." So to change the role from, "I'm her teacher, and she's got to do what I'm saying, and I've got to hover over her shoulder and make sure she's doing her homework"—to have that shift to, "Wow, I'm here to help her get what she needs done"—it was so freeing for me. You know, I can get her to the library; I can introduce her to somebody who is really excited about a subject that I don't know about. I can help her get online and research a topic or share stories that I might have on a subject. So it just

frees me up to be able to learn with her instead of feeling like I have to know everything.

Jackie's approach relieved burnout by reducing the planning time that drained so many mothers. By setting the child on an independent learning course, the facilitator strategy allowed mothers to be less dictatorial about their children's education. Because it also gave children some control, their motivation was more easily managed in this "loose," collaborative way.[35]

Mothers also felt more in tune with their children, and thus more harmony among their roles, when they trusted that their children would learn when they were "ready for it." Gretchen Forrester told me how she finally overcame Harry's reluctance to writing by dropping the subject temporarily, even though she feared he was "behind":

> GRETCHEN: I was stubborn, but I gave up after a while. And what happened was [that] I was pushing something on him, and he wasn't ready physically. Like the fine motor skills—he wasn't ready yet, and so it was really hard for him.
>
> JEN: So you think it was developmental? The reason he didn't like writing, and it was hard for him?
>
> GRETCHEN: I think there were two parts. One, it was developmental, and it was hard for him. And two, suddenly mom's coming down on him with her broom, you know, "You will write!" So I think it was both the approach—the rigidity of it—and the physical. . . . Now he loves to write. And just the other day he said, "You know, not too long ago, I did not like writing. It was really hard for me. Now, I *like* writing, and it's not hard for me." And I just thought, you know, they're ready when they're ready.

Many mothers reported, as Gretchen did, that letting their children's interests and skills guide the curriculum greatly reduced the emotional conflict they felt between their teacher and mother roles. These mothers overcame burnout by relying on their mothering instincts: as with anything, children would learn what they needed to know when they were ready for it. To these parents, learning was part of life, so education was incorporated into every aspect of their day, "like brushing your teeth or having breakfast," as one mother explained.[36]

Jackie's and Gretchen's experiences were also typical in another way: most mothers who embraced a less structured approach did so only after finding the highly structured, compartmentalizing strategy difficult, frustrating, and ineffective. Other research has revealed this pattern as well; indeed, the move to a less structured curriculum over time is one of the most consistent findings in the homeschooling research.[37] My research reveals that a less structured curriculum may help homeschoolers because it allows mothers to achieve harmony among their roles by integrating them rather than experiencing the conflict and overload that arise from compartmentalizing them.

After hearing many stories from burned-out mothers, I asked Cassandra Shudek about the difficulties of homeschooling. Her answer illustrated the importance of role integration:

CASSANDRA: [Homeschooling] just turned out to be so different than I thought it was going to be. It's so much easier and so much more fun. I thought it was going to be difficult and hard and exhausting, and it's not.

JEN: It's not exhausting?

CASSANDRA: No! It's not exhausting. [When my son was in private school], doing the whole picking up, dropping off, scheduling, volunteering, fund-raising, paying exorbitant amounts of money [*laughs*] for school, and having to work out the emotional problems that they have—*that* was exhausting and stressful and hard on the whole family. But this— this is nothing. Teaching them to read is really not much harder than teaching them to ride a bike. It isn't this difficult thing. It really, really isn't. Once you realize that it's just as easy as teaching them to walk and teaching them to feed themselves and teaching them to use the potty, you just do it. It's really not that hard. Once they're ready, they're ready, and they'll just do it.

It is clear that homeschooling mothers experienced emotional conflict. The emotional stress associated with their adjustment to the teacher role was significant, and they searched for ways to manage the problematic emotions of insecurity, frustration, and anxiety. Their initial efforts to manage these emotions took more time from their already busy lives, which intensified the temporal-emotional conflict they felt and often led to burnout. Therefore, aside from relying on their Christian faith and the knowledge they were fulfilling their sacrificial wife and mother duties, the most successful management techniques targeted mothers' time famine: soliciting husbands' contribution, forgoing housework, and destructuring their curriculum to reduce planning time. That these techniques were temporal in nature supports the findings in the literature on the household division of labor: there is a robust link between some of mothers' problematic emotions and the quantity of time they have available to them. However, my discussions with homeschooling mothers also revealed a deeper, less quantifiable connection between emotions and time. In the next chapter, I explore how homeschoolers' temporal-emotional conflict extended to their lack of personal time.

5

Losing Me-Time

The Temporal Emotion Work of Motherhood

So far, I have examined mothers' time in a variety of ways. When the mothers I studied talked about the emotional difficulties of homeschooling, time was almost always implicated in some way. When they were stressed about their children's lack of progress, it was often because they measured it against their temporal expectations, for example, as when Whitney worried that there was "no way" her son was going to complete his math book by the end of the traditional school year. When mothers became overwhelmed by the increased domestic load, it was because they did not feel they had enough time to complete their chores and educate their children. When they fretted about whether to work or stay home with their children, they considered how allocating their time in that way would make them feel. Thus, it is clear that mothers' time and emotions go hand-in-hand and weave throughout many dimensions of homeschoolers' lives and identities as mothers.

I have also shown that the majority of the sociological literature on mothers' time focuses most intensely on the specific problem of its scarcity and mothers' attempts at solutions, which revolve around objectively apportioning their time: they cut back to part-time work, leave the paid labor force entirely, solicit domestic labor from their husbands, outsource domestic labor, and combine chores with child care or their own leisure with their children's.[1] Few studies, though, have addressed how mothers tackle the problem of time scarcity by altering their subjective definitions of time. Sociologists Anita Garey's and Chris Bobel's works are exceptions, showing how the mothers they studied carved out acceptable identities for themselves by redefining time over the life course, a strategy they both call "sequencing." When mothers sequence, they compartmentalize phases in their lives according to children's development, accepting that when their children are young, they will sacrifice a great deal, although their sacrifice will attenuate as children age and become more independent.[2] Thus, as Garey points out, the time that mothers believe they should devote to mothering is intricately tied to the culturally accepted milestones of children's physical, social, and emotional development.[3] Through sequencing, mothers assure themselves that they indeed "can have it all, but not all at once."[4] Both Garey and Bobel clearly demonstrate that sequencing can help mothers deal effectively with the temporal tensions of intensive mothering, but they are less precise when discussing why it works. Though both analyses imply that sequencing helps mothers deal with the guilt, stress, and anxiety that may arise from the ways they use their time, neither engages emotions specifically to reveal exactly how these problematic feelings are assuaged when mothers redefine time through sequencing.

This chapter uncovers how homeschoolers manipulated their subjective experiences of time to manage their feelings. Even when mothers found ways to juggle all their household responsibilities and solicit domestic contributions from their husbands, it left them with their heads barely above water. Homeschoolers had no personal time or, as they called it, "me-time," which led to problematic emotions that had to be managed. Mothers first tried to allocate their time differently to carve out space in their schedules for themselves, but these quantitative time-use strategies were ineffective. As a consequence, mothers resorted to managing their feelings by manipulating their subjective experiences of time, a process I call "temporal emotion work."

Homeschooler's Strategies for Managing Time Shortage

Homeschoolers had mixed feelings about having no discretionary time. Though they were happy to live up to the ideals of good mothering by devoting a great deal of time to their children (indeed, recall from chapters 2 and 3 that this was frequently their main motivation for homeschooling), they also wished for me-time to pursue their interests. The lack of personal time created a great deal of stress, which mothers tried to alleviate by managing their time—reserving a small quantity for themselves every week. This strategy inevitably failed, however, and mothers became frustrated and resentful. To alleviate these feelings, mothers turned instead to manipulating their subjective experiences of time.

Losing Me-Time

Homeschoolers had "absolutely no time" for themselves because they were with their kids "twenty-four hours a day, seven days a week," and were "devoting every particle" of themselves to their children. Homeschoolers were often exhausted and burned out, and they discussed their lack of personal time frequently at meetings, as well as in magazines, books, and on Internet websites and listservs. Indeed, a standard question put to PATH's annual panel of experienced homeschoolers was, "How do you find time for yourself?"

Though many mothers did find ways to balance the increase in domestic labor against the decrease in available time that homeschooling engendered, even the mothers who felt the most "role harmony" (see chapter 4) still talked about lacking time for themselves. It seemed that these responsibilities—child care, housework, and homeschooling—trumped mothers' personal time, which always got pushed to the bottom of their priority lists. I heard countless mothers say that they had put their "own life on hold" to homeschool their children.[5] This refrain, an accepted truism in the subculture, not only reflected but amplified the sacrifice inherent in the ideology of intensive mothering; these homeschoolers were prepared to sacrifice themselves entirely for their children. In this respect, me-time was seen as a luxury among the mothers I talked to; it was the first thing to go and the hardest to recapture.

Yet even though homeschoolers treated time to themselves as expendable, every mother I talked to still expressed her desire for more of it, though some were more adamant than others about pursuing it. Although 71 percent of married mothers in the United States feel this way,[6] the desire for personal time was exacerbated for homeschoolers because they, often wistfully, compared themselves with mothers who sent their children to conventional schools. Pam Rausch, the white, middle-class mother of three children, ages thirteen, ten, and eight, immediately mentioned lack of personal time as a drawback to homeschooling:

I look at other mothers that send their kids off to school, and they have the day free. You know, they can have a clean house or they can have a job or whatever. They have freedom; they have time to themselves. So I think probably the biggest sacrifice for me, personally, is that I have no time for myself—I'm with [my kids] morning and night.

Despite having already dedicated years of twenty-four-hour days to being with their children, the pressure of intensive mothering in the homeschooling subculture relentlessly pushed mothers to sacrifice more. At one PATH meeting, I listened to a panel of experienced homeschoolers answer the question "How do you find time for yourself?" The first panelist worked in the garden with her children ("Did she understand the question?" I wondered in my fieldnotes); the second panelist got up at 5:00 a.m. to pray. My fieldnotes continued:

The third panelist said, quite self-consciously, "I guess I'm the spoiled brat in the group!" She then explained how *once a year* she went to a hotel "for a day and a night." "But after about two hours, I was missing the kids so much I'd call them to talk: 'Hey, there's a pool here, you guys would love it!'" So now she doesn't do that anymore.

That this mother labeled herself "spoiled," even if in a half-joking manner, reveals the degree to which self-sacrifice was integral to homeschooling motherhood; twenty-four hours per year away from her children was a luxury that other mothers—at least those on the panel—claimed they did not need.[7]

Despite these panelists' implication that they did not need time away from their children, all the mothers I talked to acknowledged the importance of personal time, yet simultaneously, most felt guilty and selfish about taking it. Therefore, they framed any pursuit of me-time in selfless terms, saying things like, "If I don't get myself filled, I can't give anything back." The cultural discourse of intensive mothering in the United States is rife with self-sacrifice, and mothers often justify self-pursuits as in the best interests of their children.[8] Homeschoolers did the same thing, but since they felt they sacrificed so much more than non-homeschoolers, such rhetoric was even more effective in neutralizing their seemingly selfish desires for me-time. They could talk about wanting time to themselves because their choice to homeschool was additional confirmation that they were intensely and constantly committed to prioritizing their children's needs over their own. Indeed, the act of talking about having no time was a way to draw attention to the sacrifices good mothers make and subsequently resulted in raising the standards for good mothering.[9] Sabrina Hernandez, the Hispanic American mother of twelve children, made this connection between sacrifice and good mothering when asked about the challenges of homeschooling:

> I stay home every day! Being around them isn't so easy. Children are hard! Working on relationships is hard. It's so easy to put them on a bus and send them to school for half a day, for a whole day and just say, "That time is mine! Phew! They're gone!" . . . But what else was I going to do with my time? Hey, I could sit down and watch soap operas in the afternoon, but what better thing to do than to give it to your children?

A few mothers admitted that they did not want to homeschool because they did not want to put their children's interests permanently above their own. Few and far between in my sample, those who acknowledged feeling this way were always second-choice homeschoolers (see chapter 2), and all connected their lack of time to a loss of self. Compared with first-choicers, second-choicers talked in much more complex terms about how home-schooling had restricted their opportunities to nurture aspects of themselves that they found important to rounding out their identities.

Darlene Rooney-Henkel, the white, middle-class mother of two, wished for an acceptable alternative to homeschooling. Recall that her eleven-year-old son had Asperger's syndrome, and though she had enrolled him in conventional school programs over the years, it never worked out; he was overwhelmed by the structure and chaos of the classroom. Darlene explained how difficult it was for her: "I am trying to resign myself to the fact that I might have to [homeschool through high school]. This has been hard for me. It's hard! It's hard as a woman to give up your own dreams for a while. I mean they're sort of put on hold to raise your kids." Compared with most stay-at-home mothers in the United States, who devote a great deal of time to their children until they reach school age, Darlene's life was going to be on hold an additional twelve years. The idea stressed and frustrated her, feelings she avowed and tried to reconcile.

Similarly, Tracy Chadwick, the white, middle-class second-choicer whose husband and father-in-law pressured her into homeschooling her eight- and four-year-olds, explained how the time required to homeschool was a problem:

> I don't want to be with my kids all day. I don't. I just don't want to do that right now. . . . And I love [homeschooling], I'm very dedicated, . . . [but] I would like personal time. 'Cause I don't get any. . . . I would pursue other

things; things that nurture me—although, this work [homeschooling] does nurture me very much—but I would see friends, and I would exercise more. I'd just recharge my batteries for when I could see my kids again.

All homeschoolers agreed that "recharging" was extremely important, but second-choicers were more vocal about wanting that recharging time to happen away from their children.

Patricia Tomlinson, the white mother of two boys and a second-choicer, had even more on her plate when I reinterviewed her in 2009. By that time, she was homeschooling her eleven-year-old and deeply engaged in helping her twenty-one-year-old, who was struggling with severe depression (more on their story in chapter 8). In addition, she was caring for her elderly parents and in-laws. She told me that because of all these responsibilities, she regretted pursuing any activity that she found self-fulfilling:

I stubbornly try to do things I like to do, which honestly feels like a penalty at this stage of my life. Whenever I try to do what I want to do, I wish I hadn't done it because it's just too much to factor it in; it just exhausts me. I'm at the stage where I have to—and it just doesn't sound right—let everybody else sort of take over my life and never do anything that I want to do. But it sort of feels that way, honestly. It feels like I've got sandwiched in between my parents and my children, and they're taking over my life. There is something extremely sacrificial about homeschooling.

Selflessness, for some homeschoolers, went beyond feeling sacrificially altruistic to feeling literally self-obliterating.[10] I asked Patricia if her lack of time made her feel like she had "lost [her] sense of self to some degree," and she responded:

Um, probably. I wonder about that sometimes. Because, honestly when somebody asks me my opinion—[yesterday my older son] asked me what I wanted to do for lunch, and I just said, "I don't know, what do you want to do?" and then I thought, "Oh, why did I do that? Why don't I have an opinion about this?" I don't, though; I honestly don't have an opinion. . . . And he did mention that, he said, "Well you should speak up for yourself!"

The problem for many mothers was the same one that sociologist Marjorie DeVault identified in her research on mothers' caring work in families: "A mother's claims for time to pursue her own projects can so easily be framed as a lack of care, and a mother's claim even to be 'a person' may be taken as 'selfish.'"[11]

Seeking Me-Time

Personal time was such a big issue, even for the first-choicers, that most mothers had much to say about how they had tried to carve it out throughout their homeschooling careers. Though attempts to do so varied a bit, most homeschoolers used similar strategies, which they tended to employ progressively. Mothers first tried to get fathers involved with the homeschooling, especially with science and math (subjects stereotyped as masculine and, therefore, perhaps thought better suited for fathers). They could study nature on a hike or complete a workbook assignment at the kitchen table. If fathers could commit to the same few hours every week, mothers could arrange their personal time dependably without disrupting the schooling schedule. However, this strategy usually failed. Mothers reported that fathers "got too busy" or "forgot" to honor their commitments, and mothers had to pick up the slack. Even when fathers did pitch in, their work with the children often did not meet mothers' standards. Liz Trudeau, a white, middle-class first-choicer who had homeschooled four children over the course of twenty years, had a typical story:

> I tried to kind of force [my husband] into the science role with [our son]. The curriculum was all right there. . . . It told you exactly what to do on Monday, what to do on Tuesday, what materials you needed a week in advance. But week after week after week he would get behind, and I was like, "Well, this isn't working." And it was a first-grade level, so it wasn't anything hard, and he still wasn't keeping up with it. [Since then] I have sometimes just said, "You need to give Mary her spelling test, and we need to go over this lesson in math with John." And I'll just say, "Do it," and he'll do it. But as far as preparing the class, as far as taking initiative, as far as saying, "What are you guys learning today?"—that's not really there. In a pinch, if I hand it to him and say, "Do this," he, for the most part, will do it. I can't even tell you whether or not he's happy about it, but he does it. So he's capable, and he will do it if I put it on him, but that's about as far as it goes.

Although some fathers were involved in the homeschooling, they were rare. Those who were unreliable and only halfheartedly invested in the homeschooling provided no relief because mothers spent additional time catching up on the work or redoing it entirely.[12] Liz was unwilling to lower her standards to gain personal time for herself because, in her view, that meant sacrificing the children's education.[13]

Faced with this circumstance, mothers lowered their expectations by asking fathers to commit to a reliable weekly schedule of child care where they could occupy the children any way they wanted. Yet again, things "came up" too often for fathers to keep the schedule, or they were reluctant to take on more parenting. Valerie Scott, the white mother with seven children, found it was "very difficult" for her husband "to change." She "nudged" him at first, "then it was like grinding the gears." After a while, she gave up. Finally, mothers lowered their expectations once more, asking fathers to commit to being home in the evenings or early mornings while the children slept.[14] Mothers found this the most dependable solution to schedule their personal time. They could go to the gym at 5:30 a.m. or, like a mother at a PATH meeting, a bookstore at night: "One night a week from nine-thirty to eleven [o'clock], I go to Barnes and Noble and read or balance the checkbook. I used to resent the kids being up after nine [o'clock]. It's my time!"

Yet this form of fathers' contribution—being on call for sleeping children—protected fathers' own personal time too. Unlike mothers' sacrifice, fathers served as warm bodies ("someone to get the kids out if there's a fire," as I wrote in my fieldnotes) rather than as engaged parents or partners who sacrificed their own time to homeschool their children. This difference in mothers' and fathers' time is an example of what sociologist Barbara Adam has called stay-at-home women's "shadow time," time that is devalued because it is "constituted as the shadows of the time economy of employment relations," and evaluated against the hegemonic conception of "the commodified time of the market."[15] The value of "free time" can also be cast in these terms: it is only defined as such when it is "wrested from employers' time";[16] therefore free time ceases to be a meaningful category for those who operate in shadow time, such as stay-at-home mothers who feel that they are "on call twenty-four-hours a day."[17] Homeschooling parents seemed to apply these principles, protecting fathers' free time while invalidating mothers' claims to it. In the process, these families created meaning systems that prioritized workplace time over domestic time, which granted fathers, but not mothers, the privilege to choose their level of family involvement. Thus, mothers sacrificed their own time to shield fathers from domestic responsibilities and preserve marital harmony (see also chapter 4).

Though most fathers did sporadically cover increments of child care time, it was still not enough, so mothers resorted to other methods of creating personal time that did not depend on their physical separation from the children. Veteran homeschoolers recommended that mothers merge their interests with their children's, a trend now common among non-homeschooling parents as well.[18] For example, Darlene took piano lessons with her daughter; Patricia integrated her love of cooking with her geography curriculum, exploring foods from different cultures. Mothers felt less stagnant when learning new things, but redefining me-time to include anything interesting that they could do with their children was fairly restrictive.[19]

Some mothers redefined me-time in the opposite way, including any time away from their children, regardless of what they were doing (as in balancing the checkbook at Barnes and Noble). Renée Peterson, who gave up her career in law enforcement, told me that she found time to herself by "getting errands done" when her children were at extracurricular activities. I asked her if grocery shopping was really time to herself, and she said:

> Well, yes! It becomes that; it does. You just make those moments. For ages I resisted getting a dishwasher because I learned to love washing the dishes. Everybody knew, just stay out of the kitchen while Mom was doing the dishes. I'd have that forty-five minutes to myself, and that was great!

Although being alone was a break Renée enjoyed, when I pressed her, she admitted that she did not find doing the dishes to be self-fulfilling. Rather, her willingness to consider forty-five minutes of household chores as personal time illustrates how homeschooling mothers redefined me-time and lowered their expectations accordingly.

Stories of fathers' resistance were widespread among the mothers I talked to, yet there was some variation not only in the degree of resistance but also in mothers' feelings about it. Conservative families, who, in my sample, were highly religious, tended to have a more traditional gendered division of labor, and thus less husband involvement. Husband contribution was slightly higher in the more gender-egalitarian families, though these wives still reported encountering a good deal of resistance. Moreover, because egalitarian wives expected more, they were more dissatisfied than traditional wives who expected, and received, less support (a pattern that parallels mothers' burnout, which I discussed in chapter 4).[20] Tracy Chadwick, the second-choicer I interviewed with her husband and father-in-law in 2002, identified as very liberal and politically progressive. When I interviewed her alone in 2009, she told me about David's disinterest in homeschooling over the years (recall from chapter 4 that David "reads the *New Yorker*" instead of doing housework after dinner):

> TRACY: I've often wondered why such a creative guy, who puts his creative energy into so many different things, hasn't put it into homeschooling as much.
>
> JEN: Have you asked him?

TRACY: Oh, lots. He usually feels like a failure as a father when I talk to him about that. But you know, [I tell myself], "it is what it is." He's so into homeschooling, it was his idea, mainly. He sees the validity and importance of it, but it's mainly been my job. And I wish that were different. . . . But I guess I'm not frustrated about it right now.

Tracy, like many mothers, had grown resigned to her husband's lack of day-to-day involvement, despite his enthusiasm for the idea of homeschooling, enthusiasm that was clear to me when I talked to him on several occasions.[21] Stevens found a similar dynamic among the homeschooling parents he interviewed. Fathers tended to talk more philosophically about the educational benefits of homeschooling (it was great in theory), whereas mothers focused more on the concrete challenges of conquering the workload (it was difficult in practice).[22]

Perhaps sacrifice is so synonymous with mothering that husbands did not understand the impact homeschooling had on mothers' time and selves. Valerie Scott's experience suggests that another way husbands and children undermined mothers' ability to find time for themselves was by interacting with them only through their one-dimensional identities as mothers:

VALERIE: [When you homeschool], you have no time by yourself. None. For Mother's Day, I always wanted a day at home, in a clean house, with nobody else here. And I love my kids—I adore them—but that just would have been bliss for me. And it was very rare, very rare.
JEN: Did you get it once a year, at least, on Mother's Day?
VALERIE: They never took me seriously, I don't think. "It's Mother's Day, Mom. Don't you want your kids around? You're a mother."

The mothers I talked to expressed a great deal of frustration with fathers' lack of contribution, but at some point, many, like Tracy and Valerie, shifted to grudging acceptance.[23] They came to terms with putting their own lives on hold for prolonged periods to homeschool their children, but the ways they accomplished this shift are worth exploring further.

Doing Temporal Emotion Work

Mothers' frustration could easily grow into resentment toward their husbands and even their children, whose demands prevented them from regularly scheduling even a small quantity of time for themselves.[24] Because

mothers' attempts to manage their objective allocation of time did not alleviate these feelings, they turned instead to managing their subjective experiences of time and their feelings about it. Because homeschoolers' problematic emotions were, at their core, time-related, mothers talked a great deal
not only about trying to change their emotions through emotion work but
also about trying to change their subjective experiences of time, a process
sociologist Michael Flaherty (drawing inspiration from Hochschild's concept) has called "time work."[25] Homeschoolers did both of these things, at
some times simultaneously, at other times reciprocally, because they found
the temporal experience of motherhood to be emotionally problematic. As I
sifted through mothers' stories, it became clear that temporality was a crucial
feature not only in the ways they experienced their problematic emotions but
also in their attempts to manage them. Therefore, I term this type of emotion
work, the type that both shapes and is shaped by temporal concerns, "temporal emotion work." To manage the temporal-emotional conflict of motherhood, homeschoolers used two types of temporal emotion work: sequencing
and savoring.

SEQUENCING: ELICITING NOSTALGIA AND ANTICIPATING REGRET

Sequencing, or the strategy of compartmentalizing phases of life according
to children's development, was a common way that homeschooling mothers performed temporal emotion work. As I mentioned at the beginning
of this chapter, Garey and Bobel have both identified sequencing as a way
for mothers to justify dedicating such a disproportionate amount of time to
their children when they are young; it is acceptable to do so because motherhood requires less sacrifice as children age and become more independent.
In this sense, sequencing constitutes Flaherty's idea of time work—it is a way
to "promote or suppress a particular temporal experience."[26] When homeschooling mothers talked about the immense amount of time they devoted
to their children, they often framed their explanations around this idea of
sequencing.[27] For example, some referred to motherhood as a "season," a biblical reference that helped them reason, as Liz Trudeau said, that "there is a
time for everything. . . . There will be time for me later to pursue anything
that interests me." However, as I explored this issue further, it became clear
that mothers' ability to accept sequencing as a rationale to "table [their] own
needs"[28] hinged on particular types of emotion work, which was the essential
link in developing and sustaining their willingness to sacrifice their interests over such a prolonged period. Therefore, I consider sequencing to be an
example of temporal emotion work—one in which a temporal strategy (in
this case, sequencing) depends on some form of emotion work.

Homeschooling mothers relied on two emotions to help them justify sequencing: nostalgia and regret. Specifically, they used these emotions to transcend the present—to cross "timeframes"[29]—into the past and the future. Nostalgia contains the dual facets of pleasure and pain: bittersweet feelings about happy times that, sadly, cannot be recaptured.[30] Yet nostalgia is an emotion that contains a temporal component because it requires retrospection. Because of this emotional focus on the past, nostalgia was quite useful to homeschooling mothers in time- and emotion-related ways.

Whitney McKee, the white working-class mother who homeschooled her eleven-year-old son for only one year, lamented the passing of time:

> You miss your baby. All those things they do and say, you cherish in your heart. I miss all that. . . . It's almost like you want to take a bite out of [that moment] and savor it and never let it out. I wanted to inhale him when he was little—I was so in love with this child. . . . It's like your life has chapters, and I'm looking back at the book and thinking, "[*Sighs*], I miss this part of the book. Do I really want to turn the page?"

Like Whitney, many mothers looked back nostalgically to help them remember that the time with their children was fleeting and could not be recaptured. They then mapped their past experience onto the future and imagined someday looking back on the present with nostalgic feelings; the present would soon move permanently into the past. Becoming nostalgic, then, taught mothers that they should be aware of the progression of time. Whitney told me that for this reason she was trying to consciously appreciate this one year of homeschooling by creating a select set of memories for the future:

> This is a grand year. This is the one when we go out into the forest to chop down a Christmas tree together. My father goes, "Why don't you just go to the store and buy one?" And I go, "Doesn't create a memory, a lasting memory." You know, everything we do together creates a legacy for my son to pass on to his children. . . . This will be the best year of our family's life. This will be the year we all look back on and wish we could relive—other than his babyhood—[because] we're all together.

Whitney's idea of a worthy memory—chopping down the family's tree instead of buying it at the store—may indicate, at least in part, that the meaning behind the memory would be unique and strong enough to elicit nostalgia in the future. Constructing particular types of memories in the present was a temporal strategy Whitney used that would allow her family to access the emotions of their special time together, which she knew was evaporating quickly. In this way, nostalgia (ironically) engendered a future-focused perspective that dampened mothers' desire for time away, especially as they imagined the end of childhood approaching.

The process of evoking nostalgia to manage the temporal tensions of motherhood was also collectively encouraged; it was part of the homeschooling subculture and discourse. For example, veteran homeschoolers gave a great deal of nostalgia-related advice about how mothers with young children should handle the unrelenting demands of homeschooling. Judith Munson, whose children were in college, sat on a panel at a homeschooling convention and advised mothers to "just relax and enjoy this time because now I wish it were back." She went on to explain how, when her children were young, she desperately wished for the day when, because of the mess, their art projects required "no more glitter!" To demonstrate how misguided those feelings were, she reached into her purse and pulled out a small vial of glitter to show the audience. "I carry this around with me now to remind me of those times. I should have appreciated it more." I talked to several mothers over the years who remembered that vial of glitter. Judith's cautionary tale packed a powerful emotional punch.

Judith's story also points to the second emotion mothers used to manage the temporal experience of homeschooling: regret. Regret comprises negative feelings about one's past actions (or lack thereof), along with the unfulfillable wish to change them. Like nostalgia, regret allowed mothers to shift time frames—to get beyond the present—mining their pasts for instances they did not want to repeat in the future. They extrapolated these past negative experiences onto the future, and that gave them the willingness to continue sequencing, to do everything they could now to avoid regret later. Following this logic, taking time for themselves in the present meant taking it away from their children, a decision they feared they would regret in the future.

When homeschooling mothers felt deeply time-starved, adopting veterans' warnings about future regret helped them marshal the emotional resources to continue sequencing. For example, recall that Darlene, whose son could not attend a conventional school because of his Asperger's syndrome, was highly dissatisfied with how much homeschooling restricted her independence. Nevertheless, she ultimately justified it:

But [the kids] grow so fast. All these women who are successful in their fields have told me, "If I had to do it over, I would have stayed home with my kids." I'm like, "Really?!" I mean, these are women I admire, who are also feminist mentors for me—I'm like, "You would?" So I keep listening to those voices and saying [to myself], "Just relax and enjoy it."

Darlene, a self-proclaimed feminist, struggled more than most of the mothers I talked to, perhaps because she was a second-choicer; homeschooling was not her preference but rather her last resort. Her biggest boost in mustering the willingness to continue, however, came from her friends' warnings about the unrelenting passage of time and the regret that would come from not appreciating it.

It is interesting to note, furthermore, that the advice Darlene tried to heed was to "just relax and enjoy it."[31] I heard numerous homeschoolers use this exact phrase (see Judith's statement earlier), and it is a telling one with respect to emotions and time. The crux of this mantra targeted mothers' problematic emotions, specifically their apparent inability to "relax" about putting their lives (to invoke another frequently used phrase) "on hold" to homeschool. Instead, they were advised to see their situation from a broader perspective, as Cassandra Shudek, the white upper-middle-class mother of four boys explained:

> Everybody tells you, "Oh, it goes by so fast!" But we don't think about that when we're tired, or have been up all night with the two-year-old. But I force myself to think about it. About when he's seventeen, and he doesn't want me to sit up with him until midnight reading the same story a hundred times. I want to really treasure it while I've got it. You know, I'm going to be a little old lady someday, all alone with [my] memories. So I think about that. I don't yearn for that day. I know it's coming. I try to appreciate what we have now, because . . . it doesn't last very long at all, in the great scheme of things.

Developing this broader perspective was a necessary temporal step to use sequencing as an emotional strategy.[32]

Evoking nostalgia and anticipating future regret were emotion management strategies that mothers used to manipulate their temporal experience and, circularly, manage some of their problematic emotions such as frustration and resentment. Nostalgia and regret were the routes to crossing time frames into the past and future, an essential shift that enabled mothers to view their lives, children, and families in the "great scheme of things." Thus, sequencing was an important form of temporal emotion work for mothers because it helped them transcend the present and transform the problematic emotions they felt there.

SAVORING: STAYING PRESENT AND CREATING QUALITY TIME

Once mothers did the temporal emotion work necessary to sequence, they then turned to a second type of temporal emotion work: savoring. On a temporal level, savoring was the opposite of sequencing. Whereas sequencing helped mothers shift to the past and future to gain a broader perspective on their mothering careers, savoring helped them stay in the here and now, narrowing their focus to become hyperaware of the present. On an emotional level, however, they were intricately connected; savoring derived from sequencing. In the process of accepting sequencing as a strategy, mothers learned an emotional lesson: their children's childhoods were evaporating daily, and mothers would regret not making the most of this time. Even with its focus on the past and future, sequencing rested on an assumption that the present was filled with precious emotional moments that should be experienced to the fullest because they would form the basis for families' nostalgia in the future. Therefore, once mothers framed their pasts and futures by sequencing, they had to figure out a way to appreciate the moment. Savoring became the main form of temporal emotion work to deal with the ephemeral nature of the present.

Homeschoolers savored because they felt like time was speeding by. One mother told me that childhood "is so temporary. It really goes by so fast. How do you put the brakes on? Slow down!" Flaherty has noted that people experience the past as "temporally compressed." In hindsight, time seems to have elapsed more quickly than when originally experienced, and because of episodic memory erosion, this effect is perpetually intensified as experiences continually recede further into the past.[33] Contrarily, we achieve "protracted duration"—time slows—when we "increase[e] the density of experience per standard temporal unit," and we do this by tightly focusing our "attention on a particular aspect of self or situation" as it is happening.[34] Through doing so, we feel like more has happened; moments become "bloated with an awareness . . . that far exceeds what they contain under ordinary conditions," and this decelerates our experience of time.[35] Homeschoolers did this type of time work. They consciously focused on the present, savoring each experience with their children, to decelerate their subjective experience of time and slow the inevitable progression of childhood. Savoring, then, is clearly a temporal strategy to prolong an experience. When homeschoolers discussed this type of time work, however, a distinct emotional component emerged. Savoring was not purely about achieving protracted duration but rather about doing so with the express purpose of sustaining and inflating pleasurable emotions in the moment.[36]

Yet mothers also wanted more than just (the feeling of) a larger quantity of time with their children; they wanted to make the most of that time, so they focused on infusing it with "quality," which meant increasing the emotional connection with their children through shared and unstructured experiences, a definition shared by non-homeschooling parents as well.[37] Homeschoolers believed that the home was the best place for these inter-actions, perhaps because much of children's structured time occurs else-where.[38] Countless mothers told me that their favorite part of homeschooling was "cuddling" or "snuggling" with their children, usually reading books on the couch, and still wearing their pajamas at lunchtime.

Not only did families need unstructured time together, but it had to be unencumbered with stress, which was especially hard for mothers with young children. Gretchen Forrester explained how the stress of family life threatened to keep her from engaging with eight-year-old Harry and her two younger boys in the way she thought she should:

> [Homeschooling] is stressful when you're distracted. Like if I'm trying to figure out, "Okay, how am I going to get the groceries, get home, answer this call, plan a meal?" . . . But they're just there, all the time, with their questions and insights and riddles. . . . And it takes a lot to be able to go, "Oh, my gosh, that's clever! How did you think of that?" when you feel like saying "Go be quiet somewhere." . . . But [it's important to be] engaged rather than being stuck in your own thoughts or distracted and being taken away from the kids. Just to be present in the moment. . . . You have to be available as a parent. You have to be willing to go the library [on a moment's notice]—not just because it's [preplanned] "library day"—but because we just saw this picture of a turtle on the beach in Mexico, and we need to know about turtles right now. Your time has to be open.

These two features of quality time—first, unstructured, open time that, second, leads to intentional engagement with children—were important because they set the stage for spontaneous connections. The quality of the time mothers spent with their children could not be forced; it had to hap-pen naturally, a feature of mainstream definitions of quality time as well.[39] Mothers talked about being constantly on guard for opportunities that might arise, either for a "teachable moment" in their homeschooling or for an instant when their children were open to emotional connection. Distraction and self-focus kept mothers from seizing these opportunities, moments that would disappear forever if they did not capitalize on them. Savoring, with its intense focus on the present and spontaneous emotional connection, served as a constant reminder of the ephemeral nature of childhood, which helped homeschooling mothers quell their desires for personal time and feel good about sacrificing it over long periods.

But how effective were sequencing and savoring as long-term strategies? Would they continue to help mothers feel better about sacrificing so much of their time and selves to homeschool their children? In the next part, I rely on the follow-up interviews, conducted six to seven years later, to examine how mothers' experiences progressed over time.

PART III

Homeschooling Motherhood over Time

The twenty-four interviews from 2002 illuminated many ways that the emotional and temporal aspects of homeschooling affected mothers' experiences. However, I wondered how mothers fared over time: How did emotions, time, and other factors affect their commitment to homeschooling throughout the years? And how did these factors influence their identities as mothers? To answer these questions, I reinterviewed sixteen of the original mothers in 2008–9, six to seven years after their initial interviews.[1]

Assessing mothers' commitment to homeschooling at the time of the second interview was not as simple as establishing who had homeschooled their children through the age of eighteen. (For ease of communicating this idea, I will call this situation "finishing" homeschooling.) Because different families were at different points in their homeschooling careers when I talked to them in 2002, some of them had finished homeschooling by 2008–9, whereas others were still homeschooling children under eighteen. Large age spreads between children also affected families' homeschooling time lines, making it difficult to use "finished homeschooling" as a gauge of their commitment.

For example, both Valerie Scott and Liz Trudeau had two "sets" of children, which meant that at the time of the second interview they were still in the thick of homeschooling, even though they had finished with the first set.

A second way to think about commitment is to consider whether children were enrolled in conventional school at the time of the second interview. Although this is a better cursory indicator, it, too, is fraught with problems due to the complexity of factors that might influence mothers' ability to continue homeschooling, such as their motivations, degree of domestic labor, children's needs, husband support, number and ages of children, religious orientation, method of educating, and financial considerations. The best I can do to unveil the parameters of mothers' commitment is to ask them about it, check in on their experiences, and have them elaborate on how different factors coalesced to create a unique context in which each mother understood her life, family, and commitment to homeschooling.

Part III of this book traces sixteen of the mothers' journeys over the six to seven years between the interviews. This is a sizable chunk of time for school-age children and their parents; it typically constitutes half of their schooling years (based on the norm of twelve grade levels) and one-third of their dependency years (based on the norm of achieving some form of adulthood by age eighteen). Because no existing research has tracked homeschooling parents over time, my goal in the follow-up interviews was to do so. In addition, no research has examined intensive mothering in a longitudinal qualitative study; thus, these interviews also contribute to that gap in the literature, albeit only for a select group who chose to homeschool their children and happened to end up in my study. Despite the limitations of my sample, the chapters in this part begin to map out how mothering and homeschooling careers may progress over time.

Chapter 6 begins this part by presenting mothers' looks back on the time between the interviews. I asked them to tell me about the successes and struggles of their journeys since I had last seen them. Chapter 7 continues chronologically and details homeschoolers' evaluations of the present: Did they think homeschooling worked for their children, and how did they know? Finally, chapter 8 features mothers' thoughts about the future: Where did they see themselves going once their homeschooling careers were over? In chapter 9, I revisit the multiple themes of emotions, time, and self and tie them together theoretically.

6

Looking Back

The Homeschooling Journey

Before I present mothers' follow-up stories, it is important to explain how the local homeschooling culture changed in the interim between the two interviews. As I mentioned in the introduction, most public schools in our county had established Parent-School Partnership (PSP) programs by 2008, in which the district provided a certified teacher to act as an academic adviser/facilitator for families, serve as a liaison between them and the school district, and organize an offering of classes for homeschooled students. Several of my interviewees had utilized these programs, and they invariably reported that it made their experiences more manageable because they no longer had to do all the work themselves. Other homeschoolers expressed staunch objection to them, however; they viewed the programs as an insidious form of government control that threatened their parental rights to educate their children as they saw fit (e.g., the stipulation that funds could not be spent on religious curricula was often seen as a form of censorship and government intrusion into family life). As a result of this controversial issue, the homeschooling community in Cedar County splintered, and PATH lost members, shrinking to about 400 families (down from about 600 in 2001). Parents who used the PSPs no longer needed the kind of support they had when they were doing it all. Of the sixteen mothers I followed up with, seven had used these programs (though four of them lived in another county and had been using them at the time of the first interview as well, as I discussed in chapter 1).

When I reinterviewed mothers, I asked them if they were still home-schooling and to explain how their experiences had unfolded since I had last talked to them. Of the sixteen, four had quit homeschooling at least once, opting instead for full-time conventional school, which their children had attended or were attending at the time of the second interview. The remaining twelve had not enrolled their children in conventional school since the first interview. Only one of these twelve had finished homeschooling entirely, eight were still homeschooling at least one high schooler, and three were homeschooling children of middle school age or younger. In short, I followed up with 67 percent of the original sample, and 75 percent of them had continued homeschooling, uninterrupted, since the first interview. Yet it is important to view these numbers in context with other factors, and the in-depth, follow-up interviews provided me with a great deal of information to do so. (I have summarized some of these factors in Table 6.1.)

The main pattern that appeared with respect to mothers' homeschooling careers concerned their first- or second-choice status. Of the sixteen mothers I reinterviewed, eleven were first-choicers and five were second-choicers. This means I reinterviewed 58 percent of the first-choicers (eleven out of the original nineteen) and 100 percent of the second choicers (five out of the original five). Mothers' designation as first- or second-choice emerged as the strongest predictor of who continued homeschooling uninterrupted and who tried other options. The patterns were strong in both directions (see Table 6.1): first-choice homeschoolers were overwhelmingly likely to continue homeschooling unin-terrupted (ten of the eleven [91 percent] did so)—a finding that was not all that surprising. Contrarily, second-choice homeschoolers were overwhelmingly likely to interrupt their homeschooling careers by enrolling their children in conventional schools (four of the five [80 percent] did so). Yet, surprisingly, they were also very likely to swing back to homeschooling (three of the four [75 percent] of those enrolled in school disenrolled and returned to home-schooling), and some even tried conventional schools a second time (two did, the third planned to). This oscillation between school and home made second-choice homeschoolers' stories over the six- to seven-year interval much more complicated than those of first-choicers.

I must add an additional note about the complexity of factors here, and that is the possibility that mothers may have switched categories between the first

Name	1st or 2nd choice homeschooler?	Enrolled in conventional school between T1 and T2?	Reason for enrolling in conventional school?	Returned to homeschooling after being in conventional school?	Reason for returning to homeschooling?	Graduated (or planned) from conventional school?
Alice Lange	1st choice	No	—	—	—	—
Annie Agresti	1st choice	No	—	—	—	—
Cassandra Shudek	1st choice	No	—	—	—	—
Gretchen Forrester	1st choice	No	—	—	—	—
Jackie Bell	1st choice	No	—	—	—	—
Leanna Livingston	1st choice	No	—	—	—	—
Liz Trudeau	1st choice	No	—	—	—	—
Pam Rausch	1st choice	No	—	—	—	—
Sabrina Hernandez	1st choice	No	—	—	—	—
Valerie Scott	1st choice	No	—	—	—	—
Whitney McKee	1st choice	Yes	Financial	No	—	Yes
Patricia Tomlinson	2nd choice	No	—	—	—	Yes
Darlene Rooney-Henkel	2nd choice	Yes	Mother's independence	Yes	Child's fit	Yes
Emily Ashton	2nd choice	Yes	Mother's independence	Yes	Child's fit	Hopeful
Tracy Chadwick	2nd choice	Yes	Mothers' independence	Yes	Child's fit	Yes
Renée Peterson	2nd choice in 2002; 1st choice in 2009	Yes	Financial	No	—	Yes

Table 6.1 Mothers' Homeschooling Journey between 2002 (T1) and 2008/2009 (T2) Interviews

and second interviews. Only one mother of the sixteen I reinterviewed did so. When I talked to Renée Peterson in 2002, she was clearly struggling to relinquish her work identity (police officer) and embrace homeschooling; when I talked to her in 2009, she explained how she had come to love homeschooling and wanted to continue all the way through her children's education. The percentages I provided earlier place Renée in the second-choice category because that is where she started out, but from here forward I recategorize her because she identified as a first-choicer at the time of the second interview.

This chapter describes who continued and who abandoned homeschooling, contextualizing mothers' experiences by examining the factors they deemed relevant to their homeschooling trajectories.

Bumps In The Road: Continuing Homeschooling

All the mothers, regardless of their first- or second-choice status, talked about several factors that affected their families over the six to seven years, creating challenges to homeschooling. One factor was fathers' lack of contribution to domestic labor. Although chapters 4 and 5 have addressed this family dynamic in depth, the issue bears repeating because mothers still talked about it in their follow-up interviews. Not all the mothers in the first round of interviews cited their domestic burden as a reason they might give up homeschooling, nor were they all dissatisfied to the same degree with their husbands' lesser participation in domestic labor. In 2002, however, several mothers did express concern that the domestic burden would be too much for them to continue homeschooling, yet none of those who had quit homeschooling by the time of the second interview said they had done so because of paltry contributions from their husbands; in fact, all sixteen mothers seemed to have become more accepting of their husbands' smaller share of household duties, rather than more resentful.[1]

Though part of this acceptance pattern might be explained by the emotion management strategies they developed along the way (see chapters 4 and 5), children's aging might also have been a factor: just as mothers had predicted, children grew to be more independent and required less intense and less constant attention (at least mothers felt this way). A mother's load lightened once children could stay home while she ran to the store, contribute more substantially to the household labor, or complete some schoolwork on their own while she did laundry or prepared dinner.

Yet although children's independence facilitated certain aspects of homeschooling, it complicated it in other ways. For example, Gretchen Forrester talked about how her children, now fifteen, eleven, and nine, had become more involved in activities outside the home, which had been eating away at the family's time together and had kept them running from one scheduled event to another. She explained the impact on the family dynamic a year earlier, which had worried her at the time:

> The kids would scream, you know, "You're the worst mom in the world!" or "I wish I was never born!" Just serious melodrama. . . . We just needed to step back and look at what exactly is going on here. And we went and saw a family counselor. . . . [I kept thinking] there's something wrong with this picture. [We discovered that] we were doing way too much. Chess club, hockey, music lessons—the list goes on. We were just constantly busy. So a lot of that stress, that yelling and screaming, was coming from the kids just needing down time! "I just need to be home! I don't need to be back [home] to go out the door again in five minutes." So part of the good thing that came from that . . . is that we looked at everything, and we cut way back on our commitments.

Gretchen's solution was to step back from the "concerted cultivation" model of filling children's time with extracurricular activities, which research has shown may impinge on family life.[2]

Another complicating factor was that mothers' lives did not always get easier as their children aged because the family was a dynamic unit of interrelated parts. When one component improved, others could deteriorate, which affected the family as a whole. Although older children gained independence, other things happened in many families to pull at mothers' time—time they would have had to themselves if everything else had remained consistent.

These changes took several forms. First, adding more children to the family kept the mothers squarely rooted in the time-intensive stage of motherhood, despite having older children as well (I will talk more about increasing family size in the chapter 8). Valerie Scott, who had seven children, one set of four and then, eleven years later, another set of three, noted the stresses of the wide age span:

> Homeschooling would get interrupted. . . . You know, you've got a baby, plus you're pregnant, then you nurse, and then you're up all night, and so you have to put some things on hold. . . . And then we kept having babies. It's hard to balance a baby on your hip and explain algebra! But then I just learned, "Hey, that's life. We'll get used to it." But that took me a little while. That took me a few years.

Unlike Valerie, Patricia Tomlinson, with her first son in college, had a harder time getting used to it, feeling like she was starting over with her eleven-year-old. She explained that the ten-year-spread between her children was intentional, but in retrospect, she asked herself, "Why did we plan things this way?" It kept her longer in the intensive and demanding version of homeschooling motherhood.

Another way family demands affected the homeschooling, even as children gained independence, was that mothers' own parents and in-laws were aging as well, and their independence was declining. Homeschooling mothers entered what has been called the "sandwich generation," in which middle-aged parents find that they are "ready for relaxation and self-indulgence, only to find that their grown children are not quite independent and their parents have moved from autonomy to a degree of dependence."[3] Several mothers talked about the additional burden their own parents or in-laws placed on them, often just at the time their children needed less attention. Patricia Tomlinson explained that she had taken on additional caregiving burdens, even though she was still homeschooling her eleven-year-old son:

> I guess it was the year after I talked to you. My husband's parents moved next door to us—most people think I'm insane when I talk about this. We had no idea [his] parents were going to buy the house next to us. . . . Then my parents moved just about two blocks away to be near us so we could coordinate things. . . . My father turns eighty this year, and I recently moved them out of their house where they had lived for forty years. I really did the [physical work of] moving [them]. My sister is in [a distant state], and she isn't really in a position to help. So that's what I've been doing. And struggling with my parents' anxiety, depression—my mother has agoraphobia—and trying to keep my head above water in that regard. . . . [My parents] are a little bit maladaptive.

In chapter 5, Patricia explained that she regretted pursuing her own interests because others' needs had taken over her life. Although mothers talked a great deal about sequencing as a strategy—devoting themselves to their children while they were young because there would be time to pursue their own interests later—other family obligations often arose and trapped them in their intensive caregiving roles.

An additional challenge for mothers was that, even though their children were aging, they themselves were, too. Several homeschoolers talked about how their own waning energy made homeschooling (and motherhood) more difficult, even as the children gained independence. Jackie Bell, the African

American first-choicer who took longer than most to embrace stay-at-home motherhood, had a third daughter the year after I talked to her in 2002. In the follow-up, we talked about how having a third child to homeschool, five years younger than her second child, required a great deal more endurance:

> I wish somebody had told me that. I wasn't just having a baby; I was having a baby, a toddler, a school-age child, a junior high schooler, high schooler, an adult, and that it just continues for the rest of your life. I would have braced myself differently.... Maybe after having two really easy kids, I thought, "Oh, you know, this won't be so bad." But [with three] you're physically outnumbered—you don't have a hand to grab each of the kids' hands—and from being outnumbered, each child gets more loud and physical [to compete for attention]. I just didn't anticipate that. I mean, it's not a bad thing. It's just I didn't expect it. And I also didn't understand, at the time, the endurance that was required. And that I'm not going to have the same kind of freshness of energy fifteen years into it as I did at three years into it.... So I wouldn't change anything, but I think I would have tried to go in with a little bit more realistic expectation.

In the follow-up interviews, mothers talked a great deal about the challenges to homeschooling they had faced in the previous seven years, yet despite these various factors, no mothers gave them as their primary reason for giving up homeschooling—indeed, all the preceding examples were from first-choicers who continued homeschooling, uninterrupted. There were two big reasons mothers cited for giving up homeschooling: money and their own independence. Yet first- and second-choicers encountered and felt these problems differently, which influenced whether they enrolled their children in conventional schools.

Roadblocks: Returning to School

By 2009, five of my original homeschoolers had sent their children to school. First- and second-choicers' experiences varied on this issue (see Table 6.1 for details).

First-Choicers' Financial Strain

The first-choice homeschoolers I was able to follow up with were very unlikely to enroll their children in conventional schools between 2002 and 2009, but when they did, it was because of money trouble. Though several mothers mentioned that financial strain arose between the first and second interviews, and they discussed its impact on the children's schooling, only two mothers talked about financial problems significant enough to enroll their children in school. One was Whitney McKee. She had known ahead of time that her family's finances would allow for only one year of homeschooling, so it was no surprise in 2009 to find that she had reenrolled Ritchie in school in the fall of 2002, about seven months after I first interviewed her. However, in retrospect, Whitney "really regretted not finishing homeschooling." I asked her what she could have possibly done differently, given the economic constraints on her family that she emphasized in the first interview:

JEN: It sounds like your hands were tied. You and your husband had to go back to work—

WHITNEY: Yes, but what kind of sacrifices—should we have made some more? Will I regret that I didn't homeschool? Yes. I'm sorry I didn't [continue homeschooling]. I wouldn't have lost my caring, loving child to hurt and anger and depression and defeat, [which he experienced in the public schools].

Though Whitney's son, by then a high school graduate, was on a course she was happy with, she explained that he had had a hard time in the public schools, dealing with "rougher" kids who were more "street smart" than he was. In addition, he had struggled with math and lost some academic confidence, one of the reasons she had wanted to homeschool him seven years earlier. In 2002, Whitney was very clear that her family was barely scraping by financially (low-wage jobs and large medical bills were big issues), and at that time, she did not consider it at all feasible for her to remain out of the workforce. But in retrospect, she second-guessed her decisions and wondered how they could have made it work. The weight of intensive mothering seemed to bear down on Whitney, making her feel guilty and regretful about her past actions—actions that seemed highly logical and rational, given the severe and very real constraints of the family's financial situation.

Renée Peterson, the ex–police officer, who was the only one of my subjects who converted to first-choice homeschooling, did so shortly after our first interview in 2002. When I talked to her in 2009, she explained that she had come to love stay-at-home motherhood because of homeschooling; through it she found a group of families she could relate to and rely on for social, academic, and emotional support.[4] However, her husband's career suffered a major setback in the economic crisis of 2008, and he lost a substantial portion of his income, a fact he hid from Renée for many months. He secretly borrowed money, and by the time Renée found out, they had accrued a massive debt. This financial stress reverberated throughout the family in different areas; the most difficult for Renée were increased marital conflict and giving up homeschooling to return to work. She had put her two children in public school just a few months before I talked to her in 2009:

> JEN: So you didn't want to go back to work. You want to keep homeschooling them.
>
> RENÉE: Yeah, I went on antidepressants and started seeing a counselor over it [*laughs*]. . . . During Christmastime and the holidays, all the money issues and all the marriage issues got brought up, and it was just like WAAA! I just couldn't even think what to make for dinner, let alone make any real decisions for the family. So, yeah, it was a huge issue. It was my identity. That's what I've been doing for the last twelve to thirteen years—I've been at home, not working, and really just focused on the kids and working things out at home. So, yeah, that was huge. To go back to work was not my idea. But it was something that had to be done.

To make matters more difficult, Renée was disappointed that her work life, which she had had a hard time giving up years earlier, was no longer in a field she was trained for, identified with, or found rewarding. This led her to wrestle with some hard questions:

> What am I basing my identity on? . . . I feel that maybe I shouldn't have so much of my identity wrapped up in this [current] job. Before I had my identity wrapped up in being a city police officer, and then I had my identity wrapped up in being a homeschool parent. But I guess it's hard for me to say, "Yes, I am a stocker at a grocery store." Oh, my gosh! College-educated and all this other stuff, and I just—you know, that is not going to be my identity [*laughs*]. I need to be okay with [thinking], "Okay this is just who I am, and that's fine." So, yeah, I'm working through some of those big life issues. And with the Prozac, choosing not to work through them [*laughs*].

Renée's experience moving into an unskilled job after years of staying at home with her children is not uncommon. Research has documented that withdrawing from the paid labor force, or even going to part-time status, reduces women's opportunities and earning power when they do return to the workforce.[5]

Whitney and Renée, first-choice homeschoolers (at least by the time of the second interview), both cited significant financial strain as the only reason for sending their children to public schools. Though other first-choicers also talked about how money problems had affected their families throughout the years, none of their stories seemed as financially desperate as Whitney's and Renée's, and none of them sent their children back to school. Thus, these data suggest that for first-choicers in my sample, severe money trouble was the only factor that compelled them to give up homeschooling.

Second-Choicers' Oscillation

Second-choice homeschoolers also talked about the challenges they had faced in the last six to seven years, but they talked about them differently. Because homeschooling was their second choice, their goal had always been to find the perfect fit for their children. Whereas first-choice homeschoolers wanted to continue homeschooling and talked about the obstacles they had had to overcome to avoid putting their children in school, second-choicers continued to search for alternatives and talked about the challenges they had faced in getting their children into schools and keeping them there. Thus, second-choicers' stories were much more complex and often marked by frequent oscillation between homeschooling and conventional school, as they struggled more overtly with weighing their own independence against their children's needs. As I will show, the intensive version of homeschooling motherhood usually prevailed.

Like some of the first-choicers, two second-choice homeschoolers (of the four who remained after recategorizing Renée in the follow-up interviews) also talked about the strong financial influence on their decisions over the years. However, the second-choicers talked about finances in the opposite way. Instead of explaining, as the first-choicers did, that lack of funds forced (or threatened) them to stop homeschooling and enter the workforce, second-choicers talked about the financial blow to their families when they had to leave the workforce to pull their children out of the conventional schools they were finally attending.

Both Emily Ashton and Darlene Rooney-Henkel had enrolled their children once they found a conventional-school fit for them, as was their hope all along, but both pulled their children out again, despite financial hardship, when school did not work out. In addition, for both of these mothers, money problems interacted with their desire for independence and career. Because their stories were quite complicated, I present them in detail here.

Emily, a second-choicer, was one of only two mothers in the original sample who worked outside of the home at the time of the first interview. She had three children and was homeschooling only her eight-year-old (middle) son because he was academically advanced but socially reserved. When I caught up with her in 2009, she explained that she homeschooled him in our state for several more years, and when she and her family moved back to her hometown in another state, she sent him to public school. All three children attended public school for two years, at which time Emily attended graduate school to get her counseling degree. She was just finishing up her licensing requirements with a paid internship and a job offer to continue there when her son entered ninth grade: "He did great in junior high, seventh and eighth grade. Then ninth grade—he started the first week at the high school . . . and he was miserable, and he asked if he could just come back [home to school]." At the same time, Emily's youngest had just entered middle school. Within the first few months, Emily and her husband noticed that their daughter was not thriving in her new environment: "She was just kind of depressed. . . . There was a little bit of bullying. And she kind of just lost her sparkle. So that, put together with my other son coming home, and we just thought, 'Okay, we're just going to do it all.'"

The decision to homeschool again was a difficult one, primarily because it meant Emily had to give up her paid work. Her son, a ninth grader, was able to work fairly independently, but when her sixth-grade daughter came home as well, Emily needed to be there. I asked her how she and her husband arrived at that decision, and she replied:

> EMILY: The decisions we made around that were that I quit my full-time job where I had been doing my internship—and I was making very good money over where I was working. I was going to leave [that job] anyway at a certain point because I had started [a] nonprofit [counseling company], but that was going to be just part-time. So we took a huge financial hit to clear up the afternoon and have me not work a full-time job. So [aside from homeschooling] I do the nonprofit, then I work a new part-time job.
>
> JEN: Is that in your field, the new part-time job?
>
> EMILY: No, not at all [*laughs*]. I work at Starbucks. I work a five fifteen to nine thirty [a.m.] shift. Then I'm home all day. Then I do the [nonprofit] counseling stuff in the evenings. So I cleared up all the afternoon to do the kids' homeschooling.

JEN: So has that been a hard adjustment on your family, to take a financial hit like that?

EMILY: The financial hit was a big hardship; we lost almost forty thousand dollars a year with my income. And I definitely haven't picked that up working morning shifts at Starbucks. So the financial strain was huge, and there is a lot of fear associated with that. But [I try to take] time to do a gratitude journal, and that keeps me focused on the gross part [big picture], and the fact that this part's temporary, and that it's not everything. But if I didn't do that, I think I would just be a mess; I would be very resentful and very cranky.

Though Emily tried to regain her time and pursue her career by putting her children in conventional schools, their needs trumped hers again, and she responded by putting part of her own life on hold, again, to homeschool. She compromised her career aspirations and took an unskilled part-time job that was unrelated to her career, but that had flexible hours so she could be there for her children, a common strategy for mothers who feel torn between work and home, though one that negatively impacts their careers and earning power.[6]

When I asked Emily if she and her husband considered having him cut back or resign from his job (recall that she told me, "*we're* just going to do it all"), she said that his income was more stable and his work less flexible (he traveled a great deal) than her fledgling company and newly blossoming career, so they decided she would be the one to cut back, a common outcome in many families when it comes to choosing which parent will stay home.[7] As many mothers conveyed in earlier interviews, Emily did substantial temporal emotion work, using sequencing (focusing on the big picture and the temporary nature of her children's educational needs) and savoring (writing in a journal to elicit gratitude for her present situation). This helped her avoid feeling "resentful and very cranky."[8]

A second mother who had had a hard time resuming homeschooling was second-choicer, Darlene, who had finally gotten her son with Asperger's syndrome integrated into an alternative public high school when he was in ninth grade. The year before doing so, she had brought her daughter home for her fifth-grade year, with the intent of sending her back to school in sixth grade when her son started in the high school. Her daughter wanted to continue homeschooling, however, and Darlene was not thrilled: "And I have to tell you, I was definitely ready to not ever homeschool again. But she wanted to homeschool. But then after a month she said, 'I'm lonely, can I go back to public school?' I'm like, 'Oh, yeah!'"

Financial troubles were plaguing the family, however. Darlene's husband, a physician in a group practice, "got shoved out of his practice, and we were in a legal battle." He could not find work locally, he was "in crisis," and she was "holding the family together." He finally found work in a nearby larger city, so they moved and enrolled the children in private high schools there (the public schools were "a mess"). At that point, Darlene "crashed" from the stress and took some time to "recoup." She "was so ready to quit home-schooling [and] so ready to get back into the workforce," but her daughter

> lasted two weeks in her [new] private school [because of clique dynam-ics]. . . . She got depressed. She went through it so badly that everybody was just like, "You've got to pull her; we've lost our Alexandra." Within two weeks! It was pretty shocking. . . . I sat in on the school, and I went, "Oh, my gosh, I see what she's seeing." And it was not fair to her, and so I pulled her and homeschooled her. She didn't want to homeschool, and I didn't want to [do it]. . . . I really wasn't ready to be tied down again; I was ready to be free. That's how I felt after nine years of homeschooling—my son, and then part-time, my daughter. . . . But you go with the flow. You do what you have to do for your kids.

Darlene resumed homeschooling because she subscribed to the "family devotion schema," a cultural philosophy that "defines an adult's personal happiness as irrelevant compared with a child's well-being."[9]

Although Darlene and her daughter adjusted well to homeschooling in the new city, Darlene soon realized that her son was having trouble in his new school as well:

> Everything was going fairly decently through Christmas, but it was clear that my son wasn't happy. I felt like he was just [merely] engaging with life. Socially he sort of went into shock. He was withdrawing. So even though people didn't think he was depressed because he seemed okay, I know him better than that.

This turn of events deeply troubled her:

> So it was a nightmare because my kids were not happy. And because my kids were not happy, I felt like a failure as a mother. I was just in crisis. I felt like I had done everything I could to find academically good, strong schools. But [the kids] were not happy. And for me, it's always been about my kids' well-being, not just their academics. So I went into crisis; I nearly

had a nervous breakdown. I froze. You hear "fight or flight"? Well I froze. You never hear that that's the third dynamic there. I finally told my husband, "You know, I can't even function anymore. I can't make a decision. You have to make a decision." Then [my son] made a statement that the thought of being at that school for another three years made him want to kill himself. And he doesn't exaggerate, so we were like, "Oh, my God." And my husband was like, "That's it. We're moving back." Because our house [back in Cedar County] hadn't sold, that was the other pressure. We were paying two mortgages and trying to juggle finances and going deeper into debt. It's like none of the stars were aligned. I was like, "I don't get it!" We tried so hard to make it work, and it wasn't working.

The family moved back to Cedar County and enrolled the children in the public schools they had been attending before they left. Fortunately, a professional opportunity opened up just at that time, and Darlene's husband found work locally. Darlene, however, did not, despite finally having the time to pursue it. She had had some leads in the bigger city, but back in Cedar County, there was nothing in her preferred fields: faith advocacy and social justice. Thus, although she was no longer homeschooling, she felt as though her children's education had trumped her career aspirations yet again. When I talked to her in 2009, her son was in his first year of college, and her daughter had another year and a half of high school. Darlene resolved to be patient just a bit longer, even though she had been looking for work for several years.

A third second-choicer whose children had oscillated between school and home was Tracy Chadwick. Recall that Tracy was very ambivalent about homeschooling when I talked to her in 2002, which stemmed, at least in part, from her husband's and father-in-law's pressure to embrace homeschooling. At that time their son, Jacob, was eight and was the focus of their educational concerns, though they did talk about what they would do for their then-four-year-old daughter, Sydney, who was enrolled part-time in a preschool. When I caught up with Tracy in 2009, Jacob was halfway through his eighth-grade year homeschooling, and Sydney was a fifth grader in public school.

For Tracy and her family, the homeschooling journey had been a "rocky road, all the way through" because "temperamentally, Jacob and I are not a great fit to be together full-time." I asked Tracy how their homeschooling had progressed since I had seen her six years earlier, in September of their second year of homeschooling, when Jacob had just started second grade. She explained:

> Let's see, Jacob [homeschooled in first grade, and then] went to public school in second grade [within a month after I talked to you], and then he

homeschooled third grade, then he went back to school in fourth grade. Because there was this periodic "I can't do this" on my part. He's very willful, and he's not able to just go with the program, whatever the program is that I've set out for that particular year. He has to argue a lot. So, he went to school in fourth grade, and it was good for the first half of the year, and then halfway through the year he just got so bored. He just was kind of like a plant that was wilting.

Jacob's teacher wanted to give him an individualized educational program (IEP) because she thought he was behind in several areas. Tracy recounted how a counselor came to observe and test him:

> TRACY: [The counselor] came back and said, "This child is very bored in the classroom"; he said that textbook learning doesn't suit him. And that he not only doesn't qualify for special-ed, he's a point from genius, and should be in the [gifted learner] program.
> JEN: Wow, was that news to you, or had you always suspected he was gifted?
> TRACY: Well, he's a high-end performer in some ways, but in the public school system, it doesn't look like that. So it's funny to figure out where he fits.

The counselor recommended Jacob go to school part-time and homeschool the remainder:

> So this was midway through fourth grade. So we took him out of school at about one o'clock in the afternoon, and then he kind of homeschooled the rest of the day. And he took the [gifted learner] test, and he didn't make it in, but that was okay. And then fifth grade he homeschooled [full-time], and then he's been homeschooling ever since. And he's in eighth grade now.

When I talked to Tracy, Jacob was applying to an alternative public high school for the next year, hoping to complete his education there. Her plan had always been to get him into school because the interpersonal dynamics with her son burned her out: "I was very clear as he got older that I cannot be this child's teacher anymore."

In the meantime, Tracy had begun working for pay. Five years earlier, when her daughter was six, Tracy had founded a "music education" company through which she gave piano and voice lessons to children. It started with her children's friends and later blossomed into a lucrative business and a rewarding career for Tracy. As the business was getting off the ground, she started to examine her daughter's education more closely because Sydney, then seven, had become "quite dissatisfied" with her learning "not going deeper" in school. At the time, Tracy was homeschooling eleven-year-old Jacob:

> And [Sydney] asked if she could homeschool, and I said, "Oh, I don't think you would like homeschooling because you're pretty social, and you'd find it isolating. And all your friends are [at school], and you have a great teacher." And she said, "I don't go to school for my friends, Mommy"—she was seven—[she said], "I go to school to learn, and this is not where I learn best." . . . And she has such a strong, even character about her, so I said, "Well, you know, I'll try it, but I don't think it's for you." So, second and third grade she homeschooled, she didn't go to public school.

Sydney went back to school in fourth grade and was halfway through her fifth-grade year in public school when I talked to Tracy in 2009. Tracy explained Sydney's experiences in the classroom:

> She's very bored in math. She really sits there and waits for everyone to catch up. It's very hard for me, having homeschooled. If she wants to do algebra, she should do algebra. If she wants to learn fractions, she shouldn't be doing multiplication. But I feel my hands are tied. I've given her to these teachers. And I have to trust them. And yet they can't meet the needs of thirty kids. They just can't. Nope. So the current challenge is that I don't want to pull her out of school; I don't want to homeschool full-time because I'm working now, and quite engaged in that. . . . So I wouldn't pull Sydney out of school. One day [a week] I would, but not five, because I've filled that time.

Tracy felt torn again, wondering how she could improve her daughter's education. In the 2009 interview she said that the "past few days" had been hard, because academically, Sydney

> is pretty disappointed, and talks about it daily, which is hard because I'm so much a homeschooler inside of me. . . . She keeps telling me how unmotivated she is at math [which is a problem] because she loves math. I'm not going to give up what I've gained in terms of my time, but I'm still going to advocate for getting her the best education I can. Even if that means we do it in the evenings.

Tracy's suggestion, that she might keep her daughter in school, yet supplement her education in the evenings, implied that she might increase her workload once more by trying to do it all.[10] Her statement also demonstrated the tensions for second-choice homeschoolers, who felt a greater need than first-choicers to balance an independent work life with sacrificing for their children. Tracy experienced a great deal of conflict between wanting to be a homeschooling mother and wanting her children in school. She told me that, even when her children were in school over the years, she would always retain her homeschooling mother identity: "I always say that I still home-school my kids, but I supplement with school."

Second-Choice Patterns

My data suggest several interesting patterns, though my sample—twelve first-choicers (after recategorizing Renée) and four second-choicers—is much too small and nonrepresentative to draw any firm conclusions about other homeschoolers or mothers in general. But these data do provide some insights that might prove useful to explore with larger, more representative samples.

First, it is really quite striking that of the four remaining second-choicers, three had such similar stories, trying numerous times to enroll their children in school but periodically returning to homeschooling. None of the first-choicers had stories like this. It seems that this oscillation was directly linked to these mothers' identities. Like first-choicers, they had high standards for their own mothering, which included seeing to their children's education, yet unlike first-choicers, they did not want to sacrifice all their own time or independent selves for such an extended period. First-choice homeschoolers were more adept at managing this tension, which they did by sequencing and savoring—strategies that helped them put their own lives on hold for prolonged periods, as I discussed in chapter 5. Yet second-choicers never achieved peace with putting their own lives on hold, and thus kept trying to find alternatives, much like many women in the contemporary United States, who feel torn between choosing work or motherhood.[11] Second-choice homeschoolers often tried the educational alternatives too soon, and as mothers, they could not watch their children "wilting" (Tracy), "withdrawing" (Darlene), or "losing [their] sparkle" (Emily) in conventional programs, so they brought them back home again.

A second similarity among second-choicers was that each of these mothers (Emily, Darlene, and Tracy) started homeschooling because of one child's needs while sending the others to conventional school, something first-choicers did not do—they homeschooled all their children when possible. Again, this pattern may be explained by mothers' second-choice status:

they started homeschooling because of fit issues; they saw that one of their children had a real educational need that could not be met by conventional programs. In contrast, first-choicers reasoned that the needs of all their children were best met by them, at home. Several first-choicers told me that they occasionally had to deny their children's requests to go to school (Angela's story in chapter 2, of how her son periodically asked her if God had released her yet, provides a good example).[12] In contrast, when second-choicers' children asked to go to school, or when mothers found a suitable program, they usually jumped at the chance.

Yet even though these three second-choicers began by homeschooling one child, at some point they all ended up homeschooling another child, whom they did not originally consider to have special needs. Moreover, it was often the case that the two children were on conflicting cycles, so mothers started to homeschool the second child (interestingly, in all three cases, a daughter) just as the first (in each case, a son) was ready to enter a conventional school. Second-choicers struggled with this situation because they were ready to regain some independence but had to sacrifice it again to homeschool the second child. First-choicers did not have this problem because they committed in advance to homeschooling all their children; they knew what was coming, so there were fewer difficult transitions to make and fewer hopes to dash with respect to their own independence and time to themselves. This finding suggests another norm of intensive mothering: mothers do not "play favorites"; they treat all their children equally. Second-choicers had begun homeschooling to meet one child's individual needs (following the norm that good mothers do so) but got caught by a second norm, to treat each child equally, which sucked them back into homeschooling. First-choicers, who homeschooled all their children from the start, were able to avoid this conflict.

7

Taking Stock of the Present

Perceptions of Success

The previous chapter presented mothers' look back on their homeschooling journey and discussed some of the struggles they encountered along the way. This chapter focuses on the second of my three purposes in conducting the follow-up interviews in 2008–9: to ask mothers to take stock of the present— where were they now? Because so many early-career homeschoolers had expressed insecurity in the first interviews, I wanted to ask in the follow-ups whether they thought homeschooling had worked for their children. Some mothers were quite certain about their answers, often because they had finished with some children or were nearing the end of homeschooling entirely. Mothers who were still "in the thick of it," as one called it, tended to be more tentative when evaluating their children's progress. Before detailing mothers' assessments of success, I will first explain where mothers were in their homeschooling careers at the time of the second interview.

Of the sixteen mothers I was able to follow up with, four were no longer homeschooling: one had finished homeschooling (Annie), and three had returned their children to school (Renée, Whitney, Darlene). Seven mothers were homeschooling only some of their children, but their other children had either finished homeschooling (five mothers: Liz, Pam, Sabrina, Valerie, Patricia) or were enrolled in school (two mothers: Tracy, Emily). Five mothers were still homeschooling all their children (Alice, Cassandra, Gretchen, Jackie, Leanna). (Table 7.1 presents more information on mothers' homeschooling status at the time of the second interview.)

Although mothers were at varied places in their homeschooling careers, all of them had thought a great deal about whether homeschooling had been the right choice for their children. Almost every mother I reinterviewed felt confident that it had. A few, however, expressed significant doubts. This chapter describes how mothers measured success and whether they thought they had achieved it. The point of this chapter is decidedly *not* to assess homeschooled children's outcomes, academic or otherwise. I simply do not have the data to do so. Instead, my data uncover mothers' perceptions of homeschooling's success, as measured by particular outcomes they saw in, and chose to relate to me about, their children.

The Proof Is in the Pudding

Homeschoolers had spent years fighting the stigma of irresponsible mothering and enumerating the ways they were not "ruining" their children, so they naturally responded to my questions about success by pointing to their children's achievements. In fact, throughout my eight years studying homeschooling, I heard dozens of mothers use the phrase "the proof is in the pudding" when talking about whether homeschooling had benefited their children. For the mothers I reinterviewed, this proof clustered around two central themes: their children's personal characteristics and professional accomplishments. In the personal realm mothers cited children's positive character traits and relationships with others as evidence that homeschooling had worked. In the professional realm they discussed children's success in academics and occupations. In chapter 3, I showed that mothers' justifications revolved around academics, character, and relationships, so it makes sense that they would be concerned with evaluating these areas in retrospect.

Personal Success: Character and Relationships

Mothers overwhelmingly talked about how homeschooling had been a successful choice for their children (though there were some who did not, and I will discuss them in turn). One way they supported their claims was by drawing on children's personal qualities, specifically their individual character

Name	1st or 2nd choice homeschooler?	Number of children in family	Number of children homeschooling	Number of children "finished" (homeschooled through 18 years old)	Number of children enrolled in school	Number of children graduated from conventional school
Alice Lange	1st choice	1	1	—	—	—
Annie Agresti	1st choice	3	—	1	—	2
Cassandra Shudek	1st choice	5	5	—	—	—
Gretchen Forrester	1st choice	3	3	—	—	—
Jackie Bell	1st choice	3	3	—	—	—
Leanna Livingston	1st choice	4	4	—	—	—
Liz Trudeau	1st choice	4	2	2	—	—
Pam Rausch	1st choice	3	2	1	—	—
Sabrina Hernandez	1st choice	12	2	9	—	1
Valerie Scott	1st choice	7	3	4	—	—
Whitney McKee	1st choice	1	—	—	—	1
Patricia Tomlinson	2nd choice	2	1	1	—	—
Darlene Rooney-Henkel	2nd choice	2	—	—	1	1
Emily Ashton	2nd choice	3	2	—	1	—
Tracy Chadwick	2nd choice	2	1	—	1	—
Renée Peterson	2nd choice in 2002; 1st choice in 2009	2	—	—	2	—

Table 7.1: Mothers' Homeschooling Status at Second Interview, 2008 or 2009

and relationships with others, as evidence that homeschooling had worked. Mothers typically provided me with specifics in these areas, for instance, telling me that their children could converse "articulately" with anyone, "of any age," and "look them in the eye."[1] These examples resonated because teenagers are stereotyped as being emotionally withdrawn, socially awkward, verbally stunted, and overly insulated within and influenced by their peer groups. Homeschoolers made it clear that they had not wanted their children to develop these qualities, so when their children did not display them, mothers had proof that homeschooling had been the right choice.

Homeschoolers had been on the defensive for years, but they felt vindicated when skeptical family members or friends finally admitted homeschooling had produced superior character in their children. Linda Kelso, for example, whose own mother had gone "ballistic" when she first heard that Linda was going to homeschool "her grandchildren," disregarded her mother's objections and homeschooled her three children anyway. She told me that her mother eventually changed her thinking, though it was years later:

> [My mother] had been working with some programs for troubled youth, and one day she called me and said, "I just realized why my grandkids are so wonderful, why I like them so much, why they are who they are." And she said, "It's because you homeschooled them." She said, "I just want to tell you that you were right, and I was wrong. You're kids are so wonderful. You did the right thing in homeschooling."

Linda and her mother both implied that without homeschooling, her children would have turned out like the troubled youth her mother had been working with. Although this may have happened, it is impossible to know because Linda did homeschool. Yet several homeschoolers used this same cognitive strategy, speculating how things could have, or surely would have, gone badly had they not homeschooled.

This type of rationale, though logically problematic, is a common human tendency. The psychological concept has a name—"counterfactual thinking"—which refers to people's penchant to think about how events could have turned out differently and to ruminate over "what-if" scenarios. This type of thinking is appealing because when we speculate about how things could have been worse, we feel better;[2] in this sense, counterfactual thinking could be considered an emotion management strategy. Of course homeschooling mothers, like the rest of us, will never know what would have happened had they made different choices, but it is clear that counterfactual thinking helped some mothers feel vindicated. Linda and her own mother used the children's prosocial character traits, which they had witnessed firsthand, to validate Linda's choice to homeschool. In this way, Linda further cemented her status as an exceptional mother who lived up to the norms of intensive mothering by raising what she saw as mature, well-adjusted children.

Many mothers also documented the character benefits of homeschooling by recounting occasions when strangers spoke highly of their children. Gretchen Forrester, whose boys were fifteen, eleven, and nine when I caught up with her in 2009, said that homeschooling had given her children an opportunity to inspire others:

> We've drawn some people into more active participation in their faith. It might not be in our church, but just by our presence and our example. I hate to say that because it seems so egotistical. But it's been one of the fruits that's come from homeschooling. People say, "How are the kids so— How do you do that?" People we don't know [say that]. [One congregation member] sent Harry a written thank-you card for his reverence as an altar server, and [it said] how much he's enhanced this person's spiritual life, just as an altar server. So it's been [*chokes up*]—those kinds of things are just like—that's just really profound [*sheds tears*]. They [my kids] are so holy. They love serving; they're all considering the vocation of priesthood.

Beyond personal character, mothers pointed to their close relationships with their children as more proof that homeschooling had worked, and this tendency was especially pronounced when children's behavior failed to demonstrate the character-development advantages of homeschooling. Louise Griggs, who sat on a panel at a statewide convention, explained how the outcome for her children, ages twenty-two, twenty, eighteen, and fifteen, was not what she had hoped for, yet she still believed homeschooling had been the right choice for her family:

> [When I decided to homeschool, I thought] my four daughters would be scholars, musicians, gardeners, and seamstresses who would sew their matching flowered dresses for their gospel quartet concerts and lead backyard children's Bible clubs while donating their freshly grown vegetables to the homeless [*audience laughs*]. They would be gourmet cooks, and of course, obedient, excellent housekeepers with a complete knowledge of Holy Scriptures. And of course someday we would be on the cover of *The Teaching Home* [Christian homeschooling] magazine [*audience laughs*]. What I got over the next nineteen years has been a messy house,

homeschool burnout, learning disabilities, hyperactivity, laziness, rebellion, sibling rivalry, pink hair, tattoos, nose-rings, heavy metal music, and a teenage pregnancy. Thankfully not all at the same time, however, and not with all of them. Yet. But would I homeschool again? You *bet* I would. I still believe the overall experience was positive, and the alternative could have been even worse. At least I truly know my children, and over the years have become their friend and confidante.

Homeschooling did not always turn out as mothers had hoped, and they often admitted it, but they usually believed that conventional school would have been worse (another example of counterfactual thinking—there is, of course, no way to know). This mother, though freely admitting that raising her daughters was fraught with challenges, did not blame homeschooling for those less-than-ideal outcomes. Rather, she credited homeschooling for helping her maintain a close relationship with her children despite those challenges.

Other mothers described how their children valued family more than they would have had they attended conventional school. Darlene Rooney-Henkel's son, who was in his first year of college, called every night to talk; Annie Agresti's daughter married but moved only a few blocks away; and Linda Kelso's children were "best friends with each other," all because of the bonds mothers had been able to develop with them (or so they perceived) through homeschooling. Sabrina Hernandez, the mother of twelve children, said, "We are a tight family. The married kids call [and] come home all the time. They're always there for each other, and I think that's something that we have taught by being consistent with the homeschooling."

I came across several people over the years who used their children's appreciation as evidence of homeschooling's success, especially if they openly declared their gratitude for their parents' sacrifice. Linda expressed this to me in our interview, but I also heard her tell this story when she was invited to a PATH meeting as a guest speaker:

> We asked [our first son] when he graduated from high school, we said, "So, okay, give us our report card. How did we do?" . . . He said, "It was great. You guys were great." He said, "The only thing I wish you would have done differently"—so we're waiting, what's he going to say?—he said, "I wish you would have sheltered me more than you did. I wish I'd been sheltered more in those early years; that I hadn't experienced some of the wounding that happened to me in [some] situations."

These types of stories were effective. One of outsiders' main criticisms of homeschooling was that parents would "ruin" their children by sheltering them from the realities of life, and that children would resent them for doing so when the real world shocked them into realizing their naïveté. Linda's example was especially poignant because her son not only did *not* resent his parents but wished they would have sheltered him more.[3]

Linda's story, furthermore, illuminates mothers' tendency to cast their own extensive sacrifice as group effort. Throughout this book, I have shown that homeschooling is a mother's project. There are many ways that mothers sacrifice a great deal more than fathers when it comes to the immense emotional, temporal, and physical workloads required to homeschool. Yet I have also uncovered the ways mothers use different strategies to obscure their disproportionate workload in the family. In this case Linda effectively used the plural pronouns "we," "us," and "you guys" to recast her years of maternal sacrifice as shared sacrifice, implying that her husband contributed to a substantial portion of the homeschooling. Though many mothers did think of homeschooling as a team effort that involved a gendered division of labor—they stayed home while their husbands toiled away in the workforce—it is interesting that, despite their years of frustration and resentment over their husbands' paltry contributions to homeschooling, some mothers shared the glory with them, giving fathers equal credit for the successes of homeschooling.

Like Linda, the vast majority of mothers I reinterviewed saw their children's relationships and character traits as proof-positive that homeschooling had been the right choice. However, problems with their children's character and family relationships caused two of the mothers to question their choice to homeschool. Neither blamed homeschooling entirely but instead attributed the challenges to their children's personalities and the nature of the teenage years.

Patricia Tomlinson, the second-choicer whose sons were ten years apart, was still homeschooling her eleven-year-old when I talked to her in 2009. Her older son, Peter, whom she had pulled out of private school when he was nine because he was so academically advanced (and got sick from the older kids poking him), was in his second year of college. I started the interview by asking Patricia how things were going, and she explained that she was in "a stage of flux right now" with homeschooling:

I'm assessing whether or not we're doing the right thing. My feeling is that we are because I think that my kids are really strong, interesting, individualistic people. But my older son has just recently gone through quite a lot of, um, well, introspection, I suppose. And depression and anxiety. And, actually, a suicide attempt. . . . I shouldn't maybe call it a suicide attempt; it was an overdose. It looked like a suicide attempt to me, but he still denies it [though] he doesn't deny being extremely depressed. . . . He did [also] have problems with an eating disorder—exercise bulimia. It's been a really hard road to try to get him to handle his depression and anxiety.

Patricia was hesitant to blame homeschooling for Peter's problems, but Peter was not. She told me about a conversation she had with him:

When he was flailing around looking for a scapegoat, one of the things he thought of was his sense of removal, you know, from popular culture. . . . He felt like a weirdo. His sense of otherness was just palpable. . . . And as we queried about it, homeschooling came up as a culprit. . . . [But] I actually think that the sense of otherness really doesn't necessarily stem from being homeschooled. I think it stems from being an introspective, introverted, highly intelligent person who has a hard time finding another person like himself. And that goes back to why we homeschooled. We homeschooled because Peter was so introverted that we wanted him to feel comfortable, and he didn't seem like he was feeling comfortable in school. . . . It's interesting because you go back-to-back. My son really believes that home-schooling has something to do with [his depression], and I believe that his temperament really has something to do with homeschooling. . . . So I'm still not convinced [that homeschooling is to blame], but it has shaken my faith a little bit. . . . It makes me second-guess myself like, "Am I being overly occlusive?" I want my kids to have all kinds of exposure to different ideas and opinions, but I don't want to come off as being occlusive. I think maybe I have. . . . There should be a margin for error—that's what I keep telling Peter. I can't be perfect. Nobody's perfect. At least I say I'm sorry.

Patricia wondered whether homeschooling was to blame for her son's struggles, and she spent a great deal of time contemplating her own fail-ure as a teacher and a mother. Yet she still felt confident that some positive things had also come out of homeschooling. For instance, she felt proud of Peter's socially progressive views, explaining that his girlfriend at college "tells him that he is the only boy she has ever met that is not sexist. . . . And when he told me that I went, 'Ahh. That was part of the plan.' That was a huge deal for me." In chapter 3, Patricia explained that one reason she pulled Peter out of school was because she was concerned that he was internalizing negative masculinity norms—becoming "closed" and emotionally reserved.

Therefore, although Patricia's faith in homeschooling had been "shaken," she drew on the positive aspects of her son's relationships and character traits to bolster her feeling that homeschooling had been very successful in some ways; it had helped her achieve at least one of her goals.

Renée Peterson, the mother who converted to first-choice homeschooling, was also trying to figure out the role homeschooling had played in her daughter's life. Renée explained that Taya had always been "challenging," which was one of the reasons she decided to homeschool in the first place. When I talked to Renée in 2002, she had been homeschooling for about four months and was trying to find a way to engage Taya, then ten years old, in schoolwork. Recall that Renée's initial weeks of homeschooling were "fantastic" because her daughter had become "a delightful kid" and "wonderful to be around." But after six weeks, Taya became difficult again. She had a "major crash and attitude problems," was "slamming doors" and talking back to her parents (see chapter 4). When I caught up with Renée in 2009, Taya had just started full-time public school as a junior because financial problems had forced Renée to return to work (though Taya had taken some classes in the school previously to supplement her homeschooling). Renée explained that Taya's behavior had been continually difficult over the years, and that she had recently decided to try "mentoring and coming alongside her" rather than trying to control her from an authoritative position:

RENÉE: I changed my parenting style with her [because] I could not control the child anymore [*laughs*]. She would be sneaking out her freshman year to see a senior boy, and [I was] chasing her to different parties, and [I was] going back and seeing what she was doing on the Internet, and just—it was time for her to own her choices and decisions rather than [for] me to control her. And we're still in that process. It's rebellion to some degree, but I can see her coming around a little bit. Now at least she's coming to me and telling me things, I mean she does terrible things and stupid things, but—

JEN: What kind of terrible things?

RENÉE: Shoplifting. Well, the police told me that one [*laughs*]. Drinking and driving, those kinds of things! But she's not pregnant; we've had lots of talks on that. Bought her friends lots of pregnancy test kits. Had lots of talks on abortion versus keeping the babies, and just issues that come up in teenagers' lives. [We've talked about] how you process a lot of those things and why you make those choices. My husband and I are not on the same page at this point.

JEN: What page is Brian on?

RENÉE: He's more on the authoritarian side of things, where [he'll say],
"She is still in our house, she has to do what I say," and "I need to
be respected," and "This is the way it is." And it causes a little bit of
strife—*a lot* of strife between us. And [strife] between him and her. . . .
But when she went to Europe [for two weeks], it was like a honeymoon
for us! It was so nice! And when she came back, within three days we
signed up for a parenting class and marriage counseling [*laughs*]. We
did! Really! But she's a great kid! She has great gifts, and she's fun to
be around, but she's a handful! And she always has been. . . . So, yeah,
homeschooling still has its issues. Kids are still going to be kids, parents are still going to be parents, and things come up. I love her dearly,
but at this point, I just need to enjoy her while she's still alive!

By the time I talked to her in 2009, Renée had reached the point of des-
peration with Taya's behavior, and her marital problems with Brian had esca-
lated, in part because of Taya's rebellious behavior, and in part because Brian
hid the truth about the family's financial problems. Her last statement, about
fearing that her daughter would not survive adolescence, was powerful; it
constitutes every mother's worst fears. Renée concluded that homeschooling
was not a cure-all, since it had not solved these problems with Taya, some of
which were the reasons she had started homeschooling seven years earlier. In
this way, children's character and relationships with others were major factors that mothers used to measure homeschooling's success.

Professional Success: Academics and Occupation

The second way mothers evaluated homeschooling was by citing their children's academic and occupational achievements. Of course academic success was a main reason mothers gave for homeschooling their children, and
one of the primary areas in which outsiders accused them of failing their
children. Thus, it makes sense that mothers would point to children's academic accomplishments as proof that homeschooling had worked.[4] All the
mothers I reinterviewed in 2008–9 noted their children's academic successes,
though, again, there is no way to tell what these children would have accomplished academically had they attended conventional schools. This problem exists in much of the research that attempts to discern the effectiveness
of homeschooling. Though it is possible to evaluate children's progress on
standardized tests, for example, and compare their scores with those of students attending conventional schools, there is no way to know how those
particular homeschooled children would have performed had they attended

a conventional school; likewise, it is impossible to know how those particular conventionally schooled students would have performed had they been homeschooled. So although there is evidence that homeschooling works academically for many children—several studies show that select groups of homeschooled students perform above average on standardized tests compared with public school students—existing research is unable to conclude that it is better (or worse) than conventional school programs.[5]

In any case, mothers explained that homeschooling had been the right choice by stating the many ways it had helped their children blossom academically. For example, Linda Kelso explained her three children's experiences when they first arrived at college and reflected on their homeschooling education:

> It was interesting, when [my sons] went to college in the early days, they came home and said, "You know what the real difference is that we're finding between homeschooled students and public school students?" They said that institutionally trained students—those that've been in public school and private school—they just want to get the grade and move on. They don't want to do any extra. They said, "Homeschooled students, we want to learn. And the grade is nice, but we actually want to learn stuff." And they had these examples of things that had happened in class, where they wanted more knowledge, because it was so interesting, [so they said to the teacher], "Give us more, we want to learn it," and everybody else is yelling at them to "Shut up, shut up! She'll put it on the test! No, we don't want to know anymore!" Because they didn't; they weren't really interested in the learning.

Mothers were gratified when their children embraced the "love of learning," as many put it, which they cited as one of their original goals in choosing homeschooling. Tracy Chadwick told me that she knew homeschooling had worked for her children because "learning is like breathing for them. They never would tell you that school and learning are the same thing. Ever. Which is disheartening, actually, because they're both in school situations now." Much of how homeschoolers measured success, as Linda and Tracy did, was through unconventional and vague indicators, such as "love of learning," rather than more accepted measures, such as grade-point averages (if the children received grades from outside sources) or standardized test achievement (which was how many parents opted to meet the legal requirement to assess their child annually).

Some mothers, however, did tout conventional academic achievements, probably because it helped them justify their unconventional educational choice. For example, one mother at a PATH meeting mentioned that she faxed her children's annual standardized test scores to their grandparents as proof that homeschooling was working for them. And despite her reservations about the role homeschooling played in her son's depression, Patricia Tomlinson pointed to the academic success of his education, as measured by expert opinion. She told me that during Peter's first year at college, a professor was surprised to learn that he had been homeschooled. The professor asked Peter who had homeschooled him, and when he answered, "My mother," the professor said, "Well, it worked!" Relying on conventional measures and expert opinion was an important way mothers showed outsiders—as well as themselves—that they were indeed preparing their children for the academic rigors they would face in high school, college, and the workforce; mothers' unconventional educational methods would indeed prepare their children for the conventional world.

Mothers who had homeschooled because their children had been slow to develop in certain areas were particularly prone to demonstrate their children's achievement in conventional terms, especially once they got older. In their view, homeschooling had allowed their children to develop at their own rate and eventually "catch up" without suffering a devastating blow to their self-esteem. Linda told me that her twenty-one-year-old son, who had not learned to read until he was twelve years old, "could have very easily been labeled. But now he functions as a twenty-one-year-old. He does everything else that everyone else in his school [college] is able to do. I mean he writes papers—long papers. He did a paper for a poli-sci class, and he tied for the highest grade." Mothers frequently related stories like this to me, where they cast their children's successes in terms of conventional academic achievements, which implied a great irony: conventional schooling would have been unable to prepare their children for conventional success as adults.

Occupational and work-related achievements were also ways mothers proved homeschooling had been successful. One mother, who sat on a panel of experienced homeschoolers at an annual state convention, answered the question "How do you know homeschooling worked for you?" by describing the recent work experience of her eighteen-year-old daughter, who had begun attending college at age fifteen:

> This week . . . we've been very aware that homeschooling has really worked for us. At eighteen, my daughter's a senior at [state university], and this summer she got a job as an intern at a company in [nearby town], where she'll be doing some electrical engineering intern work. She will be making, at age eighteen, thirty-eight hundred dollars a month, for four months,

and she thinks that's really neat [*laughs, audience laughs too*]. The first time that she admitted that she was glad that she was homeschooled was when she got to go to college when she had just turned fifteen. . . . This week her new company has flown her to [a large city in another state]. They picked her up in a limousine. The first night in [this large city], she has a two-room suite to herself with a couch and two TVs and two VCRs [*laughing from panel and audience*]. And she's with a bunch of kids from all kinds of prestigious schools like MIT and Harvard and Duke and Yale, and she is just absolutely on cloud nine this week! So she knows homeschooling worked for her, and she's thrilled with the whole experience.

Angela Welch, who decided to homeschool after hearing from God, was on the same panel and also talked about her children's financial successes and careers:

One of the things I really like, and [makes me] feel I was successful, is the fact that my children are independent, and they are self-supporting. Two girls living out of state—one in [one state] and one in [another state]. We've never paid a dollar for their education as far as college. They paid their own college. My one daughter who lives in [posh neighborhood], her rent is eight hundred dollars a month. She can do it because she makes thirty dollars an hour. So they have learned to work, they have learned to be very responsible. To me that says it all.

Both of these mothers made strong cases for homeschooling by providing their daughters' specific wages and expenses, which was not uncommon when mothers wanted to prove homeschooling's success.

Though salary and occupational prestige served as convincing evidence that homeschooling had worked, mothers also relied on less quantifiable measures such as a solid work ethic, as Angela alluded to when she noted her daughters' high levels of responsibility. At one PATH meeting, a mother explained that she knew homeschooling had worked for her two children, by then grown, because they had both been asked by coworkers and supervisors "how they got so high up at such a young age."

Even when children were not old enough to have begun occupations, some were very certain about what field they wanted to enter. Mothers saw this as a positive effect of homeschooling because it gave children the freedom to pursue their dreams and explore particular fields in depth without getting distracted by "irrelevant" curricula in conventional schools. For example, Darlene Rooney-Henkel's son, who had Asperger's syndrome, had always wanted to be a "video game program designer," a notion her husband "pooh-poohed, but I didn't." From the time her son was eleven years old, he had set his sights on attending one of the world's leading educational institutes in that field. When I followed up with her in 2009, she informed me that he had just begun his first year there. For Darlene, seeing her son achieve his dream was evidence that homeschooling had worked for him and validated the job she did as a mother.

Although some children had lifelong goals that homeschooling allowed them to pursue, others were uncertain about future career fields, a situation that worried most mothers. Liz Trudeau, who had two sets of children fourteen years apart, provided one example. Her oldest son had experienced a checkered college career, attending several universities but never finishing any. When I followed up with her in 2008, he was twenty-seven years old, expecting a baby with his wife, and working construction. Liz was uneasy about his career situation but took comfort in the achievements of her twenty-five-year-old daughter, who was clearly directed and pursuing well-defined career goals.

When children were undecided about their futures, some mothers actively discouraged college because they saw the tuition as a waste of money. Many mothers, like Annie Agresti, told me that they knew "so many people" who were undirected in college and ended up "getting into huge debt" to get a degree they would never use. For example, when Leanna Livingston's sixteen-year-old son, Paul, the first of her four children, displayed no interest in a specific future career, Leanna told me that she was actively discouraging college right away, even though both she and her husband had bachelor's degrees:

> I've always thought it would be good for the kids, the [three] boys especially, to go to the technical college, get some kind of degree in some kind of a trade or something, so that they could work their way through college, and also have a trade to fall back on if whatever else they were going into didn't work out. Now, Paul's not interested in that. I had him look through the technical college catalog a while back. They have open houses [so I said], "Let's go and just hear." [And he said], "No, no, no, no."

Most of the mothers who discouraged college for their undecided children were from less affluent families, both because they had a large number of children to support and because their husbands (the sole wage earners) were working blue-collar jobs or lower-earning white-collar jobs. These parents knew what it was like to support a family of six on an annual salary of

$50,000. Therefore, despite all their dedication to educating their children, some mothers saw college as a luxury that their children would be either unable or foolish to pursue.

Some mothers put a positive spin on children's futures when they were not college-bound. Homeschooling had taught their children to be independent learners, so they might not need college to spoon-feed them information. In addition, because of their years of homeschooling, their children were accustomed to achieving their goals in unconventional ways, so the lack of a college education might not hamper their careers. Of course, not all families with less income felt this way; some valued college above all else and encouraged their children to find and apply for scholarships. But when mothers did express these views to me, they were almost always from families that were more financially strapped and whose children did not have concrete occupational goals, whereas mothers from more affluent families were not bothered by their children's indecision.

Jackie Bell, whose husband earned a high salary ("over $100,000"), was an example. Her sixteen-year-old daughter did not know what occupational field she wanted to enter, but Jackie embraced this, crediting homeschooling for making her daughter a "Renaissance woman" who would not "feel trapped" and who "might do something for a while, and if she decides to do something different, she might just choose to do [so]." Jackie contended that because her version of homeschooling followed the children's interests, they would find it "very easy to change [career tracks] and figure out what they want to do, and then go toward that." Jackie and her husband assumed their children would go to college and were not worried about their daughter's indecision at age sixteen.

It was clear from the follow-up interviews that mothers put a great deal of thought into how homeschooling had affected their children. Mothers' accounts of their children's achievements and struggles defied the stereotypes that portray homeschoolers as irresponsible parents who do not value education and who lack concern for preparing their children for adulthood. For the most part, mothers expressed overwhelming vindication in their decision to homeschool and felt proud to have sacrificed so greatly for their children. The prolonged and intensive experience of homeschooling left its mark on their mothering identities, however, which is the topic taken up in the next chapter, as mothers looked ahead to the end of their homeschooling careers.

8

Looking Forward

Empty Desks, Empty Nests

In 2002, mothers talked a great deal about how labor-intensive homeschooling was and how it sapped them of any time for themselves. Although they often wished for a lighter domestic load and time to themselves, over the years I also heard many mothers express anxiety about the direction their lives would take at the end of their homeschooling careers. At one PATH meeting, for example, a mother said she had felt like "a ship without a rudder" since her last child had gone off to community college. Thus, in 2008–9 I made it a point to ask mothers about their future plans once they were finished homeschooling and had more time to themselves, my third goal for the follow-up interviews. As I mentioned in chapters 6 and 7, four mothers were no longer homeschooling by the time I talked to them, seven were finished homeschooling some children but not others, and five were still homeschooling all their children (see Tables 6.1 and 7.1). Therefore, at the time of the second interview, mothers' plans for the future were more immediate matters for some than others. All the mothers I talked to, however, had thought about these issues.

Mothers fell into two categories when responding to this question: those who had solid ideas about how they would move out of homeschooling, and those who wanted to extend the intensive mothering identity. Interestingly, mothers fell into these categories along first- and second-choice lines as well.

Moving On: Second-Choicers and Careers

Second-choice homeschoolers were much more likely than first-choicers to talk about their future plans in concrete ways. Throughout their home-schooling careers, they had been on the lookout for conventional educational programs that might fit their children's needs. In chapter 6, I discussed how three of the remaining four second-choicers had enrolled and disen-rolled their children in school several times, trying to find a fit, and feel-ing disappointed when it did not work out. Each of these mothers had been ready to pursue a career upon getting her children into school: Emily Ashton had gone into counseling and started her own nonprofit, Darlene Rooney-Henkel had tried to find work in faith advocacy and social justice, and Tracy Chadwick had started a music education program for children. Each of these women had specific plans to pursue her career when her children got settled.[1]

Of these three women, Emily was having the hardest time. Her career plans had once again been postponed for several more years because she had just resumed homeschooling two of her children, the youngest of whom was only in sixth grade. When I asked Emily how she felt about delaying her plans, she explained that she consciously imagined her future career path (running the counseling nonprofit) by putting together "vision boards," col-lages of inspirational words and pictures, which helped her with "dreaming-type stuff for the future" and to "keep focused [on] where it's going." This, along with the "gratitude journal" she talked about in chapter 6, kept her from becoming "very resentful and very cranky." Emily was still doing tem-poral emotion work to manage her problematic feelings, which arose because she once again put her own interests on hold to homeschool her children. Her vision boards helped her to *sequence* by imagining a future in which she would achieve her own goals, and her gratitude journal helped her to *savor* by focusing on the good things she had in her life at the moment, despite deferring her own goals.

Darlene, however, was in a different situation because her children were in school by the time I talked to her in 2009. With her son a college fresh-man pursuing video game programming and her daughter a high school junior, she was ready to ramp up her professional career. Darlene felt her independence had been a long time coming, but it hinged on her daughter's, which she carefully explained:

> I said [to my daughter], "You must get your [driver's] license because of how busy you are"—and this is how I phrased it—"I need to go on with the next stage of my life. And I need the freedom to go ahead and explore that." I wish I could be there more for her, and I'm trying to weigh that balance. . . . All the time I put into homeschooling, that was a choice I made, and I don't regret it. The only regret I have is that I didn't personally—and this was my own choice—that I did not develop a, quote, "career." But it's not too late. It's just that now that I'm fifty-three, it feels like I'm so out of date.

Darlene suspected that her time out of the labor force had made her skills obsolete and would hurt her chances on the job market. She was probably right: studies show that mothers who interrupt their careers lose earning power and opportunities in the labor market.[2] Meanwhile, Darlene, like most mothers in the United States, felt the tug of intensive mothering and was still conflicted about whether a career would allow her to "be there" enough for her daughter.[3] She had understood her choice, years earlier, as one between self (career) and family (homeschooling), and though she regretted having to make the choice, she felt that sacrificing a career to homeschool had been the right one because she had helped her son conquer the challenges of his Asperger's syndrome. As Darlene prepared to enter the job market, however, she felt guilty because her daughter was not finished with school, but Darlene forged ahead nevertheless because she had been waiting years to pursue her career passions, faith advocacy and social justice. Before she was able to get a job, however, "the economy crashed," and she lowered her sights. She "was just going to work in coffee shops that friends owned," but both closed before she was able to start. Thus she was discouraged but hopeful about the future, anxious to begin to "focus more on me as an individual and my own needs."

Second-choicers like Emily and Darlene talked a great deal about how much of their own time and independence they had given up for their children, particularly focusing on their contradictory feelings about it, a perspective that first-choicers rarely held. Though I did not sort homeschoolers into first- and second-choice based on these follow-up data, it makes sense that mothers would fall fairly neatly into these categories when talking about their satisfaction with homeschooling over the years. For example, like Darlene, Tracy, who had begun her music education business, also talked about her (second) "choice" to put her own life on hold to homeschool. And like

Darlene, she was careful to say that, although it was an intentional choice, it was not ideal:[4]

> My goal was to give [my kids] that kind of [private school] education for free. And so what got sacrificed was my own time. And again, not that I subjugated myself—I chose that—but it wasn't the best situation. It would've been better for them to be in a school all along.... And I was really clear all along that I wasn't just doing it for them, and that I *wouldn't* just do it for them. I'm not a martyr type. That's not right.... [But] I always knew that this time was short, so I was fully engaging myself in this endeavor [homeschooling]. And that later I would fully engage myself in another endeavor. I just didn't know what it was. But I knew it was coming, and it was allowed to unfold when time opened up.

In Tracy's view, homeschooling motherhood had "martyr" potential, so she had been careful over the years to meet some of her own needs through homeschooling. During the first interviews, second-choicers talked a great deal about how their lack of me-time threatened to eclipse their sense of self, and because of this, they had felt more conflicted about sacrificing so much to homeschool their children. The follow-up interviews showed that over the years, retaining an independent sense of self remained a salient issue for second-choicers, which is something that previous research on homeschooling and mothering has yet to reveal.

By the time I talked to Tracy in January 2009, she had sent her daughter back to school the previous September and was preparing for her son to attend an alternative public high school the following September. Tracy saw the light at the end of the tunnel and discussed how her life had changed since her ten-year-old daughter had gone to school and her thirteen-year-old son had become more independent:

> They're gone for long stretches of time now.... And in the meantime I've found work that I love. And that's been very healthy and important, and it's led me to grow out of homeschooling.... I mean, those days that I was homeschooling are mine now, more or less. Well, I don't want to say "mine," because I gave them to greater endeavors. But yeah, it's very good for me [to have more time to myself].... I exercise every day. My work's professional, and it's very intellectual and [involves] higher thinking skills. And I work collaboratively with other people. So there's that piece, then there's my fitness piece, there's my meaningful work piece, and it's all—I mean, I really couldn't be happier.... It's great that I did that [homeschooled], it's

great that I'm doing this [working], and when the kids leave home, I'll do something else, something more.

Tracy was excited about finally getting the opportunity to balance the work, family, and personal facets of her life. She had felt the pull of the "family devotion schema" more strongly when her children were young, and although she had not abandoned it, she was glad to begin diversifying her efforts and experiencing some of the positive emotional intensity offered by the "work devotion schema."[5] She was starting to rely less on the sequencing strategy because her children's independence and, importantly, the public school system were providing her with more time to herself, as she had hoped all along.

Second choicers like Tracy, Darlene, and Emily felt the same tension of intensive mothering that so many other mothers in the United States feel, perhaps because they had wanted professional careers and felt that homeschooling restricted their ability to pursue them. It is clear from their stories that they still understood sequencing and savoring as key processes to help them get through intensively mothering and homeschooling their children.

Extending Intensive Motherhood: First-Choicers and Family

In contrast to second-choicers' concrete, career-minded plans, first-choicers' future plans were more nebulous, at least for the nine who were still homeschooling. When I asked them in the follow-up interviews what they planned to do once they finished homeschooling, they often shrugged and said they had not given it serious consideration, or they speculated on a number of things they might be interested in doing in the future. Several mothers suggested they might volunteer for their churches someday, though they rarely specified in what capacity. Other mothers talked about returning to hobbies they had given up, such as "craft work" or playing the flute. A few said they might "get a job" to contribute to the family income, but, with the exception of one mother, first-choicers did not want to enter specific fields; they did not talk about jobs as professional careers, as the second-choicers did.

At the time of the second interview, there were three first-choicers who had begun voluntarily working outside of the home, and only part-time (this does not include Whitney and Renée, who, as I discussed in chapter 6, had both returned to the workforce unwillingly due to financial constraints and enrolled their children in school). The first was Liz Trudeau, who had become a doula (a pregnancy and birthing coach) and was the only first-choicer to cast her work professionally and locate it within a specific field. Liz had more than twenty years of homeschooling experience, and though her older children were in their twenties, she was still homeschooling her twelve- and ten-year-olds. Unlike with her first set of children, Liz had enrolled the second set in a Parent-School Partnership program through the public school system, where they took a few organized classes with other home-schooled children. Thus, Liz had regular intervals of free time, which she used at her discretion, to take on as many clients as she could comfortably handle.[6]

The other two first-choicers who had begun working did not have regu-larly scheduled help with the schooling as Liz did; thus it was much harder for them to transition to a job. Sabrina Hernandez, whose youngest of her twelve children (ages fifteen and thirteen) were still homeschooling, had recently begun bookkeeping for her older son's business when I talked to her in 2009. She started out part-time but soon had to cut back on even those hours because her younger children were not getting their work done:

> It was only three days a week, and I thought, "[The two kids] are excellent students. They do their work." . . . But they would get behind. So they still need me there, even though they're very good students. And it wasn't all their fault. I mean, working out of the house, I would come home tired. I wouldn't grade. So how could they go on if I've never graded what they did before?

Valerie Scott's story was similar. When I caught up with her in 2008, she had just bought a business but had encountered the same disruptions Sabrina had. She was trying to balance it all and, like Sabrina, was cutting back on work to be home. She was "still figuring it out" because her second set of children, who were twelve, ten, and nine, "do not like me to leave." She told me:

> I like to stay home in the morning so I can get them started. They know their goals, they know what they have to do, so they're comfortable. They've had their breakfast, they're dressed, they're ready to do school, and then if I have to go in [to work] I try only to go in for maybe two, three hours at the max.

If Valerie had to be gone for longer, she called one of her adult children to come school the younger set, or she relied on her mother, who lived next door. Even with all this family support, Valerie found it challenging to leave her children for only a few hours.

Of all my follow-up interviewees Sabrina, Valerie, and Liz, the three first-choicers who had started voluntarily working outside the home, were also the three mothers with the most experience homeschooling (more than twenty years each). In addition, Sabrina and Valerie, the two who had had more challenges transitioning to work, were also the two mothers in my study with the most children (Sabrina had twelve, Valerie had seven—four in the first set and three in the second). Unlike the second-choicers (and first-choicer Liz), Sabrina and Valerie talked about their work ventures as a way to contribute to the family income and to occupy their time as they phased out of homeschooling, rather than as a source of self-fulfillment and identity. As they tried to transition into the workforce, however, they found themselves pulled back into the home. Yet neither seemed particularly distressed by it, and both were happy to put family ahead of their new work endeavors. In this way, Sabrina and Valerie stayed highly invested in homeschooling and, in a sense, extended their intensive mothering careers rather than transition out of them. As I began to explore this issue, I found other ways first-choicers, but not second-choicers, extended intensive motherhood.

When I asked them what was in store at the end of their homeschooling careers, five of the twelve first-choicers (Liz, Alice, Annie, Valerie, and Leanna), yet none of the second-choicers, talked specifically about looking forward to grandparenthood. Though grandparenthood does not prescribe the same intensity that motherhood does, these first-choicers highlighted the caregiving aspect of it because they would have the opportunity to experience the joys of being around young children again. Liz and Alice were new grandmothers,[7] and Annie and Valerie had children who were newly married, so perhaps that was why grandparenthood was on their radar. Leanna's oldest was only sixteen, but she was already looking forward to it as well. Thus, for these women, the next phase in their lives revolved around family and relationships rather than around self-achievement in a career, as it did for second-choicers; grandparenthood was a way of extending motherhood, though dialing back the intensity a bit.

The most literal examples of extending motherhood, however, came from mothers who had had more children since I had talked to them in 2002. When I caught up with the sixteen mothers for the follow-up interviews, I was surprised to find that three of them (all first-choicers)—Jackie Bell, Leanna Livingston, and Cassandra Shudek—had had more children. Of course many of my original homeschoolers were still of childbearing age, so I should have expected that some mothers would have had more children by 2009. Naïvely, however, it never occurred to me that they would increase their family size in that time, probably because two or three children, spaced within a few years of each other, is the norm in the United States.

For these three homeschoolers, the number of years between the two youngest children was a bigger span—five or six years—than between any other children in the family. At the time of the first interview, Jackie's two daughters were 9 and 5 years old; she had another daughter a year later, who was 5 by the time of the follow-up interview (when the older two were 15 and 11). Leanna's three sons were 9, 6, and 3 at the time of the first interview; she had a daughter two years later, who was 5 at the time of our second interview (when the boys were 16, 13, and 10). Cassandra, whose four sons were 9, 6, 3, and 2 in 2002, had a 3-year-old daughter by the time I reinterviewed her almost six years later (her boys were then 15, 12, 9, and 8).

Of these three mothers, only Jackie expressed ambivalence about her third pregnancy, which she discovered about a month after our first interview:

> It was quite a surprise! . . . Because I was like, "Okay, I'm going to be turn-ing forty, my youngest is going to be six," and I could really step out and do some things of my own. And then I found out I was pregnant. That was okay, too. But at the time Benny was [writing a screenplay and producing an independent film], and so we were pretty much living off of savings at that point. So it was a tough decision to make, but it was good. We were really happy.

Though I did not ask her for clarification (I felt it was too personal an issue to probe at that point in the interview), Jackie's statement about the "tough decision" seemed to imply that she and her husband had considered termi-nating the unexpected pregnancy. At the very least, her statement implied some ambivalence about whether to extend her intensive mothering career, and "start parenting all over again," as she later stated. This ambivalence became clearer the more we talked about how the pregnancy changed her plans for the future:

> I had wanted to find a way to volunteer and be a part of the community. . . . These are things that I felt, as an adult human being, I wanted to contrib-ute, . . . but it didn't happen right then. You can imagine how having a baby shifted that. But the seed was sown, and I knew in my own mind that I needed to do that eventually.

When Jackie's youngest was about three years old (the other two were thirteen and nine), she was able to begin some community volunteer work, which, over the next two years, progressed to her active participation in a campaign to support marriage equality. She explained the shift in her experience:

> Before I was pretty much doing things for the kids, and I was just put-
> ting on hold any interests that I had. And by doing this kind of volunteer
> work [on a marriage equality act], it was really fulfilling for me, just to
> feel like I could do something that I could call my own, that had nothing
> to do with kids, nothing to do with homeschooling, nothing to do with
> anybody but me. I was self-motivated to do it. It was a long time coming
> because my kids are spread out age-wise. . . . And as I've been doing that,
> it has had a really wonderful effect on my kids' learning. My kids see me
> self-actualizing, and it has sped up their own self-actualization process. . . .
> I don't want to feel like they are my life in the sense that if I'm not doing
> something for them, then I don't have any merit.

Jackie was unique among the first-choice homeschoolers in that she envi-
sioned the future as one in which she would transcend the intensive demands
of homeschool mothering and "self-actualize" by pursuing her own interests
(although she still rationalized her own self-actualization as ultimately ben-
eficial to her *children's* self-actualization). In talking about her own goals and
sense of identity, Jackie sounded more like the second-choicers, even though
homeschooling had been her first choice. However, Jackie had always occu-
pied this peripheral position in the first-choice/second-choice continuum;
recall that her decision to give up her career and stay at home with her children was fraught with intense deliberation from the beginning, though she
eventually embraced the choice wholeheartedly (see chapter 2).

The vast majority of first-choicers, however, were not as torn as Jackie about
negotiating a balance between intensive mothering and pursuing their self-
interests. Indeed, most first-choicers embraced a version of motherhood that
led them to want to extend the experience. One way they did so was by planning to have more children (as opposed to Jackie's unplanned pregnancy). By
doing so, they intentionally reset their mothering-career clocks, so to speak,
and went back to square one.[8] Both Valerie and Liz said that they had had
their second set because they missed parenting young children once their first
set moved into their teens. Several other mothers expanded their family size,
and thus extended their mothering careers, by putting the decision "in God's
hands." Two mothers offered particularly poignant stories to this effect.

When I interviewed Cassandra Shudek in 2008, her youngest of five
children, born several years after the first interview, was three years old.

Cassandra's experience in adding to her family stood in stark contrast to Jackie's ambivalence at her surprise pregnancy and is much more in line with other first-choicers' philosophies. Cassandra articulated this rationale well and at length:

> CASSANDRA: I would love to have more kids, but geez, I'm forty-six, I don't
> know how likely that is. . . . The norm in the culture today is, what,
> two-point-six kids? So after I had [my second child] everybody
> expected me to get sterilized! But I just didn't feel comfortable with
> it [even though] everyone was saying how horrible it was, how it was
> stealing my youth. And that I wouldn't be able to fulfill myself, with all
> my talents and gifts and education and everything. But I just didn't buy
> it. So we took the big risk, and we decided to completely go off birth
> control and just trust God with the outcome. We lost a lot of friends
> because of it. They thought I was insane. My mom actually thought
> I was mentally ill because I had [my fifth child]. [And before I lost a
> baby last year], she thought that I was probably clinically depressed
> and having some sort of psychotic episode, and that I needed to be
> committed because I was having another baby at [age] forty-five.
>
> JEN: So you lost friends? For having more than two children? Or for late
> childbearing, or what?
>
> CASSANDRA: I've found that women hold their birth control really close,
> and it's a really personal issue. So for me to say, "I'm going off, and
> I'm just going to have faith that God knows what he's doing; I'm not
> afraid," I think it was something that they just couldn't support because
> they were afraid of getting pregnant. I talked to so many friends, even
> Christians, [who said] it was the one thing they would never, *never*
> give up. Because for them it was the means by which they could have
> control over their finances, over their future, over their bodies, you
> know, over the relationship with their husband. And for them to give
> that up seemed like the worst possible thing in the world.

Cassandra pointed to several ways that reproduction and disempowerment are intricately connected for women. She implied that most women see motherhood as completely sacrificial, representing a loss of control over self-hood on even the most fundamental levels, such as the physical body and intimate relationships. Even her Christian friends were unwilling to deepen their subordination and powerlessness by extending their intensive mothering careers indefinitely, and they believed (according to Cassandra) that anyone who would voluntarily do so was clearly "psychotic." The friendships could not withstand the stigma of unchecked childbearing:

> It was as if they could no longer identify with me, I guess. So I just had to accept that and wish them well. And it's been hard. Nobody came to [my fifth child's] birthday party. There were no baby showers, no visitors. So it's been isolating in some ways, but it's also just caused me to try and figure out why I believe what I believe. . . . We'd love to have more [children]. More to love. For us, it's like saying there's too many flowers in the world, or too many sunsets. They're so beautiful! They're so wonderful to be around, I can't imagine saying that I have enough. . . . Even [U.S. House of Representatives Speaker] Nancy Pelosi said yesterday that sterilization and abortion and birth control are the way to economic recovery. And I'm just trying to figure out how babies became the enemy to our culture.[9] I just can't view children that way. I love them, and I see them as a blessing. And I wish I had more to give the world; I do. So maybe we'll adopt.

Although Cassandra saw herself as an outsider, even among her more traditionally minded friends (she identified herself and her friends as "conservative Christians"), there were other first-choicers who also told me about their decision to put their families in God's hands, such as Sabrina Hernandez, whose decision to give up birth control after her third child resulted in adding nine more to her family.

Gretchen Forrester was another mother who talked in depth about extending intensive motherhood, though her situation was a bit different and even more complicated. When I talked to her in 2009, her boys were fifteen, eleven, and nine, but she and her husband had recently experienced a change of heart about family size. The subject came up when I asked her what she would do after she was finished homeschooling. She replied:

> GRETCHEN: I don't know. Maybe I'll have more kids! . . . I just love kids; they're amazing. I don't think I'd actually be able to bear them because I'm forty-one. But I'm not closed to [the idea of] having more. And that's a recent thing. [My husband and I] just had a real awakening. It's like, "Wow, why did we stop? What were we thinking?" I mean, obviously we were thinking, "Three's enough. Family's perfect. Money? Fine. Car seats? Good." It was this whole fabricated checklist that we met. . . . I don't think we really thought about it. I think we just went through the motions. But it's not very Catholic, either, so we've come around spiritually about the decision we've made. I wouldn't want to

feel like I had gone against my calling in life or been so selfish as to not be doing what I was supposed to.

JEN: What would be selfish about that? Not giving more of yourself to more children?

GRETCHEN: Well, basically taking the decision about whether or not we were open to life out of God's hands. The church doesn't say, "Have as many kids as you can"; the church says you have to be "open to life." . . . There's good reasons to space out having children, or put off hav-ing children. But we took the surgical alternative which is *so* against the teachings of the church. . . . And nobody—none of the Catholic parents were like, "Are you sure?" . . . I was thirty-two. It's pretty young. . . . And just last year, when I met [my friend], the mother of the thirteen kids, one of the first things she said to me was, "How come you only have three kids and you're Catholic?" And I told her straight up, "I'm really embarrassed to tell you that I had my tubes tied. I don't know what I was thinking." And I just regret the decision we made.

As Gretchen's children aged, she and her husband began to question their previous family-size choices. I had known Gretchen for about a year before I interviewed her in 2002 (when her boys were eight, four, and two), and at that time money was a constant concern for the family. Her husband owned a business, which experienced a number of setbacks that year, and they bud-geted carefully so that she could continue to stay home with the children. So I was surprised to hear that, seven years later, at age forty-one, she was worried she had gone "against [her] calling in life," which could have been to have more children.

As time passed between our interviews, Gretchen had begun to feel more regret, guilt, and embarrassment because she knew she had gone against the church's teachings by not being "open to life," even though she was in her early forties, a stage in life that typically marks the end of women's reproduc-tive years. As we continued to talk, Gretchen explained that she had only recently discovered the great distress the tubal ligation had caused her over the years:

JEN: So you regret the decision to have your tubes tied?

GRETCHEN: Yeah. I've been suffering [since I did it], but I didn't know I was for like eight years. And I look back on it [and I can see that] even right after [my third child] was born, it was black—it was different from the other childbirths—it was dark. . . . Part of it is that I was under a little bit more stress because I had two young kids at home.

But looking back on it now, I think it [the dark feeling] was definitely related to having just been sterilized. I did the wrong thing. And so I was suffering. . . . I was really sad. And it wasn't postpartum depression either; it was just really dark. I think on some level I was grieving the loss of never having another. I was holding [my baby], who was beautiful, and thinking, "This is the last one." I wasn't thinking, "Oh, this is wonderful! I could do this every day! I could have one of these every year!" [Instead I knew] when he weaned, it was the last time I ever nursed. And when he potty trained, I knew it was the last. Done! And I'm never having another child.

In retrospect Gretchen understood her experiences differently.[10] She realized that she had never wanted to be "sterilized," and she understood her sadness and other "dark" feelings to be the result of putting a limit on her mothering career. Recall from chapter 5 that many mothers did temporal emotion work to savor the identity and experience of motherhood, as well as to avoid feeling regret once their children were grown. One obvious way to extend their mothering careers was by having more children, but Gretchen's choice had precluded her ability to do so, and she felt immense regret—the emotion most mothers feared would arise if they did not prioritize intensive mothering at every opportunity. Unable to stop time and savor motherhood as long as she wanted, Gretchen felt overwhelming regret and guilt about limiting her mothering career.

Meanwhile, Gretchen was unaware that her husband had also been struggling with the fallout of their choice nine years earlier. She explained:

On his own, Tyler was also dealing with the spiritual results. Coming to terms with that decision and wanting to repent. . . . Then he went to confession. He had never confessed having a part in the sterilization. So the priest in the confession suggested [surgical] reversal. . . . And [Tyler talked to me about it, and] we came to it in prayer and were really both on the same page. He was like, "Whatever you decide. You're the one who has to go through the surgery. I don't want to be like, 'Yeah, let's do it!' That's easy for me to say. But I'm totally supportive. We can make it happen financially." Because that was my big holdup. I didn't want to ask to do it because it was eight thousand dollars. He had to come up with eight thousand dollars out of nothing. But we did it; I had a reversal. We went to [another state]. There's a tubal reversal clinic there. That's all they do. And it wasn't to get pregnant. It was to be open to life. So if God would want us to bring new life to the world, we would be open to it. It's our way of making amends.

As Gretchen's story unfolded, her dedication to extending intensive motherhood (even just potentially) became clear. Her willingness to "ask" her husband to spend $8,000, which she was not sure they could afford, fly to another state, and have major surgery under general anesthesia indicated how strongly she felt about this issue and how badly she wanted to put things right with the church. Doing so eased her problematic feelings and gave her a sense of peace:

> I could see [getting pregnant] just being the fulfillment of what was supposed to be. But if it doesn't happen, it wasn't what was meant to be. So that's a long answer to your question of what will I do after [my third child] goes to college. But it would be disingenuous for me to say anything else like, "Oh, I'm going to become an artist; I might take up photography." Now that we're open to life, who knows what will happen.

Gretchen's striking comparison of her real desire for the future (having another baby) with the alternative (taking up a hobby) highlighted the supreme value motherhood held for her. Clearly, she had a tremendous emotional investment in the intensive mothering aspect of her identity and went to great lengths to extend and savor the experience.

The prospect of reaching the end of their homeschooling careers evoked different emotions for different groups of mothers. The second-choicers felt excited about the next phase of their lives, whereas the first-choicers expressed more nostalgic feelings and a greater desire to extend their mothering careers. Both groups, however, clearly recognized that the diminishing temporal and emotional demands of homeschooling would greatly affect their identities, not only as homeschoolers but as mothers as well.

9

Savoring Motherhood

Throughout this book, I have explored the experiences of homeschooling mothers. I have examined how mothers made decisions to homeschool, responded to outsider criticism, handled the increased domestic labor, dealt with losing me-time, understood their journey in retrospect, viewed their children's successes, and planned for the future. Several themes have run throughout the course of this study: the self and identity, emotional culture, and the temporal dimensions of mothering. Some of these themes intersect, and I turn now to analyze these intersections theoretically.

The Emotional Culture of Good Mothering

Emotions such as guilt, resentment, frustration, pride, joy, and love are central to the experience of intensive mothering, yet little sociological research has placed maternal emotions at the center of analysis. One of the goals in this book has been to focus on how homeschoolers in particular use their emotional experiences to understand themselves as good mothers, and, in doing so, to suggest how some of these processes may map onto the emotional culture of intensive mothering more generally. In the early chapters, I showed that two important elements of homeschoolers' emotional culture greatly impacted their identities: how they felt about staying home with their school-age children, and how they constructed good mother identities when outsiders labeled their emotions as deviant. These two areas represent mothers' identity struggles both internally and externally.

Internal Identity Struggles: Managing Emotions with Choices and Epiphanies

Mothers arrived at their decision to homeschool in various ways, and as I noted in chapter 2, their motivations related to how they felt about stay-at-home motherhood. Second-choicers' stories revealed a great deal of conflict as they struggled to reconcile their feelings about, first, staying at home and, later, homeschooling. These mothers tended to feel dissatisfied and coerced by outside pressures—children's needs and husbands' wishes—to sacrifice their own time and interests to homeschool their children. Compared with first-choicers, second-choicers experienced greater emotional conflict and had a harder time making their stay-at-home and homeschooling choices.

Sociologists have discussed mothers' choices in depth, mostly with respect to middle-class mothers' decision to work in the paid labor force or stay at home with preschool-age children. Several scholars have investigated how "choice rhetoric"[1] has been folded into the mothering discourse as a way to help middle-class mothers justify their decision to put their "career goals on hold" to stay home.[2] Though choice rhetoric helps mothers couch their decision to leave paid work as one in which they freely exercise their agency to dedicate themselves to full-time motherhood, research has shown that the language of choice actually conceals a "choice gap," one that is created by workplace practices that are so incompatible with family life that they push women out of careers by making them choose between work and family.[3] In doing so, the rhetoric effectively obscures structural inequality in the workplace by individualizing the problem of work-family conflict and providing mothers with a culturally valid justification to give up their career identities.[4] The data provided by my second-choicers confirm the way many mothers talk about choice in order to manage their identities. However, my data further suggest that the discourse of choice is not only a strategy to manage identity but also one to manage emotions.

The second-choicers I studied clearly used the language of choice to convey and manage their conflicting emotions about putting their own lives "on hold" for their children. When they recounted their initial decision to home-school, they spoke of their genuine desire to sacrifice for the good of their children while simultaneously lamenting the career identities they would be giving up. They cast their decision to homeschool as an emotional com-promise in which they chose to live with the dissatisfaction of relinquish-ing their career plans rather than with the guilt of sacrificing their children's well-being. Furthermore, my follow-up interviews showed that this emo-tional conflict continued to arise over the years, affecting second-choicers greatly. Chapters 5, 6, and 8 demonstrated that second-choicers felt highly ambivalent about their years of sacrifice and struggled with regret, disap-pointment, and frustration along the way, repeatedly trying and often failing to integrate their children into conventional programs.

This emotional struggle is salient in other research on intensive moth-ering, yet the emotional facets have not been analyzed as emotions per se. Blair-Loy's work stands as a partial exception. She noted similar feelings among some of the women she interviewed, who had left elite careers to stay home with their children because they embraced the "family devotion schema," a cultural model that promises mothers meaningful and fulfill-ing lives through a single-minded focus on family caregiving. This schema directs mothers to pursue "an almost ascetic life path of transcending self-centeredness for the sake of others' well-being" in return for an intense emotional connection with their children.[5] Although some of Blair-Loy's stay-at-home subjects were happy with their decision to embrace the fam-ily devotion schema, a substantial portion felt disillusioned and conflicted, which were difficult emotions to experience. Blair-Loy concluded that these women's experiences of motherhood required "profound emotion work,"[6] though she did not present the strategies they used to accomplish it, some-thing that Hochschild discussed in detail when developing the concept of emotion work.[7]

My data fill this gap in the literature on mothers' emotions by showing exactly how second-choicers' homeschooling careers required continuous and prolonged emotion work, and revealing that they performed it, in part, by drawing on maternal choice rhetoric. When second-choicers reflected on their difficult journey through their homeschooling careers, they were care-ful to explicitly remind me (and, by way of doing so, remind themselves) that they had chosen freely. For example, recall from chapter 8 that Darlene told me, "The only regret I have is that I didn't personally—and this was my own choice—that I did not develop a, quote, 'career'"; and Tracy qualified her discontent over the years by saying, "Not that I subjugated myself—I chose [homeschooling]—but it wasn't the best situation." By analyzing mothers' emotional struggles in their choice between career and family, my research shows how the rhetoric of choice operates as an emotion management strategy to help some homeschooling mothers, and probably other intensive mothers as well, feel better about sacrificing their own interests for their children. In this way, it is clear that choice rhetoric is integral to the emotional culture of intensive mothering and may operate as an indispensable emotion management strategy for some women, though one that may be fairly ineffective, given the ongoing dissatisfaction that many mothers experience.

In contrast, it is interesting that very few of the first-choicers I studied invoked the rhetoric of choice. Jackie came closest when describing her "evolution" in embracing stay-at-home motherhood, but the remaining first-choicers did not talk about the emotional conflict in having to choose between work and career; for them, going back to the paid labor force was not enticing. It would be a mistake, however, to assume that first-choicers experienced no emotional turmoil about staying at home with their children or about homeschooling; while this may be the case for some mothers, others may have expressed little emotional conflict when I talked to them because they had already successfully managed any problematic feelings related to staying home and homeschooling.

Indeed, digging deeper into the data reveals that this was the case for most first-choicers, who related their moments of clarity when they suddenly "knew in their hearts" that staying home and homeschooling were the right courses of action. Their emotional epiphanies, which spontaneously appeared out of the blue (or from God), helped them manage the emotional contradictions of intensive mothering by reinforcing a model of motherhood that rested on a set of intense, "natural" maternal emotions. Recall that Judith phoned her boss from the hospital to resign from her job because of the sudden and intense emotional attachment she felt to her new baby; and recall that Angela "had no peace" about the question she "kept pondering" ("What does God want you to do?") until the moment she heard about homeschooling, which produced "a burst of enthusiasm within me!" Mothers felt so certain they were on the right path that their entry into stay-at-home mothering and homeschooling seemed "choiceless"; as Valerie said upon having her epiphany, "How can you *not* [homeschool]?" By providing first-choicers with a clear answer and solid conviction, emotional epiphanies relieved the conflict that accompanies choice by obscuring the act of choosing. Choices can be wrong; "knowing" is infallible.[8]

It is possible, then, that first-choicers did much less emotion work around their identities as stay-at-home mothers and homeschoolers because their epiphanies more successfully managed their emotional conflict, and this emotional harmony facilitated long-term, intensive involvement with their children. Though first-choosers experienced their share of emotional conflict in other areas, they felt at peace with their decisions to stay at home and to homeschool, which helped them embrace their homeschooling mother identities more easily than second-choosers.

My findings also suggest that maternal emotional epiphanies may serve an important function in the emotional culture of intensive mothering more broadly. When Bobel found that the natural mothers she studied talked a great deal about how their instincts and feelings led them to "choose" natural mothering, she noted the irony in understanding choice this way: "This forced-choice paradigm directly contradicts the natural mother's discourse of free choice.... Did these women freely choose ... or did their 'hearts' choose for them?"[9] My research suggests that one way to answer this question is to consider the emotional conflict that choice rhetoric engenders for some women; though it purports to solve the emotional conflicts of intensive mothering, for some homeschooling mothers, and probably some other intensive mothers as well, choice rhetoric actually intensifies the conflict. Maternal emotional epiphanies, in contrast, function as a way to resolve that conflict because they allow mothers to escape the emotional turmoil involved in choosing one path at the expense of the other; they absolve mothers from making a choice. Mothers appeal to their "instinct" and "know in their heart" that they are on the right path, and in a historical moment when the ideology of intensive mothering ensures that a woman "can never fully do it right,"[10] this kind of validation for maternal desires, emotions, and practices is crucial. This finding reveals that the emotional culture of intensive mothering contains a toolbox of emotion management strategies, from choice rhetoric to emotional epiphanies, which mothers can apply discriminately, interactively, and with different degrees of success, to manage the variety of emotional conflicts that occur with different mothering dilemmas.

External Identity Struggles: Combating the Stigma
of Maternal Emotional Intensity

In addition to the internal identity conflicts first- and second-choosers grappled with, homeschoolers also struggled with their identities externally because they were accused of irresponsible mothering for keeping their children out of conventional schools, as I discussed in chapter 3. Strangers, friends, and even family members often implied (or stated outright) that they were "ruining" their children by depriving them of the opportunity for "normal" development in four areas: academic, social, moral, and relational. Within each of these four areas, outsiders labeled mothers as having a specific emotional problem, which they assumed misguided them into homeschooling. Children would suffer academically because their mothers were arrogant, and they would fail to develop social skills because mothers were overprotective. Mothers' self-righteousness would prevent their children from accepting mainstream morals, and their hyperengagement would hamper children's developing independence. Thus, homeschoolers' stigma as maternal deviants was anchored in what outsiders perceived to be their *emotional* deviance, in this case, holding "too much" of the "right" maternal emotions—confidence, protectiveness, moral conviction, and attachment.

To combat the charges of maternal deviance, then, mothers developed four justifications, each targeting one of the (alleged) overly intense emotions, which helped them construct identities as good mothers. The main way they did so was by drawing heavily from the ideology of intensive mothering to cast their strong emotions as appropriate and in line with those that responsible mothers feel. Examining this deviant emotional intensity, as well as the ways mothers tried to justify it, exposes important elements of the emotional culture of intensive mothering and explicates the integral role it plays in many mothers' experiences.

Previous research has identified some of the emotions integral to the cultural ideal of mothering, although it has not analyzed them as emotions per se or as part of the emotional culture of motherhood. For example, love, concern, and willingness to sacrifice are the most important emotions of good mothering, while greed, selfishness, and laziness are all characteristic of bad mothers. Generally, these emotions cluster around the theme of sacrifice (and its antithesis, selfishness), the core feature in defining good mothering in contemporary U.S. culture.[11] By identifying the unacceptably intense feelings of arrogance, overprotectiveness, self-righteousness, and hyperengagement, my research reveals a wider variety of emotions and their acceptable limits than the previous research on intensive mothering has identified.

In examining homeschooling mothers' accounts for their alleged emotional deviance, my research also shows how individual mothers may interpret the emotional mandates of good mothering, evaluate themselves against it, and work to decrease the "emotive dissonance"[12] they may experience. In some ways, my homeschoolers were like other mothers, drawing on a subcultural discourse to account for their emotional deviance, as did the mothers in sociologist Verta Taylor's study, who labeled their deviant emotions, such as anxiety and resentment, as symptomatic of postpartum illness.[13] Yet, unlike Taylor's subjects who excused their deviant emotions by attributing them to a biological process out of their control, homeschooling mothers justified their deviant emotions by endorsing them.

This comparison illustrates that excusing and justifying maternal emotional deviance have very different implications for the social construction of intensive mothering. Excuses allowed Taylor's subjects to reinforce the mainstream emotional culture of mothering; although they denied responsibility for their feelings, mothers agreed, for the most part, that they were inappropriate and undesirable—the "wrong" emotions: resentment, guilt, depression, anger, shame, anxiety, fear, detachment, and disappointment. That these mothers went so far as to label themselves ill is testament to how incompatible these emotions are with the emotional culture of mothering.

Homeschoolers, in contrast, were accused of having "too much" of the "right" emotions—confidence, protectiveness, moral conviction, and attachment—which allowed them to use the discourse of good mothering not only to show that they held the "right" emotions but also to argue that mothers can never feel "too much" of these important emotions. Thus, homeschoolers' vision advocated feeling more of the emotions that good mothers feel. Yet, in justifying these intense emotions, homeschoolers not only defended their identities as good mothers but also elevated the standards for good mothering, ultimately promoting an emotional culture of intensive mothering that was even more difficult to live up to than the mainstream (already intensive) version.

By illuminating the ways that maternal deviance may be cast as emotional deviance, this study broadens our knowledge about the variety of maternal emotions considered important as well as deepens our understanding about how they operate in defining intensive mothering. Moreover, my research demonstrates that some of the ways mothers account for emotional deviance may constrict the parameters of acceptable mothering practices, intensify emotional expectations, and further trap women within the narrow confines of the emotional culture of intensive mothering.[14]

The Temporal-Emotional Conflict of Good Mothering

The emotional culture of homeschooling motherhood had a significant impact on mothers' feelings and identities as they progressed through their homeschooling careers. Yet one constant source of emotional conflict involved time, not only how much mothers had and how they used it but also the meanings they gave to the temporal experience of homeschooling motherhood.

Objective Time: Domestic Labor and Burnout

Chapter 4 demonstrated that mothers who began homeschooling had to find a way to incorporate the teacher role into their repertoire of other roles, and as they did so, most passed through three stages of role strain—ambiguity, failure, and conflict/overload—each of which engendered more intense emotions and time-consuming management techniques than the previous stage. Though veterans advised newcomers to destructure and incorporate learning into everyday life, new homeschoolers ignored them because they thought teaching involved setting a structured curriculum, achieving affective neutrality toward students, and compartmentalizing education apart from other aspects of life. They clung to dominant definitions of teaching and education (the only ones they knew) in an effort to manage their fears about shortchanging their children. Mothers wanted to reassure themselves that they were educating the right way, but compartmentalizing their roles was so labor- and emotion-intensive that they experienced a great deal of time stress and emotional burnout. When mothers felt conflict and overload among their multiple roles, they were forced to confront their priorities by allocating their time accordingly. Those who overcame burnout did so by achieving role harmony: they downgraded housework and integrated the mother and teacher roles, which helped them manage their dwindling time (although, as I have shown, mothers' time allocation did not relieve all of their stress).

The homeschoolers in my study experienced similar time stress and employed many of the same time management strategies as other (non-homeschooling) mothers do. Sociologist Suzanne Bianchi and her colleagues addressed parents' time use in their comprehensive study of American family life over the last decades of the twentieth century, noting that both mothers and fathers have less time for raising children and running a household because more women are in the workforce than ever before. Their research found that "time deepening," or multitasking, has become a way that parents have tried to juggle their multiple responsibilities to give them a sense of having more hours in the day. Married fathers, married mothers, and single mothers have all roughly doubled their multitasking hours, so in this sense, both mothers and fathers feel more time pressure with respect to their multiple roles. However, Bianchi and her colleagues found that mothers—both married and single—were significantly more likely to feel time pressure than fathers. Mothers reported that they multitask "most of the time" and feel "always rushed," even when their objective reports of multitasking equaled those of fathers. The authors concluded that emotions are implicated more in mothers' time pressure than fathers', saying that "fathers are simply not as likely to always feel rushed" and that "mothers may actually do two things at once at the same rates as fathers, but they feel as if they must almost constantly be on the move to keep the family afloat."[15]

The explanation Bianchi and her colleagues offer is that the nature of mothers' work is more complex because they are the active household managers. This work is complicated and must be carefully choreographed to meet everyone's needs, and this complexity stresses mothers more than fathers. In other words, although fathers and mothers in individual families may be equally likely to experience role strain, the nature of mothers' roles is qualitatively different—perhaps more likely to contain role conflict and ambiguity, as my research has uncovered—than fathers'. Because roles that conflict operate at cross purposes, and those that are ambiguous are hard to perform, these forms of role strain could be harder to manage than just having too much to do (role overload). My research supports and extends this hypothesis, at least for the homeschooling mothers in my study, to suggest that role ambiguity and role conflict constitute distinct forms of time stress, which may be more likely to lead to emotional burnout than role overload.

This proposition also explains my finding that mothers who integrated their roles managed burnout more effectively than those who compartmentalized. Mothers who thought of teaching as just one aspect of their more important mother role better navigated the competing role demands than mothers who compartmentalized and juggled each role equally. By prioritizing motherhood and recognizing that teaching was an essential part of mothering, these homeschoolers reconciled the competing emotional demands of the professionalized teacher role and the personalized mother role, and in doing so, they eradicated the conflict between the two. Furthermore, mothers who overcame burnout were no longer multitasking, which Bianchi and her colleagues have shown increases time stress. Instead of juggling their differentiated, compartmentalized roles, mothers who integrated their roles were able to achieve their goals with more focus and consistency, which reduced their time stress and burnout.

Yet the fact that mothers with husband support were the ones likely to integrate their roles, whereas mothers without support were not, adds another layer of complexity to the analysis. It is possible that the unsupported homeschoolers did not integrate their roles because the inequality inherent in their marriages kept them from doing so. Redefining the demands of each of their roles, such as doing less housework, could easily change the balance of power in their unequal relationships, an option traditional husbands would likely oppose.[16] Although redefining and integrating their roles would reduce the time stress they felt as mothers, teachers, and homemakers, husband resistance would increase the stress they felt as *wives*, which might be no relief at all. Thus, my research indicates that if the substantial work of homeschooling is not shared alongside household and caregiving labor, it may deepen gender inequality and make women's family life even more temporally and emotionally demanding. When fathers do not acknowledge mothers' immense workload and time famine, mothers may normalize them and, in doing so, once again ratchet up the standards for intensive mothering to historically unprecedented levels.[17]

Subjective Time: Temporal Emotion Work and Time-Sensitive Identities

Aside from the burnout that threatened homeschoolers who tried to compartmentalize their roles, the temporal experience of motherhood was also emotionally problematic for homeschoolers because even when they were able to find ways to tame their vast domestic loads, they still had no me-time. This temporal situation affected them emotionally in two ways, as I showed in chapter 5. First, mothers had so little time to themselves that they felt a great deal of stress and dissatisfaction. Though they attempted to alleviate these feelings by trying to allocate their time differently—a quantitative solution—the demands of homeschooling and their husbands' paltry contributions to it prevented them from reserving enough reliable me-time, which left them feeling frustrated and resentful. Mothers' attempts to manage these feelings, however, led them to focus on another temporal tension: the idea that their children's childhoods, and thus their own identities as intensive mothers, were evaporating daily; they were at the mercy of the unrelenting progression of time. This temporal realization led them to sequence and savor, qualitative strategies that capitalized on their anxiety about the impermanence of childhood and granted them not only the temporal ability to put their own lives on hold for prolonged periods but, importantly, the emotional ability to do so willingly. The ways homeschoolers used sequencing and savoring to reconcile the emotional and temporal tensions of intensive mothering are examples of a process I have called "temporal emotion work."

My research uncovers some of the theoretical links between emotion work and temporality, not only by introducing the concept of temporal emotion work but also by showing that it can be used as a tool in self-construction. Charmaz has shown that thinking about the "self in time" is an important part of identity.[18] Her work with the chronically ill demonstrates that one way people use time is by anchoring the self in different "timeframes"—past, present, or future—defining their real selves as the person they were before their illness, the ill person they are in the present, or the person they will be once they go into their next cycle of remission. Charmaz weaves emotions into this analysis to show how ill people's temporal conception of self has emotional consequences, implying that (in Flaherty's terms) "time work" can be used to manage emotions as well as construct a sense of self-in-time. However, ill people's particular emotion management techniques are not the central focus of Charmaz's research, and thus she does not fully explore the role of emotions in crossing time frames. Other research, however, has highlighted emotions more directly to show how people link past and present to construct a continuous self over time. For example, sociologist Melinda Milligan has noted that nostalgia acts as an emotional bridge to help people who are experiencing "identity discontinuity" to transition to a new identity by allowing them to integrate emotions from the old one.[19] Although Milligan does not engage the literature on temporality, it is clear from her work that nostalgia can be used to do time work—to "promote or suppress a particular temporal experience"[20]—which in turn helps a person construct a stable sense of self over time.

My data confirm this role of nostalgia but also suggest that there are other specific emotions, such as regret, along with emotional processes, such as sequencing and savoring, that may aid in doing time work and constructing a continuous self over time. The emotions of nostalgia and regret were the route to other time frames, at least for homeschoolers, allowing mothers to transcend the present and construct their past and future selves through the sequencing strategy. In this way, it is clear that emotion work can influence time work. My data also show, however, that the relationship is reciprocal: time work can influence emotion work. Savoring was not only about slowing down time but about doing it so mothers could elicit the positive emotions that increased their appreciation of the time they spent with their children.

Though these data are specific to homeschooling mothers' experiences, they imply some "theoretical generalizability"[21] for the relationship between emotion work and time work. My research suggests that there may be a subclass of emotions, which I will call "temporal emotions," that can only be felt by crossing time frames, and thus may be more useful (than nontemporal emotions) in constructing a continuous self over time. While all emotions can be felt in the present, remembered in the past, or anticipated in the future, there are a few, such as nostalgia, regret, disillusionment, ambition, hope, optimism, and dread, that cannot be felt without bridging the present to either the past or the future. For example, regret requires accessing memories from the past; dread depends on anticipating events in the future. These emotions contain an inherent temporal component—whenever they are felt it is always relative to the past or future. As such, it is possible that the ways we use temporal emotions have a particularly important effect on construct-ing a continuous self over time. Although scholars have shown that past emotional experiences can be used as a template for understanding present emotions,[22] my research goes further, identifying the category of temporal emotions that require a person to transcend the present. Because accessing the past or imagining the future is a mandatory feature of feeling temporal emotions, it is possible that they have a greater effect on the construction of a continuous self over time than nontemporal emotions. If it is indeed true that people construct both a "self-in-emotion"[23] and a "self in time,"[24] it stands to reason that temporal emotions would be particularly powerful tools that tie our experiences together as we try to construct a continuous emotional self; they allow us to perform time work and emotion work simul-taneously and reciprocally, thereby lending more credence to our subjective experiences by giving our feelings continuity and durability, which may sig nificantly contribute to an enduring sense of self.

The prevalence of temporal emotion work among homeschooling moth-ers leads to another significant contribution of this research: that intensive motherhood may be what I will term a "time-sensitive identity"—an iden-tity governed by the unrelenting progression of time—which is an aspect of intensive mothering that has yet to be fully explored. My research dem-onstrates that homeschoolers' ability to sequence and savor rested on the assumption that childhood (and, by extension, motherhood) has a distinct end point; they believed they would cease being mothers—or at least a par-ticular kind of mother—once their children reached adulthood. Previous research on more heterogeneous groups of mothers also supports this con-clusion, showing that advice manuals and mothers themselves define moth-ering almost exclusively as it applies to dependent-age children.[25] The dearth of literature (scholarly or popular) on mothering adult children is further evidence that our dominant definition of good mothering—intensive moth-ering—has an expiration date, and this assumption affects mothers' identities as they progress through the experience. Chapter 8 demonstrated this well by highlighting several ways some mothers tried to prolong their mothering careers.

Yet extending this idea beyond the limits of the mothering career suggests that a time-sensitive understanding of intensive mothering may shape wom-en's identities over the life course. Sociologists Laura Hamilton and Eliza-beth Armstrong's work, for example, gives empirical support for this idea. They show how the middle-class expectation for college women's personal growth and individual achievement (the "self-development imperative") conflicts with the gendered expectation that women should want to be in romantic relationships with men (the "relationship imperative"). One way the middle-class women in their study managed this tension was by staying out of committed relationships during the college years. Doing so allowed them to focus instead on the self-development imperative before getting into "greedy" relationships that would prevent them from pursuing their own interests. Though Hamilton and Armstrong's point is to show that different strategies lead to a host of other conflicts and are influenced by social class, their work also reveals the ways anticipating the time-sensitive identity of intensive mothering may shape young women's decisions in the premothering years. Indeed, one of their subjects articulated this well, saying that college was "the only time in your life when you should be a hundred percent selfish. . . . I have the rest of my life to devote to a husband or kids or my job . . . but right now, it's my time."[26] Thus the middle-class expectation that these heterosexual women held about their futures as intensive mothers shaped their identities years in advance—I will call it the "presequencing" phase—laying the emotional groundwork for the extreme self-effacement inherent in the middle-class expectation of intensive mothering. Thus, my research suggests that defining intensive mothering as time-sensitive may powerfully affect women's identities across the life course. During the mothering years, it maintains the gender order in most heterosexual families by teaching mothers to suppress their frustration and resentment and to accept their subordinate positions relative to their husbands and children. Yet the idea may also be embedded in a variety of gender norms (such as those Hamilton and Armstrong identified), molding women's identities along these emotional and temporal trajectories throughout other phases of their lives.

Although my data illustrate that intensive mothering is defined as time-sensitive among homeschooling mothers (and possibly among middle-class women more generally), they also, again, suggest some theoretical generalizability for other identities that have clear temporal boundaries. It is reasonable to speculate that the degree of control over when a particular identity is going to begin or end may significantly alter the experience. Specifically, lacking control over when one enters or exits an identity—that of college athlete or prisoner, for example—may intensify any problematic emotions associated with the shift. This intensification, which may spring directly from the lack of control over the temporal end points, could require additional emotion work. Indeed, Charmaz has shown that for many chronically ill people, "feeling trapped by an uncontrollable future also traps [them] in a dialectic of negative emotions," which in turn affects their identities.[27] Contrarily, identities that have controllable end points (e.g., some volunteer positions or occupations), though perhaps emotionally difficult in other ways, may be less sensitive to the emotional dynamics of starting, stopping, or progressing through them. Sociologist Jenna Howard's work with people who were "recovering" from a "disorder" gives empirical support for this idea, showing that when people intentionally disidentified with the label, wresting control over the identity and its limitations, they felt less "inner conflict."[28] This suggests that control over temporal boundaries may be one important factor in the degree of emotional turmoil brought about by identity shifts. Thus it stands to reason that time-sensitive identities, because they strip the individual of control over entering and exiting, may require additional (and perhaps a different type of) emotion work than those with temporal boundaries that are easier to control.

This analysis of homeschooling mothers' experiences not only shows several ways that the temporal-emotional conflict is part and parcel of the ideology of intensive mothering but also suggests that what underlies the temporal and emotional tensions, at least in part, is a definition of childhood, and by extension intensive mothering, as time-sensitive. This temporal assumption was the most salient feature in homeschooling mothers' experiences and had the biggest impact on their identities. It drove the ways they interpreted their past, present, and future and, through temporal emotion work, helped them construct identities as good mothers over time. Although previous research has emphasized sacrifice (and its antithesis, selfishness) as the prominent theme in contemporary definitions of motherhood in the United States, my research suggests that underlying this drive to sacrifice, at least among homeschooling mothers, and possibly among other intensive mothers, are the problematic emotions that arise from defining intensive mothering as a time-sensitive identity and the compulsion to perform the corresponding temporal emotion work of savoring motherhood.

NOTES

NOTES TO INTRODUCTION

1. The National Household Education Surveys Program, using small but nationally representative samples, estimates that homeschooling in the United States has increased from 2.2 percent of the school-age population in 2003 to 2.9 percent in 2007.
2. Stevens (2001) reports the rise in homeschooling numbers over recent decades.
3. Gaither (2008) has examined the history of homeschooling in depth.
4. To protect my subjects' privacy, I use pseudonyms for all names of people, places, and organizations; in some cases, I have changed identifying characteristics.
5. Typically, the term "homeschooler" can refer to parents who homeschool or children who are homeschooled. For my purposes here, I have tried to reserve the term "homeschooler" for the parents in homeschooling families (unless otherwise indicated); I try to use the term "homeschooled children" to distinguish my discussion of the children in these families.
6. Since the late 1980s, researchers have examined how homeschooled children compare with their conventionally schooled peers on achievement tests and social skills, as well as how they fare as adults. The little research that exists on these topics shows that homeschooled children compare quite favorably. However, the studies do not rely on representative samples of homeschooled children (and there is no way to obtain such a sample), so the findings tell us nothing conclusive about all, or even most, homeschooled children in how they *compare* with conventionally schooled children. I take up this issue further in chapter 7, but for now it is safe to say that research shows that most homeschooled children do just fine; whether they would do *better* in conventional schools is an impossible question to answer. The existing research on homeschooled children's achievement is limited. Rothermel (2004) provides a summary of the research that has examined homeschooled children's academic achievement (see also Ray [1988, 2000b]; Wartes [1988]), and Medlin (2000) and Shyers (1992) have both examined homeschooled children's social skills, albeit with greatly limited samples and procedures. Van Pelt, Allison, and Allison (2009) followed up with some previously homeschooled adults in Canada, fifteen years after they participated in a study as homeschooling children.
7. According to U.S. census data from 2000, 600 families constituted between 3 and 4 percent of the *households* with children under eighteen in Cedar County. At that time, the U.S. Department of Education estimated that between 1 and 2 percent of school-age *children* were homeschooled nationally; thus, it appeared that homeschooling in our county in the beginning years of my research was indeed quite prevalent—at least twice the national rate, and probably much higher, since most families ("households") homeschooled more than one child. For the most credible estimates on the prevalence of homeschooling when I began this research, see Lines (1998) and the National Household Education Surveys Program (2003).

8. Quoted in Hochschild (1983:231).

9. For discussion of how emotions change across cultures and throughout history, see Cancian and Gordon (1988); Stearns (1994).

10. For discussion of how our ideas of emotions are gendered, see Cancian and Gordon (1988), Hochschild (1983), Kanter (1977), Kimmel (1996), Lois (2003), and Pierce (1995).

11. Bianchi, Robinson, and Milkie (2006) provide a thorough review of the research on the divisions of labor in the home.

12. See Charmaz (1991).

13. See Blum (1999) for discussion of breastfeeding norms in the United States in recent decades.

14. See Blair-Loy (2003), Blum (1999), and Lareau (2003) for discussion of class bias in the norms of good mothering.

15. See Hays (1996).

16. Quoted in Hays (1996:8).

17. See Zelizer (1985) for a discussion of children's economic value at the end of the nineteenth century.

18. Quoted in Hays (1996:8).

19. An additional facet of our idea of good mothering in the contemporary United States is that we define it almost exclusively as it applies to dependent-age children. There is a dearth of scholarly or popular literature on being a mother to adult children, although mothering continues even when children age, move out of the house, get jobs, have families, get married, get divorced, retire, and grow older. But as a culture, we are not very concerned with that type of mothering; we do not consider the impact that a mother has on adult children to be as important as her impact on dependent-age children. (Consider for a moment that this might not be true.) Yet this belief—true or not—greatly influences our behavior as well as a multitude of other interrelated beliefs about what it means to be a good mother. Hays (1996) has discussed the ways that mothering is defined in terms of dependent-age children. See also Bobel (2002) and Garey (1999).

20. Researchers have shown that these standards are not as strict or as omnipresent for fathers. The idea of good fathering, though changing incrementally, is still largely about providing financially; thus, those cultural messages pale in comparison with those aimed at mothers when it comes to intense involvement in a wide range of parenting arenas. Both Blair-Loy (2003) and Walzer (1998) discuss the expectations of fathers compared with mothers.

21. Quoted in Hays (1996:133). In addition, Blair-Loy (2003), Blum (1999), Bobel (2002), Garey (1999), and Stone (2007) are just a few researchers who have also documented the contradictions between the sacrificial tenets of good mothering and the self-empowering ideas of feminism. Stevens (2001) has discussed this issue with respect to homeschoolers specifically.

22. For discussion of the ways mothers adhere to and depart from the ideology of good mothering, see Blair-Loy (2003), Blum (1999), Bobel (2002), Garey (1999), Stone (2007), and Walzer (1998).

23. Blair-Loy (2003), Garey (1999), Gerson (1985), and Stone (2007) have examined good mothering as it relates to paid work; Bianchi, Robinson, and Milkie (2006) and Hochschild (1989) discuss how mothering relates to household labor; and Klassen (2001), Luker (1984), and Walzer (1998) tie good mothering to reproductive choices.

24. See Lareau (2003).

25. See Griffith and Smith (2005).

26. See Stevens (2001).

27. For discussion of the ways mothers try to reconcile the competing demands of mothering and womanhood, see Stone's analysis of mothers who left elite occupations to stay home with their children. She found a "professionalization of domesticity," in which mothers came to "regard motherhood as a second career, pursuing it with the same intensity and commitment they formerly applied to their professions" (2007:168–69). Similarly, the mothers Webber and Williams (2008b:16) studied considered their part-time work status to be the "best of both worlds" because it allowed them to balance their worker and mother identities.

28. Quoted in Stevens (2001:72).

29. Quoted in Stevens (2001:83).

30. In a small study, Aurini and Davies (2005) discuss homeschooling parents' identities specifically, concluding that the choice to homeschool stems from the "ideology of intensive parenting." Parents employ an "expressive logic" to reason that homeschooling is the best way to obtain an individualized educational program for the "precious child."

31. The Home School Legal Defense Association (HSLDA) categorizes different states' homeschooling laws based on their restrictiveness (see http://www.hslda.org/laws/default.asp). Though this organization purports to work on behalf of all homeschoolers, it is dominated by evangelical Christians with conservative political and social agendas. From their website, under "About HSLDA": "Home School Legal Defense Association is a nonprofit advocacy organization established to defend and advance the constitutional right of parents to direct the education of their children and to protect family freedoms. Through annual memberships, HSLDA is tens of thousands of families united in service together, providing a strong voice when and where needed." Then, under the frequently asked question, "Is HSLDA a Christian Organization?" follows this response: "HSLDA's mission is to protect the freedom of all homeschoolers regardless of their faith background. HSLDA officers, directors and employees are followers of Christ who seek to provide the very highest levels of service in defending homeschooling freedom and equipping homeschoolers. HSLDA membership is open to all who choose to exercise their fundamental parental right to educate their children at home." See Stevens (2001) and Gaither (2008) for further discussion of the role of the HSLDA's political and religious agenda in the rise of the homeschooling movement in the United States.

32. Studies have been unable to capture accurate demographics of the homeschooling population as a whole because of the difficulty in obtaining a representative sample. (I elaborate on these difficulties in the notes to chapter 1.) The research that comes closest, however, clearly shows that homeschooling is not a monolithic movement. Homeschoolers are from all races, though are typically white; socioeconomic statuses, though are usually middle-class or above; hold a variety of religious orientations, though most often are evangelical or mainstream Protestant; and have larger-than-average families. Despite popular perception, there is a great deal of variation among homeschoolers. The one area with the least demographic variation among homeschoolers is in gendered family structure. Fathers and single parents do homeschool, but overwhelmingly homeschooling is performed by at-home mothers in two-parent, heterosexual families with a father serving as the single wage earner in the paid labor force. In trying to capture homeschoolers' demographic characteristics via survey research, Bauman (2002), Mayberry et al. (1995), the National Household Education Surveys Program (2003, 2007), Ray (2000b), and Wagenaar (1997) have obtained the best response rates and have used a variety of sampling methods to locate different enclaves of homeschoolers, though the resulting samples are far from perfect. For discussion of the diversity found in self-selecting samples of different homeschooling communities, see Collom and

198 << NOTES TO CHAPTER 1

Mitchell (2005), Klein and Poplin (2008), Mayberry et al. (1995), and Stevens (2001). For discussion of homogeneity in homeschoolers' family structure, see Aurini and Davies (2005), Bauman (2002), Mayberry et al. (1995), and Stevens (2001).

33. Jackie most closely approximated the "natural mothers" studied by Bobel (2002), several of whom also homeschooled as part of their natural mothering ideology. See also Klassen's (2001) study of home-birthing mothers, some of whom also homeschooled their children.

NOTES TO CHAPTER 1

1. See Guba and Lincoln (1994) and Prus (1996) for detailed discussions of the ontological and epistemological issues in field research.

2. See Blumer (1969), Glaser and Strauss (1967), and Lofland et al. (2006) for detailed discussions of the strengths and weaknesses of ethnographic research.

3. See Glaser and Strauss (1967). In addition, Blumer (1969), Lofland et al. (2006), and Prus (1996) discuss similar issues relating to the generalizable aspects of field research.

4. For discussion of the ways trust and rapport with subjects are essential components of the field research process, see Lofland et al. (2006).

5. Biernacki and Waldorf (1981) discuss the advantages and disadvantages of snowball sampling.

6. Of the nine mothers my undergraduate students located and interviewed, I was later able to meet four of them and talk to two more on the phone for the follow-up interviews in 2008–9.

7. I cannot know how similar my homeschooling sample was to the population of homeschoolers in the United States because, as I mentioned in the notes to the introduction, researchers have yet to obtain a representative sample of them to study. To obtain such a sample, researchers would need to randomly select homeschoolers from some kind of list of all homeschoolers, so that each family on the list had an equal probability of being selected. Researchers like random selection because, even though the families selected may not represent the population as a whole, random selection makes it possible to estimate the degree to which they do not. Researchers can then make claims about homeschoolers in general from studying only a portion of them because they can confidently report the margin of error in their findings. Therefore, having an existing list from which to select homeschooling families would be ideal. However, no such list exists. Different states have vastly different reporting laws, so records are not comparable across states; furthermore, because homeschooling is stigmatized to some degree, and because *some* homeschoolers hold antigovernment ideologies, some families do not report themselves at all. As with many stigmatized populations, random samples are impossible to obtain because people hide their activity. Researchers have tried, however, to put together samples of homeschoolers that may best approximate the population as a whole, given the available options. In the 1980s, Mayberry (1988) mailed surveys to homeschooling magazine subscribers—a biased list to begin with but possibly one of the best ways to target a fairly diverse group of homeschoolers. And in 2003 and 2007, the National Household Education Surveys Program surveyed randomly selected Americans about education, and a very small percentage of the respondents were homeschoolers. Compounding the sampling problem, much survey research on homeschoolers has resulted in extremely low response rates. For example, Klein and Poplin (2008) conducted a survey of homeschoolers in virtual charter schools but obtained only a 10 percent response rate (they distributed 1,422 surveys, but only 146 were returned). It is likely some key aspects of the homeschooling population were overlooked, since the data

collected failed to represent 90 percent of the sample. Kunzman (2009a) critiques some of the methodological problems of earlier research on homeschooling and, for further explanation, points the reader to Welner and Welner's (1999) comprehensive critique of the methodological bias in much homeschooling research. See Stevens (2001) for a discussion of some of the ways researchers have tried to study homeschoolers through survey research. For specific examples of research using some of these sampling techniques, see Mayberry et al. (1995), Ray (2000b), and Wagenaar (1997).

8. Homeschoolers' faith orientations are a main focus of much research on homeschooling. The issue has been addressed in two forms: as a demographic characteristic and as a *motivation* for homeschooling. Looking purely at the demographic numbers, and taking into account the problems with obtaining a representative sample (which I detailed in the previous note), it appears that the proportion of evangelical Christians in my research roughly mirrored what we do know (however imperfect) about the homeschooling population in the United States. The question of how homeschoolers' faith may be the motivation for them to homeschool is a much more complicated issue that cannot be accurately captured through survey research, mostly because motivations overlap greatly and faith underlies many of them. I will take up this issue in detail in chapter 2 when I discuss mothers' initial reasons for homeschooling.

9. My subjects' social class was difficult to assess for several reasons. Generally sociologists use a combination of factors, such as family income, education level, and occupational prestige, to measure social class. However, there is no accepted method for doing so, and different measures may be more or less suitable for different populations. One problem I faced in categorizing my subjects as working-class, middle-class, or upper-middle-class was that family income often contradicted parents' education levels or occupational prestige. My sample contained mostly college-educated mothers who chose to stay out of the workforce and rely solely on their husbands' income. When the husband was college-educated as well, and earned a high salary, it was easy to categorize the family as middle-class or upper-middle-class. But when the husband was not college-educated, and worked a blue-collar job, it was harder to assign social class. Perhaps if the mother was in the workforce, her college education would have garnered the family a higher income and propelled it into a higher socioeconomic category. However, when the earning *potential* in the family was middle-class, but the salary *earned* fell into the realm of the working class (because educated mothers stayed out of the paid labor force), the categories blurred. In the end, I assigned my subjects a social class status by assessing the education levels of both parents, family income (which I collected for fifteen of the twenty-four families), occupation, and the degree to which the family seemed to be economically comfortable, a qualitative measure that often emerged throughout our interviews. See Krieger, Williams, and Moss (1997) for a comprehensive discussion of the difficulties in measuring social class.

10. For discussion of rapport in studying racist activists, see Blee (1998); in studying child protective services, see Reich (2003); in studying public health workers, see Dickson-Swift et al. (2009).

11. For discussion of how lack of rapport can skew understanding, see Holland (2007). For discussion of how lack of rapport can prevent subjects from sharing their stories, see Reich (2003).

12. Conceding to ignorance is one strategy to keep interviewees talking, though it often results in stripping the interviewer of his or her power (Hoffman 2007) and occasionally demotivates subjects to answer further questions (Reich 2003).

13. Jorgensen (1989) and Lofland et al. (2006) have noted that it is typical for fieldnotes to become more focused as researchers' time in the setting accumulates and they become more selective with their observations.
14. See Blumer (1969).
15. See Geertz (1973).
16. See Glaser and Strauss (1967).
17. See Taylor (1991).
18. For discussion of how researchers take on different roles in the setting, depending on their own knowledge, comfort, and abilities, see Lofland et al. (2006).
19. See Adler and Adler (1987) and Lofland et al. (2006) for discussion of how researchers' membership roles affect the data they are able to obtain.
20. Van Maanen (1991:40) contends that when researchers become "caught up in the same life situation and circumstances" as their subjects, they develop a rich and "empathetic" understanding of their subjects' lives.
21. See Adler and Adler (1987).
22. For discussion of how motherhood in particular may facilitate understanding in some research settings, see Reich (2003).
23. Kleinman and Copp (1993) discuss the important role researchers' feelings play in understanding our data. They argue that emotions and the emotion work we find ourselves doing in the field are important cues to understanding our subjects' lives. In this sense, researchers' emotions are valuable sources of data that should be analyzed. See also Dickson-Swift et al. (2009), Hoffman (2007), and Holland (2007).

NOTES TO INTRODUCTION TO PART I

1. See Gordon (1989).
2. See Wharton (2009) for a review of research that shows how types of occupations, gender, and race affect emotion management (specifically, that which is done for a wage, or "emotional labor"). For analyses of how race affects beliefs about emotions and how we act on them, see Kang (2003) and Wingfield (2010); for gender, see George (2010), Hochschild (1983), Lois (2003), and Pierce (1995) as examples. DeVault (1999) discusses how beliefs about gender, social class, race, and sexual orientation may affect emotion work in families specifically.
3. See Hochschild (1983).
4. Quoted in Thoits (1990:181).
5. That very little research has examined the emotional culture of good mothering is curious, given that particular emotion norms (and thus deviance) are fundamental to contemporary definitions of femininity in various arenas such as work (e.g., Hochschild 1983; Pierce 1995), self-help groups (e.g., Irvine 1999), voluntary associations (e.g., Lois 2003), and families (e.g., Cancian and Gordon 1988; DeVault 1991; Erickson 1993; Hochschild 1989).
6. Quoted in Hays (1996:57).
7. A great deal of the mothering research has illuminated the importance of emotions, yet little research has made emotions a central feature of the analysis. Several scholars have focused on mothers' emotions as being indicators of good mothering: Bobel has shown how mothers rely on their intuition, making choices that "feel right" (2002:91; see also Blum 1999; Garey 1999). Other research has highlighted the highly emotional experience of motherhood: Walzer (1998) found that the new mothers she interviewed were constantly in a state of "mother worry," which was driven by their concern with meeting the exceptionally high standards of good mothering;

and Klassen's (2001) study demonstrated how home-birthing mothers were criticized for considering their own emotional experience when deciding to give birth outside of a hospital environment. But little work has examined the specific feelings mothers rely on, or what they do when they feel the wrong feelings—something that Hochschild (1983, 1990) discussed in detail when developing the concept of emotion work. Taylor's (1995) research on postpartum depression, however, stands out as an exception, showing how the new mothers she studied drew on larger cultural beliefs about the physiology of "deviant" emotions to define themselves as good mothers, despite their anxiety about mothering and resentment toward their babies. Researchers in the sociology of mental health have also examined emotions in the family, but from a slightly different perspective. One interesting finding that has come out of this body of research is that the stresses of parenthood override the emotional fulfillment of having children. On balance, negative emotions prevail in Americans' parenting experiences, resulting in parents being more likely to experience "symptoms of depression (feelings of sadness, loneliness, restlessness, and fear) than non-parents their own age" (Simon [2008:42]; see also Evenson and Simon [2005]). Although this research helps us to see how emotions are important factors in raising children and that culture—and the emotional beliefs it promotes about parenthood—plays a strong role in what parents feel, this literature provides little discussion of the expectations of mothering specifically, or of how individual mothers interpret the cultural messages about raising children.

8. See Hochschild (1983).

9. Though Blair-Loy's (2003:90) work with women in elite careers uncovers the "moral and emotional" dimensions of choosing between work and family and the "profound emotion work" they had to do to come to terms with their choice, her analysis gives scant attention to the specific emotions they found problematic and the ways they tried to manage them.

10. See Blair-Loy (2003), Bobel (2002), Garey (1999), and Stone (2007) for discussion of how middle-class mothers' emotions influence their choice to work in the paid labor force or stay home with their children.

11. For research that has compared mothers' experiences across social class, see Blum (1999), Garey (1999), Griffith and Smith (2005), Hays (1996), and Lareau (2003).

NOTES TO CHAPTER 2

1. For discussion of mothers being more likely to leave the paid labor force than fathers, see Bianchi, Robinson, and Milkie (2006). For discussion of the gendered configuration of homeschooling families, see Aurini and Davies (2005:470), who found that the presence of a "non-working adult in the household" is the "strongest predictor of homeschooling." See also Bauman (2002), Mayberry et al. (1995), and Stevens (2001).

2. Patricia Tomlinson and Renée Peterson left the paid labor force after their second children were born; Maria Rojas and Whitney McKee worked in the paid labor force unwillingly.

3. Scholars have also analyzed society-wide issues with regard to homeschooling, such as the consequences for the public education system (e.g., Apple 2000; Hill 2000; Lubienski 2000; Ray 2000a) and how homeschooling has developed as a social movement (e.g., Bates 1991; Collom and Mitchell 2005; Stevens 2001).

4. Klassen's (2001) study of home-birthing parents reveals a similar anti-government-control philosophy among her subjects.

5. Van Galen (1988) was the first to typologize homeschoolers by their motivations, dichotomizing them into "ideologues" and "pedagogues." Mayberry (1988) later elaborated, adding "socio-relational" and "new age" concerns to the typology of motivations, and recently

Fields-Smith and Williams (2009) discovered "ethnological" reasons among the black families they studied. Other researchers have uncovered relatively similar findings, although they have labeled their homeschoolers' motivations slightly differently (see Bates 1991; Collom 2005; Knowles 1991; Pitman 1987; Stevens 2001).

6. Mayberry and her colleagues' (1995) work added another layer of complexity, illustrating that most homeschoolers have overlapping reasons, a pattern other research has continued to confirm (see Apple 2004; Collom and Mitchell 2005; Klein and Poplin 2008). For example, some highly religious subjects may also (or instead) categorize their main reasons as pedagogical or relational, which blurs the boundaries between motivational categories. For more discussion on homeschoolers' motivations, see Arai (2000), Brabant, Bourdon, and Jutras (2003), Knowles (1988), Mayberry (1988, 1992), and Mayberry and Knowles (1989). See Kuntzman (2009b) for the most recent explanation of the complexities of homeschooling motivations.

7. A number of studies have focused on the role of faith in homeschooling, particularly with respect to parents' motivations. In addition to the difficulty in obtaining a representative sample (as I discussed in the notes for chapter 1), faith-related motivation is impossible to assess through survey research, as evidenced by the widely disparate statistics that exist on the topic. For example, the National Household Education Surveys Program (2007) collected data from a small number of homeschoolers as part of a larger, representative sample of Americans. Of these homeschooling respondents, 83 percent reported that they homeschooled "to provide religious or moral instruction" (up from 72 percent in 2003), but only 36 percent gave this as their "most important" reason. With such a vast difference between these two percentages, it is hard to say how "religious" homeschoolers are. Clearly, some of the answer is influenced by how the questions are asked. A few studies have tried to measure homeschoolers' faith-related motivations. One survey listed parents' possible reasons for homeschooling as "dissatisfaction with traditional schools," "religious motives," "protection from unwanted influences," and "maintenance of the family unit" (Chapman and O'Donoghue 2000:24); another asked parents to rank such motivations as "better socialization through family and community life," "Godly prescription," "parents in a better position to educate," "parental responsibility," "peer dependence," "negative experiences in school," and "curriculum enrichment" (Brabant, Bourdon, and Jutras 2003). In Fields-Smith and Williams's (2009:379) interview-based study on black homeschooling parents, twenty-one out of twenty-four parents said that "religious beliefs influenced their decision" to homeschool, whereas fifteen said that homeschooling was a "complement and support to their religious beliefs," and six said that God had "led them" to homeschool. The problem with measuring motivations in these ways, especially when trying to draw conclusions about the role of religion, is that many of the motivations provided on surveys may be measuring some aspect of faith they do not intend. For example, parents may be concerned about "peer dependence" for reasons that are specifically faith-based—or not. Yet researchers often decide which of these measures reflect parents' religious motivations, and which do not (see Brabant, Bourdon, and Jutras [2003] for an example of how such motivations are sorted into categories), and then make claims such as "motivations directly related to God and religion rank at the lowest level of importance" (Brabant, Bourdon, and Jutras 2003:126), contradicting findings such as those I reported earlier, which suggest the polar opposite. See Apple (2004) for a discussion of how religion may underlie many of the motives that other researchers assume are distinct from faith, such as wanting a closer relationship with their children, dissatisfaction with schools, and instilling "morality" and "character" in their children. The most credible studies indicate that evangelical Christian homeschoolers

constitute a disproportionately large portion of the homeschooling population, though by no means all of it. See Stevens (2001) for discussion of the role of faith in the development of the homeschooling movement.

8. See Hays (1996), Blair-Loy (2003), Garey (1999), Stone (2007), and Webber and Williams (2008a) for examples of how the decision to stay at home with young children is integral to the emotions involved in intensive mothering.

9. Stone (2007) found a similar pattern regarding mothers' decisions to work or stay home. Some of her subjects—high-achieving women who left the workforce to stay home with their young children—left work immediately after their babies were born, whereas others left after a few years of trying to reconcile the tensions between work and family.

10. Other research has documented this same dynamic among a wider variety of mothers; they are surprised and transformed by their level of attachment to their babies and in some cases suddenly realize they want to stay home rather than return to work as they had planned. See Blair-Loy (2003), Garey (1999), and Stone (2007).

11. Quoted in Bobel (2002:26).

12. My thanks to Lori Peek for her insight into this important point about the social context of mothers' emotional epiphanies.

13. Quoted in Stone (2007:78).

14. In her research with high-achieving women who had left the workforce to become stay-at-home mothers, Stone (2007) found that about one in ten in her sample did so because they had always wanted to stay home with their children. In her research on abortion activists, Luker (1984) found that the pro-lifers held similar stay-at-home gender ideologies.

15. See Stevens (2001).

16. In their study of black homeschoolers, Fields-Smith and Williams found that the majority of mothers did not have a predisposition to stay-at-home motherhood. In fact, leaving the workforce was very difficult, especially for those who had college degrees, because they felt disapproval from older relatives who could not understand why they would give up their financial independence. In addition, mothers felt that leaving their careers was betraying the black community; it represented an "abandonment of hopes and dreams of two generations . . . [and] of the rewards obtained from a long struggle toward equality in the workplace" (2009:381).

17. Bobel (2002) also found some of the natural mothers she studied did not understand her questions because they violated the assumptions they held about motherhood.

18. Other researchers have uncovered mothers' difficulty articulating their feelings or intuition about different aspects of the mothering experience (see Bobel 2002; Stone 2007).

19. Quoted in Blair-Loy (2003:82, 170). In addition, Walzer (1998) speculated that this "natural, universal, and unchanging" perspective of motherhood explained some of the behavior of the new parents she studied. And Bobel's (2002) research on natural mothers and their child-rearing philosophies has uncovered this naturalized view of motherhood as well. In his research on homeschooling parents, Stevens (2001) found some natural mothers among the homeschoolers he studied. However, his data show that the natural mothers were from the secular side of homeschooling, a pattern that did not emerge from my data.

20. Interestingly, Stone uncovered a similar delayed decision about staying at home. Some of her subjects left their elite careers to stay home once their children entered school. They found that the demands of cultivating their children's social and human capital increased as they got older, and they felt that "outsourcing" this labor to their "less well-educated nannies and au pairs, most of whom were from very different class, race, ethnic, and of course educational backgrounds," was unacceptable (2007:50).

21. See Fields-Smith and Williams's (2009), and Stevens's (2001) work for similar stories of how God called mothers to homeschool.

22. See Emerson and Hartman (2006) for a discussion of how fundamentalist Christianity promotes traditional gender roles and patriarchal families.

23. There were three epiphany first-choicers in my sample; two were evangelical, and one was not religious. There were five second-choicers in my sample; one was evangelical, two identified as some variation of progressive Christian, and two were "not at all religious."

24. The women in elite careers that Blair-Loy (2003) studied often felt the pull of contradictory emotions when trying to reconcile family and career. Research on homeschoolers is more equivocal. Stevens's (2001) research uncovered hints of this ambivalence among a few of the homeschoolers he interviewed, whereas Arai (2000) found that the majority of homeschoolers he studied first explored educational alternatives, such as private schools, before settling on homeschooling.

25. See Aurini and Davies (2005) for discussion of the "expressive logic" that compels some parents to homeschool their children.

26. Both Blair-Loy (2003) and Stone (2007) found that some of their subjects also felt "invisible" when they left their careers to be stay-at-home mothers.

27. Research on homeschoolers' income confirms that most occupy middle income brackets (Bauman 2002).

NOTES TO CHAPTER 3

1. For discussion of how people internalize a deviant identity as a result of others' treatment of them, see Becker (1963), Degher and Hughes (1991), and Nack (2008).

2. Quoted in Scott and Lyman (1968:46).

3. Quoted in Scott and Lyman (1968:47).

4. "Saving face" is Goffman's ([1955] 1982) term for the ways that people try to repair a punctured self-presentation. For further discussion of how people try to align their identities and behavior with cultural expectations, see Stokes and Hewitt (1976).

5. A host of studies have indirectly revealed good mothering norms by examining the ways mothers account for violating them. Murphy showed how new mothers may feel deviant for departing from the medical recommendation for infant feeding. The mothers she studied felt the need to account for their decision to quit breastfeeding earlier than recommended (2000), when they chose not to breastfeed at all (1999), and even when they anticipated while still pregnant that they might "fail" at breastfeeding (2004). Other researchers have relied on Sykes and Matza's (1957) "techniques of neutralization" to illuminate ways mothers neutralize stigma. For example, Heltsley and Calhoun (2003) uncovered the rhetoric that helped mothers of child beauty pageant contestants deflect charges of bad mothering, and Copelton (2007) examined how mothers-to-be accounted for violating "nutritional norms" during pregnancy.

6. No studies have specifically analyzed how mothers account for emotional deviance. Because the homeschoolers I studied used justifications, but not excuses, to account for the maternal emotional deviance others attributed to them, an accounts framework is theoretically helpful in understanding their experiences. Moreover, analyzing emotional deviance more broadly further specifies theories of accounts and other forms of "aligning actions" (Stokes and Hewitt 1976). By focusing solely on how people manage their deviant "behavior," "actions," and "conduct," these theories have neglected deviant emotions entirely.

7. Some of Bobel's (2002) natural mothers were homeschoolers and experienced similar criticism from friends and family members. The black homeschoolers that Fields-Smith and Williams (2009) studied were often criticized by outsiders as well.

8. For discussion of the mandates of good mothering, specifically that mothers know their children better than anyone and respond to all their needs, see Blum (1999), Brown, Small, and Lumley (1997), Hays (1996), and Lupton and Fenwick (2001).

9. Providing for a child who has special needs—whether advanced or delayed—is not an uncommon reason for homeschooling (see Knowles 1988; Mayberry 1988).

10. See Scott and Lyman (1968).

11. See Lareau (2003).

12. Fields-Smith and Williams (2009) found that race bias and other institutional norms in conventional schools created problematic environments for black students, especially boys, which was the primary reason the black families they studied homeschooled.

13. Research showing that gendered and racial stereotypes in schools disadvantage girls, particularly those of color, have been widely disseminated in popular culture. See, for example, Orenstein (1994). In addition, the middle-class black parents in Lareau's (2003:181) study encountered some of the same conflicts, which pitted their class privilege against the "racial exclusion and insensitivity" of the predominantly white environments of their children's school and extracurricular activities. As a result, the middle-class black mothers in Lareau's study had to be more vigilant than their white counterparts. Jackie and her husband, by forgoing conventional schools entirely, avoided this problem.

14. Quoted in Hays (1996:7). Blum (1999) also discusses the protective norms of motherhood.

15. Quoted in Blum (1999:36).

16. Quoted in Hays (1996:78).

17. For discussion of how having concern for and protecting children's health and physical safety are requirements of good mothering, see Brown, Small, and Lumley (1997), Lupton and Fenwick (2001), Murphy (2000), and Tardy (2000).

18. See Goffman (1971).

19. Hays (1996), Murphy (2000), and Wall (2001) have all discussed the importance of good mothers' focus on children's moral development.

20. Garey (1999), Hays (1996), and Snyder (2007) have all specifically discussed the norm of mothers "being there" for their children.

21. Other studies have found that many parents homeschool, at least in part, because they do not believe that their conservative evangelical Christian beliefs will be upheld by the public school system; see, for example, Collom (2005), Knowles (1988, 1991), Mayberry (1988, 1993), Mayberry and Knowles (1989), Mayberry et al. (1995), Pitman (1987), Stevens (2001), and Van Galen (1988).

22. Kunzman (2009a:315) explains that many Christian homeschoolers believe that it is their "God-given right and responsibility" to educate their children, and that instilling godly "character" is the primary goal in doing so. See also Stevens (2001).

23. See Sykes and Matza (1957).

24. For discussion of good mothers' role in safeguarding their children's budding moral development, see Bigner and Yang (1996), Brown, Small, and Lumley (1997), and Hays (1996).

25. Apple (2001) has written about the evangelical movement in the United States, noting how a key component of evangelicals' ideology is an absolutist belief in their own moral superiority.

26. Apple's (2001) analysis of evangelical Christian rhetoric has uncovered its distinctively militant language.

27. Several studies have found that some parents homeschool because they do not believe their liberal, progressive ideology will be upheld by the public school system; see Knowles (1991), Mayberry et al. (1995), Stevens (2001), and Van Galen (1988).

28. Bobel's natural mothers felt this stigma of hyperengagement as well and, like my homeschoolers, justified it based on the primacy of the "mother-child bond." They admitted that "*mothers need their children* to meet their own daily emotional needs," a "taboo subject" by mainstream standards because it suggests that such mothers are "overidentified" and using "their children in morally and psychologically suspect ways" (2002:137, emphasis in original). In this way, Bobel's natural mothers and my homeschoolers were like Klassen's (2001:214) home-birthing mothers, who considered "their own physical and emotional health" and refused "to accept a model of maternal sacrifice that eclipses the mother in touting the virtues of a mother's love."

29. For discussion of homeschooling for family-related reasons, see Collom (2005), Knowles (1988, 1991), Mayberry (1988, 1993), Mayberry et al. (1995), Stevens (2001), and Van Galen (1988).

30. See Blum (1999) and Bobel (2002) for discussion of the natural mothering rhetoric present in La Leche League; see Hays (1996), Murphy (1999), and Bobel (2002) for analyses of mainstream good-mothering rhetoric.

31. See Blum (1999).

32. In addition to Blum (1999), Bobel (2002), Hays (1996), and Wall (2001) have also discussed the ways that mothers' intense emotional bond with their children is assumed to be innate, ubiquitous, and unparalleled.

33. For discussion of how institutional education encroaches on family life, see Lareau (2003) and Griffith and Smith (2005).

34. For discussion of the ways mothers feel responsible for maintaining their children's ties to other family members, see DeVault (1991), Hays (1996), and Seery and Crowley (2000).

NOTES TO INTRODUCTION TO PART II

1. The "second shift" is Hochschild's (1989) term. For a summary of the gendered division of household labor, see Coltrane (2000). See also Bianchi, Robinson, and Milkie (2006).

2. See Blair-Loy (2003), Hochschild (1989), Stone (2007), and Webber and Williams (2008a) for discussion of how lack of husband contribution toward domestic chores and child care affects wives.

3. Quoted in Bianchi, Robinson, and Milkie (2006:92).

4. Likewise, in her study of new parents, Walzer (1998) found that mothers felt they lost more leisure time than fathers, which Walzer showed is often due to the ideology of intensive mothering and the guilt mothers feel for not dedicating that time to their children. The fathers Walzer studied did not feel this guilt.

5. Walzer found that the new mothers she studied "experienced stress about the time they *didn't* spend with their children, while many fathers were stressed by the time they *did* spend with their children" because other things "were not getting done" (1998:23, emphasis in original). For discussion of how mothers react to fathers' insufficient contribution to household labor, as well as how it affects the relationship, see Coltrane (2000), Hochschild (1989), and Webber and Williams (2008b).

NOTES TO CHAPTER 4

1. For discussion of the gendered division of household labor, see Bianchi, Robinson, and Milkie (2006), Coltrane (2000), and Hochschild (1989). For discussion of the gendered division of emotional labor in families, see Erickson (1993, 2005).

2. See Hochschild (1983). In addition, though many studies on emotional labor focus on customer service employees, other researchers have focused quite a bit on "care work" and burnout, such as that performed by teachers (see Brissie, Hoover-Dempsey, and Basler 1988) and nurses (see Theodosius 2008).

3. More recent research has identified conditions under which emotional labor is unlikely to produce self-alienation and burnout (see Wharton 2009 for a thorough review.)

4. The Maslach Burnout Inventory was developed by Maslach (1982).

5. Quoted in Hochschild (1983:68).

6. Erickson's (1993) work is a notable example. She found that husbands' contributions to "family emotion work" were more important to marital well-being than their combined contributions to housework and child care. Two other studies are further exceptions: Kulik (2002) found that poor health, low religiosity, and inequality in gender roles contributed greatly to marital burnout among older Israeli couples; Gottschalk (2003) showed how children of Holocaust survivors became emotionally exhausted as they tried to manage their parents' posttraumatic feelings and meet their difficult emotional expectations. If such intense parent-child interactions can drain children, it makes sense to study how they may affect parents.

7. Goode introduced the concept of role strain in 1960, yet since then, researchers have identified three subtypes: "role ambiguity" exists when role expectations are unclear (Rizzo, House, and Lirtzman 1970); "role conflict" arises when one role's demands directly interfere with another's (Hecht 2001); and "role overload" occurs when there are too many role demands given the time allotted (Hecht 2001).

8. The Maslach burnout literature has consistently found role strain to be positively associated with burnout.

9. Many homeschoolers in Stevens's (2001) study were also very worried that they would fail to teach their children adequately. In their study of black homeschooling parents, Fields-Smith and Williams (2009) also found that parents doubted their own capabilities.

10. For discussion of the ways that insecurity leads to burnout among professional teachers, see Cordes and Dougherty (1993), Friedman and Farber (1992), Greenglass and Burke (1988), and Ray and Miller (1991).

11. See Hochschild (1983).

12. This short honeymoon period was typical for mothers using the structured, "school-at-home" method of teaching, which the vast majority implemented at the start. It is important to note, though, that I did interview two mothers (Gretchen and Cassandra) who used a flexible pedagogical style from the start, something other mothers only adopted later, as I will discuss. However, even mothers who were unstructured at the beginning were not immune to experiencing the challenges of homeschooling, which only meant that their honeymoon period—perhaps a year or two—was longer than that of structured mothers.

13. Chin (2000) found very similar emotional dynamics in her study of parents helping their children apply to elite private schools.

14. See Lois (2001).

15. Bullock and Waugh (2004), Copp (1998), and Hochschild (1983) have shown that service workers who manage others' emotions are more prone to burnout than those who do not;

Gottschalk (2003) and Mac Rae (1998) have noted this phenomenon among people who must frequently manage family members' emotions.

16. See Maslach (1982) for an extended treatment of the components of burnout syndrome.

17. Quoted in Hochschild (1990:123).

18. Maslach's (1982) theory posits that burnout begins with emotional exhaustion. DeVault (1991) has identified this type of constant cognitive and emotional work as the "provisioning" work of motherhood, which is largely invisible. See also Griffith and Smith (2005) for a discussion of how organizing children's lives around the school schedule is itself work.

19. Quoted in Mayberry et al. (1995:49).

20. See Hecht (2001) for analytical discussion of role conflict and role overload.

21. Paid caregivers also feel tension between personal caring and professional neutrality (e.g., Bullock and Waugh 2004; Copp 1998; Murray 1998).

22. Goode (1960) showed that role compartmentalization is a common response to role conflict.

23. Fields-Smith and Williams (2009), Mayberry et al. (1995), McDowell (2000), and Stevens (2001) have found that mothers often feel overwhelmed with the amount of work involved in homeschooling their children.

24. See Orzechowicz (2008).

25. In her study of transgender men doing housework, Pfeffer (2010) found that their female partners often justified their disproportionate burden of household labor by citing some idiosyncratic aspect of their own personalities, such as being a "neat freak," which is similar to what Tracy did when she explained her unusually large stores of energy. See also Blair-Loy (2003), Hochschild (1989), and Stone (2007) for further examples of how women justify their husbands' scant contributions to household labor.

26. Mayberry et al. (1995) found that most homeschooling mothers in their studies eventually moved away from highly structured curricula because they took too much time and seemed unnecessary to get children to learn.

27. In their study of mothers who worked for pay part-time, Webber and Williams (2008b) found that those who worked out of their home shouldered a larger proportion of the household labor than their husbands because there was no physical boundary between their paid and unpaid work. As a result, these mothers were more likely to feel inadequate in both roles.

28. See Maslach (1982) for an elaborate explanation of burnout progression.

29. The religious parents in Stevens's (2001) research also relied on their faith in God to help them feel confident about their choice to homeschool.

30. My thanks to Martha Copp for pointing out the ways mothers used rhetorical devices to obscure their proportionally greater family responsibilities relative to their husbands'.

31. In his study of homeschooling parents, Stevens quoted Mary Pride's well-known Christian homeschooling book that similarly encouraged mothers to deny the problematic emotions that arose from their immense domestic burden. Pride says, "Loving our children means just *enjoying* them and not fretting about the time it takes to serve them" (quoted in Stevens 2001:98, emphasis in original).

32. Kulik (2002) found that inequality in gender roles is a major factor in marital burnout.

33. See, for example, Hochschild's (1989) study of married couples for an analysis of how gender ideology may affect household division of labor.

34. Forgoing housework to spend more time with children is a philosophy that Stevens (2001) found among his homeschooling subjects and Bobel (2001:140) found in her research

on members of the pro-breastfeeding group La Leche League, who embraced the slogan "people before things." See also Stone (2007).

35. See Lois (2001).

36. In his study of conservative Christian homeschoolers, Kunzman (2009b) also found that parents considered parenting and teaching to be inextricably linked, a finding other research on homeschoolers has uncovered as well (see Mayberry et al. 1995; Stevens 2001).

37. For discussion of homeschoolers' move to a less structured curriculum, see Charvoz (1988), Knowles (1988), Mayberry et al. (1995), Stevens (2001), and Van Galen (1988).

NOTES TO CHAPTER 5

1. For discussion of how mothers manage time by cutting back to part-time work, see Blair-Loy (2003), Garey (1999), and Webber and Williams (2008a, 2008b). For discussion of mothers leaving the paid labor force entirely to manage their time, see Blair-Loy (2003), Bobel (2002), and Stone (2007). For discussion of how mothers manage time by soliciting domestic labor from their husbands, see Hochschild (1989), Walzer (1998), and Webber and Williams (2008b). For discussion of how mothers outsource domestic labor, see Romero (1992) and Treas and de Ruijter (2008). For discussion of mothers combining chores with child care or their own leisure with their children's to manage their time, see Bianchi, Robinson, and Milkie (2006) and Lareau (2003).

2. Similarly, Webber and Williams (2008a) found that the mothers they studied cut their work hours to part-time to spend more time with their children, which the mothers considered to be a temporary strategy while their children were young.

3. See Garey (1999).

4. Quoted in Bobel (2002:24).

5. A few of the homeschoolers Stevens (2001) studied also referred to putting their own needs aside to homeschool their children.

6. Bianchi, Robinson, and Milkie (2006) found that 71 percent of married mothers in the United States desired more personal time.

7. In her study of mothers' caring work of "feeding the family," DeVault (1991:118) found a similar dynamic: the mothers she studied felt "spoiled" when served by someone else, whereas the fathers in her study felt "entitled."

8. For discussion of how the cultural discourse of good mothering centers around the idea of self-sacrifice, see Blair-Loy (2003), DeVault (1991), Garey (1999), and Hays (1996).

9. Stevens (2001) also found that homeschoolers talked about their sacrifice and, in doing so, intensified the standards for good mothering. I will explore this topic in chapter 9.

10. Interestingly, in her study of women who left elite careers to stay home with their preschool-age children, Stone (2007:139) found that about one-third of the mothers increased their leisure time and were able to get "back in touch with me as a person," whereas other mothers lost all their personal time and found the situation difficult to deal with.

11. Quoted in DeVault (1991:156).

12. Ten of my twenty-four interviewees specifically mentioned their dissatisfaction with their husbands' contributions to the schooling. Twelve others were dissatisfied with husbands' support for their total domestic load, though several of them preferred that their husbands steer clear of the schooling.

13. Moreover, when mothers strictly defined their identities according to the ideology of intensive mothering, which includes setting extreme child-rearing standards and asserts that mothers' caregiving is far superior to anyone else's, fathers' contributions to homeschooling

could never measure up. Furthermore, when mothers allowed parenting practices that they viewed as substandard, it could threaten their own identities. Walzer (1998) found that the new parents she studied also fell into this gendered dynamic, and when husbands did contribute, it was often under the direction of their wives.

14. Garey (1999) and Webber and Williams (2008b) also found some families in which fathers' most reliable contribution to child care was during sleep time.

15. Quoted in Adam (1995:94).

16. Quoted in Adam (1995:96).

17. Quoted in Adam (1995:95).

18. Bianchi, Robinson, and Milkie (2006) found that parents have incorporated children into their own leisure time in recent decades.

19. See DeVault (1991) for similar examples of how mothers define increments of time with their children as their own leisure time.

20. For discussion of how wives' level of dissatisfaction is linked to their expectations regarding husbands' housework, see Hochschild (1989).

21. Some of Blair-Loy's (2003) subjects, mothers who had left elite careers to stay home with their children, were also at first frustrated but eventually felt resigned to their husbands' lack of contribution to caregiving.

22. See Stevens (2001).

23. See Hochschild (1989) for discussion of this same dynamic in the household division of labor literature, which details the strategies some wives use to either reduce or escalate marital conflict when husbands, either intentionally or neglectfully, deny their bids for respect and gratitude.

24. In her study of new parents, Walzer (1998) found that mothers often resented fathers' availability of leisure time, and Webber and Williams (2008b) found that when some of the mothers they studied cut their work hours to part-time, their own leisure time decreased while their husbands' leisure time *increased*, which led mothers to feel frustrated and over-whelmed. Similarly, some of the mothers Blair-Loy (2003) studied resented their husbands for their lack of contribution to family caregiving.

25. See Flaherty (2003).

26. Quoted in Flaherty (2003:19).

27. Many mothers, not just homeschoolers, frame their maternal sacrifice in sequencing terms because the concept is part of many motherhood discourses (see Bobel 2002; Garey 1999).

28. Quoted in Bobel (2002:7).

29. See Charmaz (1991).

30. For a definition and sociological discussion of nostalgia, see Davis (1979).

31. In her study of natural mothers, Bobel (2002) also heard homeschoolers say "just relax and enjoy it."

32. Stone also found that thinking about their children getting older and anticipating potential regret in the future was one way mothers justified leaving elite careers to stay home with their children. She found that the "prevailing feeling" the mothers in her study expressed "was one of no regrets" (2007:155). See also Blair-Loy (2003).

33. Though this process has been shown to be a feature of how people generally experience time (see Flaherty 1999), it is possible that the effect was exacerbated for homeschooling mothers. It is reasonable to speculate that sequencing, with its heavy dependence on nostalgia and regret, led homeschoolers to experience the sensation of temporal compression more acutely than people who spend less time scrutinizing the past.

34. Quoted in Flaherty (2003:23)

35. Quoted in Flaherty (1999:95).
36. Flaherty (1999:154) has suggested that the specific term "savoring complex" may well describe the temporal process of purposely trying to achieve protracted duration, though he has yet to develop this term more fully with respect to emotions (see also Flaherty 2003; 2011:31–35). I borrow from him here in labeling this form of temporal emotion work as "savoring."
37. Snyder (2007) has found that parents feel quality time with children is best achieved through emotional connection that occurs in unstructured time.
38. Lareau (2003) has shown that much of children's structured time occurs outside of the home, especially for middle-class children.
39. Both Bianchi, Robinson, and Milkie (2006) and Snyder (2007) have shown that parents believe quality time with children cannot be forced.

NOTES TO INTRODUCTION TO PART III

1. In chapter 1, I explain why I did not reinterview the other eight mothers.

NOTES TO CHAPTER 6

1. Of course not all mothers were in the same stage of their homeschooling careers, so their feelings about husbands' domestic contributions at the first or second interview cannot be compared as though they were—some mothers may have already come to terms with the division of labor by the first interview, whereas others could have been still trying to work it out.
2. In her study of middle-class parents' drive to provide their children with opportunities that will enhance their cultural capital, Lareau (2003) identified several ways that extracurricular activities can spin out of control and keep family members from spending time together.
3. Quoted in Miller (1981:419).
4. Some of Blair-Loy's (2003) subjects, mothers who left elite careers to stay home with their preschoolers, also had a hard time adjusting initially but learned to enjoy being home after finding a supportive group of other stay-at-home mothers.
5. For discussion of women's opportunities as they relate to leaving the paid labor force and going to part-time work, see Risman (1998) and Webber and Williams (2008b).
6. For discussion of how some mothers compromise their careers, taking "secondary," low-paying jobs not in their occupational field to be more available for their children, see Webber and Williams (2008b).
7. For discussion of how mothers are more likely than fathers to compromise their careers, as well as how parents arrive at these decisions, see Blair-Loy (2003), Garey (1999), Stone (2007), Walzer (1998), and Webber and Williams (2008a, 2008b).
8. See Garey (1999:44) for discussion of how the mothers she studied struggled with "reconciling their positive feelings about being workers with cultural expectations about what it means to be a good mother."
9. Quoted in Blair-Loy (2003:75).
10. Lareau (2003) has discussed middle-class parents' tendency to watch children's classroom progress closely, to frequently intervene if they feel their children are "bored," and to feel entitled to ask the teacher to accommodate their children on an individualized basis to challenge them at the right academic level. Tracy struggled with these ideas, wanting those outcomes for her children (because that is what good mothers do), yet knowing the structure of mass education did not allow for individual accommodation at every turn.

11. For discussion of the tension mothers feel between work and family, see Blair-Loy (2003), Garey (1999), Stone (2007), and Webber and Williams (2008a, 2008b).

12. This did not happen often, but when mothers did go against their children's wishes, it was much more likely to be first-choicers. In addition, it is important to point out that no mothers reported that their children hated homeschooling and constantly begged to go to school. It was more common that children would go through stages where they wondered if they should be in school instead, or asked to go because they did not understand what they were missing. For example, in a few cases, mothers reported that the most enticing aspect of conventional school for their children was riding the school bus.

NOTES TO CHAPTER 7

1. See Lareau (2003) for discussion of how children's ability to interact with other children and adults, as evaluated by middle-class standards, is used as a measure of successful socialization and considered to be the result of effective parenting. See also Simon (2008),

2. For further discussion of counterfactual thinking, see Epstude and Roese (2008).

3. Duggan (2010) found that a small sample of homeschooled students attending a community college were likely to credit their homeschooling for their academic knowledge and abilities, rate themselves high in mathematical ability and reading comprehension, and express high drive to succeed. Duggan compared homeschoolers' answers with those of conventionally schooled students and found that homeschoolers rated themselves higher in all these areas, a finding that holds dubious value. (In note 5 I will address the limitations of comparing across groups.)

4. See Griffith and Smith (2005) and Lareau (2003) for discussion of how academic success is considered a reflection of good parenting.

5. A number of studies have compared homeschooled students' test scores with those of their conventionally schooled peers. There are several significant drawbacks in this research, however. First, it is impossible to obtain comparable groups because of the unknown differences between homeschoolers and conventionally schooled students. For example, if a higher percentage of homeschoolers than conventional schoolers have parents who value education (though this is not necessarily true), it is impossible to disentangle the cause of higher test scores among homeschoolers. Is it that their parents emphasize the value of education, or is it that learning at home works better than learning at school? The same rationale holds for any difference that might exist between homeschooled and conventionally schooled children: socioeconomic status, parents' education levels, race—the list of potential causal factors goes on. A second limitation of these studies is that the homeschoolers who take the tests (or are evaluated in other ways, depending on the research) do not represent all homeschoolers. For example, the test results of the homeschoolers attending a private charter school cannot tell us anything about the test-taking abilities of homeschoolers who were not in that study (which is to say, most of them). As another example, the people who choose to participate in the research are systematically different from those who decline, which creates a selection bias that invalidates any meaningful comparisons between the two groups. Some studies have made claims about homeschoolers after receiving only a 10 percent response from surveys disseminated via the Internet (e.g., Klein and Poplin 2008). It is highly likely that failing to collect data from 90 percent of the targeted audience skews a study's conclusions in ways that we cannot know. Third, the tests researchers have relied on may not be good indicators of academic achievement. This limitation is particularly true

of the studies that claim to show positive social skills among homeschoolers compared with their conventionally schooled peers. How does one measure social skills?

Let me provide just one example of these problems that plague the research in comparing homeschooled students' achievements with those of conventionally schooled students. In 2004, Rothermel conducted a study comparing home-educated and school-educated students in the United Kingdom on a test called Performance Indicators in Primary Schools. She found that homeschooled students outperformed the conventionally schooled students by quite a bit. However, there were only thirty-five students in her study, and they were selected in the following way: a survey was disseminated to 5,000 homeschooling families, who were accessed through sources such as support networks and Internet discussion lists (creating a selection bias); 1,000 families responded (a 20 percent response rate—creating a second selection bias); 419 of those families "were themselves selected" (2004:278) from the 1,000 (a third level of selection bias), and thirty-five children were selected from these 419 families to take the standardized test (compounding selection bias for a fourth time). The test scores of these thirty-five children were then averaged and compared with the national average of the students in conventional schools taking the same test. Although Rothermel acknowledges, "Whether these [thirty-five] children were representative of home-educated children generally is impossible to know" (2004:279), with the drastic attenuation of participants and severe self-selection procedures at four different points in the research process (yielding a sample of thirty-five students from the originally biased pool of 5,000 families), the sample Rothermel used is almost certainly skewed exponentially. Because there is no way to know for sure just how skewed the sample is, it is scientifically invalid to claim that it reveals anything meaningful about homeschooled students' achievement compared with students who are conventionally schooled. I must mention one last problem with this particular study: the homeschooled students who were tested were between four and five years old; they were tested again ten months later, when most were between five and six years old. It is hard to know how much impact "education"—at school or home—can have on children so young, who have barely started any academic work. What does this tell us about how effective homeschooling is *compared with conventional school*? I would argue, resoundingly, nothing. Careful researchers acknowledge these limitations in the research, but the upshot is that there are no studies that can compare homeschooling to conventional schooling. To truly determine the causal relationship between type of schooling and academic performance (or social skills), researchers would need to design a controlled experiment in which they randomly assign students to a homeschool or conventional-school program. Then the students in each group would receive the same treatment as the others in their group except for the type of schooling. Randomly assigning students into these groups would allow the researchers to calculate the likelihood of statistical error and the impact of other causal forces (for instance, the education level of parents). Researchers would then use the same standardized assessment tool in every group to evaluate students' progress. Those results (given some other caveats, such as using valid measures) could give us a meaningful comparison of homeschooling and public schooling. Needless to say, conducting such an experiment is not feasible because it would affect real people's lives in such a major way. To sum up: the problem in evaluating homeschoolers' success is in *comparing them with conventionally schooled students*. There is ample evidence that many homeschoolers thrive and go on to achieve great things academically, occupationally, personally, and relationally. So it is clear that homeschooling is highly effective for many children—I do not dispute this finding—but we cannot meaningfully compare their accomplishments with those of conventionally schooled students.

For research that has tried to evaluate homeschoolers' academic success (some of which has carefully acknowledged these methodological limitations), see Collom (2005), Klein and Poplin (2008), Ray (1988, 2000b), Van Pelt, Allison, and Allison (2009), and Wartes (1988). For further discussion of problems in the research, see Kunzman (2009a) and Welner and Welner (1999).

NOTES TO CHAPTER 8

1. The fourth second-choicer, Patricia Tomlinson, had continued to homeschool without interruption—her children were twenty-one and eleven at the time of the second interview—and she did not have concrete future plans.
2. For discussion of how women lose earning power and opportunities by interrupting their careers, see Risman (1998).
3. For discussion of mothers' conflict between careers and children, see Blair-Loy (2003), Garey (1999), and Hays (1996).
4. Some of the mothers studied by Webber and Williams (2008a:761) also talked anxiously about how they had "no regrets" about their "choice" to put their "career goals on hold" and move to part-time work so they could be there for their children.
5. See Blair-Loy (2003). In addition, some of Garey's (1999) subjects also felt that balancing work and family helped them achieve a more positive sense of self.
6. Liz's job consisted of coaching women through their pregnancies, labors, births, and post-partum periods. Thus although the labor and birthing components were unpredictable, Liz was able to schedule her pre- and postnatal clients with regularity.
7. Though Alice had been homeschooling her grandson for years, she considered herself to be more of a mother than a grandmother to him because he and his father lived with her, and his biological mother was "out of the picture." Her other son had just had a baby, however, and she was looking forward to a more traditional grandmother-grandchild relationship with him.
8. Bobel (2002) suspected that some of the natural mothers she studied wanted more children to extend their mothering identities as well.
9. Bobel (2002:133) also found that some of the natural mothers she studied thought that "a culture that casts mothers and children in opposition" was a problem.
10. One of the home-birthing mothers studied by Klassen (2001) also retrospectively attributed her depression to a negative set of circumstances surrounding the birth of her child.

NOTES TO CHAPTER 9

1. See Williams (2000).
2. Quoted in Webber and Williams (2008a:761)
3. See Stone (2007).
4. For discussion of how choice rhetoric obscures structural inequalities in the workplace, see Blair-Loy (2003), Bobel (2002), Gerson (1985), Stone (2007), and Webber and Williams (2008a).
5. Quoted in Blair-Loy (2003:54).
6. Quoted in Blair-Loy (2003:90).

7. See Hochschild (1983, 1990).

8. My thanks to Joanna Gregson for this last phrase to sharpen my point about the distinction between choosing and "knowing."

9. Quoted in Bobel (2002:95).

10. Quoted in Hays (1996:133).

11. For discussion of the norms of good mothering, see Blair-Loy (2003), Blum (1999), Bobel (2002), Copelton (2007), Hays (1996), and Murphy (2000).

12. See Hochschild (1983).

13. See Taylor (1995).

14. The emotional deviance data also lead to some theoretical insights about deviant identity management, an analysis I have not included here. See Lois (2009) for a discussion of how emotional messages may be embedded in deviant accusations, providing a hidden "layer" in the accounting process to explain why individual excuses and justifications are not always interchangeable in neutralizing stigma.

15. Quoted in Bianchi, Robinson, and Milkie (2006:137).

16. For discussion of how husbands are likely to oppose their wives' requests for a more equitable division of household labor, see Hochschild (1989).

17. These data also lead to some theoretical insights about how burnout operates in private life, an analysis I have not included here. See Lois (2006) for a discussion of how the emotion norms in personal relationships, in particular that between mother and child, conflict with the most effective ways workers manage emotions on the job to forestall burnout.

18. See Charmaz (1991).

19. See Milligan (2003). For further discussion of nostalgia, see Davis (1979). For discussion of the role emotions plays in the development of a continuous self, see Hochschild (1983).

20. Quoted in Flaherty (2003:19).

21. See Glaser and Strauss (1967).

22. Charmaz (1991), Hochschild (1983), and Mattley (2002) have all shown that past emotional experiences can be used as a template for understanding present emotions.

23. See Hochschild (1983).

24. See Charmaz (1991).

25. For discussion of how our definitions of motherhood seem to apply exclusively to dependent-age children, see Bobel (2002), Garey (1999), and Hays (1996).

26. Quoted in Hamilton and Armstrong (2009:602).

27. Quoted in Charmaz (1991:251).

28. See Howard (2006).

BIBLIOGRAPHY

Adam, Barbara. 1995. *Timewatch: The Social Analysis of Time*. Cambridge: Polity Press.

Adler, Patricia A., and Peter Adler. 1987. *Membership Roles in Field Research*. Newbury Park, CA: Sage.

Apple, Michael W. 2000. "The Cultural Politics of Home Schooling." *Peabody Journal of Education* 75:256–71.

———. 2001. "Bringing the World to God: Education and the Politics of Authoritarian Religious Populism." *Discourse: Studies in the Cultural Politics of Education* 22:149–72.

———. 2004. "Away with All Teachers: The Cultural Politics of Home Schooling." In *Pedagogy of Place: Seeing Space as Cultural Education*, ed. David M. Callejo Perez, Stephen M. Fain, and Judith J. Slater, 149–73. New York: Peter Lang.

Arai, A. Bruce. 2000. "Reasons for Home Schooling in Canada." *Canadian Journal of Education* 25:204–17.

Aurini, Janice, and Scott Davies. 2005. "Choice without Markets: Homeschooling in the Context of Private Education." *British Journal of Sociology of Education* 26:461–74.

Bates, Vernon L. 1991. "Lobbying for the Lord: The New Christian Right Home-Schooling Movement and Grassroots Lobbying." *Review of Religious Research* 33:3–17.

Bauman, Kurt J. 2002. "Homeschooling in the United States: Trends and Characteristics." *Education Policy Analysis Archives* 10(26). Retrieved June 14, 2010. http://epaa.asu.edu/epaa/v10n26.html.

Becker, Howard S. 1963. *Outsiders: Studies in the Sociology of Deviance*. New York: Free Press.

Bianchi, Suzanne M., John P. Robinson, and Melissa A. Milkie. 2006. *Changing Rhythms of American Family Life*. New York: Russell Sage.

Biernacki, Patrick, and Dan Waldorf. 1981. "Snowball Sampling: Problems and Techniques of Chain Referral Sampling." *Sociological Methods and Research* 10:141–63.

Bigner, Jerry J., and Raymond K. Yang. 1996. "Parent Education in Popular Literature: 1972–1990." *Family and Consumer Sciences Research Journal* 25:3–27.

Blair-Loy, Mary. 2003. *Competing Devotions: Career and Family among Women Executives*. Cambridge: Harvard University Press.

Blee, Kathleen M. 1998. "White-Knuckle Research: Emotional Dynamics in Fieldwork with Racist Activists." *Qualitative Sociology* 21:381–99.

Blum, Linda M. 1999. *At the Breast: Ideologies of Breastfeeding and Motherhood in the Contemporary United States*. Boston: Beacon Press.

Blumer, Herbert. 1969. *Symbolic Interactionism: Perspective and Method*. Englewood Cliffs, NJ: Prentice-Hall.

Bobel, Christina G. 2001. "Bounded Liberation: A Focused Study of La Leche League International." *Gender & Society* 15:130–51.

———. 2002. *The Paradox of Natural Mothering*. Philadelphia: Temple University Press.

Brabant, Christine, Sylvain Bourdon, and France Jutras. 2003. "Home Education in Quebec: Family First." *Evaluation and Research in Education* 17:112–31.

Brissie, Jane S., Kathleen V. Hoover-Dempsey, and Otto C. Basler. 1988. "Individual, Situational Contributors to Teacher Burnout." *Journal of Educational Research* 82:106–12.

Brown, Stephanie, Rhonda Small, and Judith Lumley. 1997. "Being a 'Good Mother.'" *Journal of Reproductive and Infant Psychology* 15:185–200.

Bullock, Heather E., and Irma Morales Waugh. 2004. "Caregiving around the Clock: How Women in Nursing Manage Career and Family Demands." *Journal of Social Issues* 60:767–86.

Cancian, Francesca M., and Steven L. Gordon. 1988. "Changing Emotion Norms in Marriage: Love and Anger in U.S. Women's Magazines since 1900." *Gender & Society* 2:308–42.

Chapman, Anne, and Tom A. O'Donoghue. 2000. "Home Schooling: An Emerging Research Agenda." *Educational Research and Perspectives* 27:19–36.

Charmaz, Kathy. 1991. *Good Days, Bad Days: The Self in Chronic Illness.* New Brunswick, NJ: Rutgers University Press.

Charvoz, Adrienne. 1988. "Reactions to the Home School Research: Dialogues with Practitioners." *Education and Urban Society* 21:85–95.

Chin, Tiffani. 2000. "'Sixth Grade Madness': Parental Emotion Work in the Private High School Application Process." *Journal of Contemporary Ethnography* 29:124–63.

Collom, Ed. 2005. "The Ins and Outs of Homeschooling: The Determinants of Parental Motivations and Student Achievement." *Education and Urban Society* 37:307–35.

Collom, Ed, and Douglas E. Mitchell. 2005. "Home Schooling as a Social Movement: Identifying the Determinants of Homeschoolers' Perceptions." *Sociological Spectrum* 25:273–305.

Coltrane, Scott. 2000. "Research on Household Labor: Modeling and Measuring the Social Embeddedness of Routine Family Work." *Journal of Marriage and Family* 62:1208–33.

Copelton, Denise A. 2007. "'You Are What You Eat': Nutritional Norms, Maternal Deviance, and Neutralization of Women's Prenatal Diets." *Deviant Behavior* 28:467–94.

Copp, Martha. 1998. "When Emotion Work Is Doomed to Fail: Ideological and Structural Constraints on Emotion Management." *Symbolic Interaction* 21:299–328.

Cordes, Cynthia L., and Thomas W. Dougherty. 1993. "A Review and an Integration of Research on Job Burnout." *Academy of Management Review* 18:621–56.

Davis, Fred. 1979. *Yearning for Yesterday: A Sociology of Nostalgia.* New York: Free Press.

Degher, Douglas, and Gerald Hughes. 1991. "The Identity Change Process: A Field Study of Obesity." *Deviant Behavior* 12:385–401.

DeVault, Marjorie L. 1991. *Feeding the Family: The Social Organization of Caring as Gendered Work.* Chicago: University of Chicago Press.

———. 1999. "Comfort and Struggle: Emotion Work in Family Life." *Annals of the American Academy of Political and Social Science* 561:52–63.

Dickson-Swift, Virginia, Erica L. James, Sandra Kippen, and Pranee Liamputtong. 2009. "Researching Sensitive Topics: Qualitative Research as Emotion Work." *Qualitative Research* 9:61–79.

Duggan, Molly H. 2010. "Is All College Preparation Equal? Pre–Community College Experiences of Home-Schooled, Private-Schooled, and Public-Schooled Students." *Community College Journal of Research and Practice* 34:25–38.

Emerson, Michael O., and David Hartman. 2006. "The Rise and Fall of Religious Funda-mentalism." *Annual Review of Sociology* 32:127–44.

Epstude, Kai, and Neal J. Roese. 2008. "The Functional Theory of Counterfactual Thinking." *Personality and Social Psychology Review* 12:168–92.

Erickson, Rebecca J. 1993. "Reconceptualizing Family Work: The Effect of Emotion Work on Perceptions of Marital Quality." *Journal of Marriage and Family* 55:888–900.

———. 2005. "Why Emotion Work Matters: Sex, Gender, and the Division of Household Labor." *Journal of Marriage and Family* 67:337–51.

Evenson, Ranae J., and Robin W. Simon. 2005. "Clarifying the Relationship between Parent-hood and Depression." *Journal of Health and Social Behavior* 46:341–58.

Fields-Smith, Cheryl, and Meca Williams. 2009. "Motivations, Sacrifices, and Challenges: Black Parents' Decisions to Home School." *Urban Review* 41:369–89.

Flaherty, Michael G. 1999. *A Watched Pot: How We Experience Time.* New York: NYU Press.

———. 2003. "Time Work: Customizing Temporal Experience." *Social Psychology Quarterly* 66:17–33.

———. 2011. *The Textures of Time: Agency and Temporal Experience.* Philadelphia: Temple University Press.

Friedman, Isaac A., and Barry A. Farber. 1992. "Professional Self-Concept as a Predictor of Teacher Burnout." *Journal of Educational Research* 86:28–35.

Gaither, Milton. 2008. *Homeschool: An American History.* New York: Palgrave Macmillan.

Garey, Anita Ilta. 1999. *Weaving Work and Motherhood.* Philadelphia: Temple University Press.

Geertz, Clifford. 1973. *The Interpretation of Cultures.* New York: Basic Books.

George, Molly. 2010. "Interactions in Expert Service Work." *Journal of Contemporary Eth-nography* 37:108–31.

Gerson, Kathleen. 1985. *Hard Choices: How Women Decide about Work, Career, and Mother-hood.* Berkeley: University of California Press.

Glaser, Barney, and Anselm Strauss. 1967. *The Discovery of Grounded Theory.* Chicago: Aldine.

Goffman, Erving. [1955] 1982. "On Face-Work." In *Interaction Ritual: Essays on Face-to-Face Behavior,* 5–45. New York: Pantheon.

———. 1963. *Stigma.* Englewood Cliffs, NJ: Prentice-Hall.

———. 1971. *Relations in Public.* New York: Harper and Row.

Goode, William J. 1960. "A Theory of Role Strain." *American Sociological Review* 25:483–96.

Gordon, Steven L. 1989. "Institutional and Impulsive Orientations in Selectively Appropriat-ing Emotions to Self." In *The Sociology of Emotions: Original Essays and Research Papers,* ed. David D. Franks and E. Doyle McCarthy, 115–35. Greenwich, CT: JAI Press.

Gottschalk, Simon. 2003. "Reli(e)ving the Past: Emotion Work in the Holocaust's Second Generation." *Symbolic Interaction* 26:355–80.

Greenglass, Esther R., and Ronald J. Burke. 1988. "Work and Family Precursors of Burnout in Teachers: Sex Differences." *Sex Roles* 18:215–29.

Griffith, Alison I., and Dorothy E. Smith. 2005. *Mothering for Schooling.* New York: Rout-ledge Falmer.

Guba, Egon G., and Yvonna S. Lincoln. 1994. "Competing Paradigms in Qualitative Research." In *Handbook of Qualitative Research,* ed. Norman K. Denzin and Yvonna S. Lincoln, 105–17. Thousand Oaks, CA: Sage.

Hamilton, Laura, and Elizabeth A. Armstrong. 2009. "Gendered Sexuality in Young Adulthood: Double Binds and Flawed Options." *Gender & Society* 23:589–616.

Hays, Sharon. 1996. *The Cultural Contradictions of Motherhood*. New Haven: Yale University Press.

Hecht, Laura M. 2001. "Role Conflict and Role Overload: Different Concepts, Different Consequences." *Sociological Inquiry* 71:111–21.

Heltsley, Martha, and Thomas C. Calhoun. 2003. "The Good Mother: Neutralization Techniques Used by Pageant Mothers." *Deviant Behavior* 24:81–100.

Hill, Paul T. 2000. "Home Schooling and the Future of Public Education." *Peabody Journal of Education* 75:20–31.

Hochschild, Arlie R. 1983. *The Managed Heart: Commercialization of Human Feeling*. Berkeley: University of California Press.

———. 1989. *The Second Shift*. New York: Avon.

———. 1990. "Ideology and Emotion Management: A Perspective and Path for Future Research." In *Research Agendas in the Sociology of Emotions*, ed. Theodore D. Kemper, 117–42. Albany, NY: SUNY Press.

Hoffman, Elizabeth A. 2007. "Open-Ended Interviews, Power, and Emotional Labor." *Journal of Contemporary Ethnography* 36:318–46.

Holland, Janet. 2007. "Emotions and Research." *International Journal of Social Research Methodology* 10:195–209.

Howard, Jenna. 2006. "Expecting and Accepting: The Temporal Ambiguity of Recovery Identities." *Social Psychology Quarterly* 69:307–24.

Irvine, Leslie. 1999. *Codependent Forevermore: The Invention of Self in a Twelve-Step Group*. Chicago: University of Chicago Press.

Jorgensen, Danny L. 1989. *Participant Observation: A Methodology for Human Studies*. Newbury Park, CA: Sage.

Kang, Miliann. 2003. "The Managed Hand: The Commercialization of Bodies and Emotions in Korean Immigrant-Owned Nail Salons." *Gender & Society* 17:820–39.

Kanter, Rosabeth Moss. 1977. *Men and Women of the Corporation*. New York: Basic Books.

Kimmel, Michael. 1996. *Manhood in America: A Cultural History*. New York: Free Press.

Klassen, Pamela E. 2001. *Blessed Events: Religion and Home Birth in America*. Princeton: Princeton University Press.

Klein, Carol, and Mary Poplin. 2008. "Families Home Schooling in a Virtual Charter School System." *Marriage and Family Review* 43:369–95.

Kleinman, Sherryl, and Martha A. Copp. 1993. *Emotions and Fieldwork*. Newbury Park, CA: Sage.

Knowles, J. Gary. 1988. "Parents' Rationales and Teaching Methods for Home Schooling: The Role of Biography." *Education and Urban Society* 21:69–84.

———. 1991. "Parents' Rationales for Operating Home Schools." *Journal of Contemporary Ethnography* 20:203–30.

Krieger, N., D. R. Williams, and N. E. Moss. 1997. "Measuring Social Class in U.S. Public Health Research: Concepts, Methodologies, and Guidelines." *Annual Review of Public Health* 18:341–78.

Kulik, Liat. 2002. "Marital Equality and the Quality of Long-Term Marriage in Later Life." *Ageing and Society* 22:459–81.

Kunzman, Robert. 2009a. "Understanding Homeschooling: A Better Approach to Regulation." *Theory and Research in Education* 7:311–30.

———. 2009b. *Write These Laws on Your Children: Inside the World of Conservative Christian Homeschooling*. Boston: Beacon Press.

Lareau, Annette. 2003. *Unequal Childhoods: Class, Race, and Family Life*. Berkeley: University of California Press.

Lines, Patricia M. 1998. *Home Schoolers: Estimating Numbers and Growth*. Washington, DC: National Institute on Student Achievement, Curriculum, and Assessment, Office of Educational Research and Improvement, U.S. Department of Education.

Lofland, John, David Snow, Leon Anderson, and Lyn H. Lofland. 2006. *Analyzing Social Settings: A Guide to Qualitative Observation and Analysis*. 4th ed. Belmont, CA: Wadsworth.

Lois, Jennifer. 2001. "Managing Emotions, Intimacy, and Relationships in a Volunteer Search and Rescue Group." *Journal of Contemporary Ethnography* 30:131–79.

———. 2003. *Heroic Efforts: The Emotional Culture of Search and Rescue Volunteers*. New York: NYU Press.

———. 2006. "Role Strain, Emotion Management, and Burnout: Homeschooling Mothers' Adjustment to the Teacher Role." *Symbolic Interaction* 29:507–30.

———. 2009. "Emotionally Layered Accounts: Homeschoolers' Justifications for Maternal Deviance." *Deviant Behavior* 30:201–34.

Lubienski, Chris. 2000. "Wither the Common Good? A Critique of Home Schooling." *Peabody Journal of Education* 75:207–32.

Luker, Kristin. 1984. *Abortion and the Politics of Motherhood*. Berkeley: University of California Press.

Lupton, Deborah, and Jennifer Fenwick. 2001. "'They've Forgotten That I'm the Mum': Constructing and Practising Motherhood in Special Care Nurseries." *Social Science and Medicine* 53:1011–21.

Mac Rae, Hazel. 1998. "Managing Feelings: Caregiving as Emotion Work." *Research on Aging* 20:137–60.

Maslach, Christina. 1982. *Burnout: The Cost of Caring*. Englewood Cliffs, NJ: Prentice Hall.

Mattley, Christine. 2002. "The Temporality of Emotion: Constructing Past Emotions." *Symbolic Interaction* 25:363–78.

Mayberry, Maralee. 1988. "Characteristics and Attitudes of Families Who Home School." *Education and Urban Society* 21:32–41.

———. 1992. "Home-Based Education: Parents as Teachers." *Continuing Higher Education Review* 56:48–58.

———. 1993. "Effective Learning Environments in Action: The Case of Home Schools." *School Community Journal* 3:61–68.

Mayberry, Maralee, and J. Gary Knowles. 1989. "Family Unity Objectives of Parents Who Teach Their Children: Ideological and Pedagogical Orientations to Home Schooling." *Urban Review* 21:209–25.

Mayberry, Maralee, J. Gary Knowles, Brian Ray, and Stacey Marlow. 1995. *Home Schooling: Parents as Educators*. Thousand Oaks, CA: Corwin.

McDowell, Susan A. 2000. "The Home Schooling Mother-Teacher: Toward a Theory of Social Integration." *Peabody Journal of Education* 75:187–206.

Medlin, Richard G. 2000. "Home Schooling and the Question of Socialization." *Peabody Journal of Education* 75:107–123.

Miller, Dorothy A. 1981. "The 'Sandwich' Generation: Adult Children of the Aging." *Social Work* 26:419–23.

Milligan, Melinda J. 2003. "Displacement and Identity Discontinuity: The Role of Nostalgia in Establishing New Identity Categories." *Symbolic Interaction* 26:381–403.

Murphy, Elizabeth. 1999. "'Breast Is Best': Infant Feeding Decisions and Maternal Deviance." *Sociology of Health and Illness* 21:187–208.

———. 2000. "Risk, Responsibility, and Rhetoric in Infant Feeding." *Journal of Contemporary Ethnography* 29:291–325.

———. 2004. "Anticipatory Accounts." *Symbolic Interaction* 27:129–54.

Murray, Susan B. 1998. "Child Care Work: Intimacy in the Shadows of Family-Life." *Qualitative Sociology* 21:149–68.

Nack, Adina. 2008. *Damaged Goods? Women Living with Incurable Sexually Transmitted Diseases*. Philadelphia: Temple University Press.

National Household Education Surveys Program. 2003. National Center for Education Statistics. Retrieved May 28, 2004. http://nces.ed.gov/nhes/homeschool/.

———. 2007. National Center for Education Statistics. Retrieved June 20, 2010. http://nces.ed.gov/pubs2009/2009030.pdf

Orenstein, Peggy. 1994. *School Girls: Young Women, Self-Esteem, and the Confidence Gap*. New York: Anchor.

Orzechowicz, David. 2008. "Privileged Emotion Managers: The Case of Actors." *Social Psychology Quarterly* 71:143–56.

Pfeffer, Carla A. 2010. "'Women's Work'? Women Partners of Transgender Men Doing Housework and Emotion Work." *Journal of Marriage and Family* 72:165–83.

Pierce, Jennifer L. 1995. *Gender Trials: Emotional Lives in Contemporary Law Firms*. Berkeley: University of California Press.

Pitman, Mary Anne. 1987. "Compulsory Education and Home Schooling: Truancy or Prophecy?" *Education and Urban Society* 19:280–89.

Prus, Robert. 1996. *Symbolic Interaction and Ethnographic Research: Intersubjectivity and the Study of Human Lived Experience*. Albany, NY: SUNY Press.

Ray, Brian D. 1988. "Home Schools: A Synthesis of Research on Characteristics and Learner Outcomes." *Education and Urban Society* 21:16–31.

———. 2000a. "Home Schooling for Individuals' Gain and Society's Common Good." *Peabody Journal of Education* 75:272–93.

———. 2000b. "Home Schooling: The Ameliorator of Negative Influences on Learning?" *Peabody Journal of Education* 75:71–106.

Ray, Eileen Berlin, and Katherine I. Miller. 1991. "The Influence of Communication Structure and Social Support on Job Stress and Burnout." *Management Communication Quarterly* 4:506–27.

Reich, Jennifer A. 2003. "Pregnant with Possibility: Reflections on Embodiment, Access, and Inclusion in Field Research." *Qualitative Sociology* 26:351–67.

Risman, Barbara. 1998. *Gender Vertigo: American Families in Transition*. New Haven: Yale University Press.

Rizzo, John R., Robert J. House, and Sidney I. Lirtzman. 1970. "Role Conflict and Ambiguity in Complex Organizations." *Administrative Science Quarterly* 15:150–62.

Romero, Mary. 1992. *Maid in the U.S.A.* New York: Routledge.

Rothermel, Paula. 2004. "Home Education: Comparison of Home- and School-Educated Children on PIPS Baseline Assessments." *Journal of Early Childhood Research* 2:273–99.

Scott, Marvin, and Stanford Lyman. 1968. "Accounts." *American Sociological Review* 33:46–62.

Seery, Brenda L., and M. Sue Crowley. 2000. "Women's Emotion Work in the Family: Relationship Management and the Process of Building Father-Child Relationships." *Journal of Family Issues* 21:100–127.

Shyers, Larry E. 1992. "A Comparison of Social Adjustment between Home and Traditionally Schooled Students." *Home School Researcher* 8:1–8.

Simon, Robin W. 2008. "The Joys of Parenthood, Reconsidered." *Contexts* 7:40–45.

Snyder, Karrie Ann. 2007. "A Vocabulary of Motives: Understanding How Parents Define Quality Time." *Journal of Marriage and Family* 69:320–40.

Stearns, Peter N. 1994. *American Cool: Constructing a Twentieth-Century Emotional Style.* New York: NYU Press.

Stevens, Mitchell L. 2001. *Kingdom of Children: Culture and Controversy in the Homeschooling Movement.* Princeton: Princeton University Press.

Stokes, Randall, and John P. Hewitt. 1976. "Aligning Actions." *American Sociological Review* 41:838–49.

Stone, Pamela. 2007. *Opting Out? Why Women Really Quit Careers and Head Home.* Berkeley: University of California Press.

Sykes, Gresham M., and David Matza. 1957. "Techniques of Neutralization." *American Sociological Review* 22:667–69.

Tardy, Rebecca W. 2000. "'But I *Am* a Good Mom': The Social Construction of Motherhood through Health-Care Conversations." *Journal of Contemporary Ethnography* 29:433–73.

Taylor, Steven J. 1991. "Leaving the Field: Research, Relationships, and Responsibilities." In *Experiencing Fieldwork: An Inside View of Qualitative Research*, ed. William B. Shaffir and Robert A. Stebbins, 238–47. Newbury Park, CA: Sage.

Taylor, Verta. 1995. "Self-Labeling and Women's Mental Health: Postpartum Illness and the Reconstruction of Motherhood." *Sociological Focus* 28:23–47.

Theodosius, Catherine. 2008. *Emotional Labour in Health Care: The Unmanaged Heart of Nursing.* London: Routledge.

Thoits, Peggy A. 1990. "Emotional Deviance: Research Agendas." In *Research Agendas in the Sociology of Emotions*, ed. Theodore D. Kemper, 180–203. Albany, NY: SUNY Press.

Treas, Judith, and Esther de Ruijter. 2008. "Earnings and Expenditures on Household Services in Married and Cohabiting Unions." *Journal of Marriage and Family* 70:796–805.

Van Galen, Jane A. 1988. "Ideology, Curriculum, and Pedagogy in Home Education." *Education and Urban Society* 21:52–68.

Van Maanen, John. 1991. "Playing Back the Tape: Early Days in the Field." In *Experiencing Fieldwork: An Inside View of Qualitative Research*, ed. William B. Shaffir and Robert A. Stebbins, 31–42. Newbury Park, CA: Sage.

Van Pelt, Deani A. Nevan, Patricia A. Allison, and Derek J. Allison. 2009. "Fifteen Years Later: Home-Educated Canadian Adults." Canadian Centre for Home Education. Retrieved June 22, 2010. http://www.hslda.ca

Wagenaar, Theodore C. 1997. "What Characterizes Home Schoolers? A National Study." *Education* 117:440–44.

Wall, Glenda. 2001. "Moral Constructions of Motherhood in Breastfeeding Discourse." *Gender & Society* 15:592–610.

Walzer, Susan. 1998. *Thinking about the Baby: Gender and Transitions into Parenthood.* Philadelphia: Temple University Press.

Wartes, Jon. 1988. "The Washington Home School Project: Quantitative Measures for Informing Policy Decisions." *Education and Urban Society* 21:42–51.

Webber, Gretchen, and Christine Williams. 2008a. "Mothers in 'Good' and 'Bad' Part-Time Jobs: Different Problems, Same Results." *Gender & Society* 22:752–77.

———. 2008b. "Part-Time Work and the Gender Division of Labor." *Qualitative Sociology* 31:15–36.

Welner, Kariane Mari, and Kevin G. Welner. 1999. "Contextualizing Homeschooling Data: A Response to Rudner." *Education Policy Analysis Archives* 7(13). Retrieved July 28, 2010. http://epaa.asu.edu/epaa/v7n13.html.

Wharton, Amy S. 2009. "The Sociology of Emotional Labor." *Annual Review of Sociology* 35:147–65.

Williams, Joan. 2000. *Unbending Gender*. New York: Oxford University Press.

Wingfield, Adia Harvey. 2010. "Are Some Emotions Marked 'Whites Only'? Racialized Feeling Rules in Professional Workplaces." *Social Problems* 57:251–68.

Zelizer, Viviana A. 1985. *Pricing the Priceless Child: The Changing Social Value of Children*. New York: Basic Books.

29.

ABOUT THE AUTHOR

Jennifer Lois is Associate Professor of Sociology at Western Washington University and author of *Heroic Efforts: The Emotional Culture of Search and Rescue Volunteers.*